PENGUIN BOOKS

CONFESSIONS OF A SECULAR
FUNDAMENTALIST

Born in Lahore in 1941, Mani Shankar Aiyar received his education
at the Doon School, Dehra Dun; St. Stephen's College, Delhi; and the
University of Cambridge, UK. He joined the Indian Foreign Service
in 1963 and served in Brussels, Hanoi, Baghdad and as India's first-
ever Consul General in Karachi. From 1985 to 1989, he was Joint
Secretary to Prime Minister Rajiv Gandhi. He made the transition
from the civil service to politics in 1989 and was elected to the Lok
Sabha from the Mayiladuturai constituency of Tamil Nadu in 1991,
and again in 1999 and 2004. In May 2004, he was named Minister
of Petroleum and Natural Gas, and of Panchayati Raj.

He is also a well-known author and columnist who, for a decade
from 1989 to 1999, penned the popular weekly column 'Mani-Talk'
in *Sunday* magazine, later resumed in the *Telegraph* of Kolkata. He
has also written for a number of English, Hindi and Tamil journals.
His books include *Remembering Rajiv* (1992), *One Year in Parliament*
(1993), *Pakistan Papers* (1994) and *Knickerwallahs, Silly-Billies and
Other Curious Creatures* (1995).

Mani Shankar Aiyar is the founder-president of the Society for
Secularism.

PRAISE FOR THE BOOK

'A delightfully readable book... deals with substantial issues with
unusual elegance' —*Frontline*

'Gives a sound picture of how the "secular" mind functions... Well-
argued, surprisingly sober' —*Free Press Journal*

'An excellent addition to public discourse on a subject that needs far
greater analysis and advocacy than it has so far received in South
Asia' —*Hindu*

'A deft tour-de-force' —*Time Out Mi*

GW00778381

Confessions of a Secular Fundamentalist

Mani Shankar Aiyar

PENGUIN BOOKS

PENGUIN BOOKS
Published by the Penguin Group
Penguin Books India Pvt. Ltd, 11 Community Centre, Panchsheel Park, New Delhi
110 017, India
Penguin Group (USA) Inc., 375 Hudson Street, New York, New York 10014, USA
Penguin Group (Canada), 90 Eglinton Avenue East, Suite 700, Toronto, Ontario,
M4P 2Y3, Canada (a division of Pearson Penguin Canada Inc.)
Penguin Books Ltd, 80 Strand, London WC2R 0RL, England
Penguin Ireland, 25 St Stephen's Green, Dublin 2, Ireland (a division of Penguin
Books Ltd)
Penguin Group (Australia), 250 Camberwell Road, Camberwell, Victoria 3124,
Australia (a division of Pearson Australia Group Pty Ltd)
Penguin Group (NZ), cnr Airborne and Rosedale Roads, Albany, Auckland 1310,
New Zealand (a division of Pearson New Zealand Ltd)
Penguin Group (South Africa) (Pty) Ltd, 24 Sturdee Avenue, Rosebank, Johannesburg
2196, South Africa

Penguin Books Ltd, Registered Offices: 80 Strand, London WC2R 0RL, England

First published in Viking by Penguin Books India 2004
Published in Penguin Books 2006

Copyright © Mani Shankar Aiyar 2004, 2006

All rights reserved

10 9 8 7 6 5 4 3 2 1

ISBN-10: 0143 062050; ISBN-13: 9780143062059

The views and opinions expressed in this book are the author's own and the facts are as
reported by him which have been verified to the extent possible, and the publishers are
not in any way liable for the same.

While every effort has been made to trace copyright holders and obtain permission, this
has not been possible in all cases; any omissions brought to our attention will be remedied
in future editions.

Typeset in *Adobe Garamond* by SÜRYA, New Delhi
Printed at Chaman Offset Printers, New Delhi

To my mother
S. Bhagyalakshmi (1910–1988)
—religious *and* secular

'It is all very well for the likes of Sapru and me to talk pompously and in a superior way of our tolerance in matters of religion but neither of us has any religion worth talking about.'

—Jawaharlal Nehru, letter to Mahatma Gandhi, dated 10 March 1933, *Selected Works of Jawaharlal Nehru*, vol. 5, pp. 459–460, cited by Sunil Khilnani in his Nehru Memorial Lecture, 2002

'The holy word of God is on everyone's lips...but we see everyone projecting their own versions of God's word, with the sole purpose of using religion as a pretext for making others think as they do.'

—Baruch de Spinoza (1632–1677), displayed in the Holocaust Museum, Berlin

'If any person raises his hand to strike down another on the ground of religion, I shall fight him till the last breath of my life, both as the head of the Government and from outside.'

—Jawaharlal Nehru as quoted by S. Gopal, *Jawaharlal Nehru: A Biography*, from the *National Herald* report on 4 October 1951

Contents

Contents

Author's Note

This book was prepared in the expectation that it would be published in the summer of 2004 leading to the elections to the fourteenth Lok Sabha that were to be held in September–October 2004. However, after the manuscript was submitted to the publishers in January 2004, the BJP-led NDA government brought forward the elections to April–May 2004. That did not help the BJP. They and their partners lost. And in their place, the Congress-led United Progressive Alliance took office in May 2004—and to my surprise, I was made a Cabinet minister. It is, therefore, incumbent on me to clarify that the views expressed in this book are entirely mine in my personal capacity and do not necessarily reflect the views of the party to which I belong nor the government of which I have the honour to be a member. What I have to say binds only me as a concerned citizen of this great country.

A substantial portion of this book has been freshly written but I have also drawn extensively on my writings in several journals over the last fourteen years. I have pinched a few lines from Rajiv Gandhi. I am sure he will not mind.

Author's Note

Prologue:
A Conversation with Arun Shourie

Mani Shankar Aiyar (MSA): What are your personal religious beliefs? Are you, like I am, an atheist, an agnostic, or do you, like Shahabuddin, profess a religious faith?

Arun Shourie (AS): Conditioned by the suffering that I have seen, I cannot reconcile myself to the idea of an all-powerful, all-knowing and compassionate God. But I am an ardent idolater. As for religious practices, I meditate every day for about one hour, guided almost entirely by Buddhist scriptures.

MSA: Would you describe your personal religious faith as Buddhist?

AS: By practice, Buddhist; by culture, Hindu.

MSA: Your ideological beliefs, would you say, are Hindu in origin but the rites that you follow are Buddhist?

AS: The rites that I follow are Hindu, in the sense that I would go to the temple, celebrate *raksha bandhan* or Diwali...I would also go to dargahs, because of idolatry. But in the sense of a religious ideology, or a body of ideas, I would be closest to the ideas of the Buddha—his explanation for suffering and the way to mitigate it. I've derived great sustenance from it.

MSA: Is that because the Buddha did not concern himself with the question of whether or not there is a God?

AS: Yes. It is just the fact of suffering—that it is there, that no great personal purpose is served by it for which this is inflicted. While we cannot erase the objective source of suffering, we can work on our own reactions to it to be able to bear it and be of service to others.

MSA: So what attracts you to that religion is that it enables you to cope with the human condition. It eschews any attempt at an all-pervasive explanation, unlike Islam which attempts an all-pervasive explanation …

AS: There is no comparison between the two. There is an entire tradition, the Eastern tradition other than Confucius, where the inner dialectics …

MSA: You said Eastern tradition. You do not regard the Middle East as part of the East?

AS: No. I'd like to distinguish this Eastern tradition from the Semitic tradition like Judaism, early Christianity especially Christianity of the Church, and Islam and Marxism-Leninism. That is one tradition, the premises of which are completely destructive.

MSA: And those premises you don't accept. You even find them offensive.

AS: No, not personally offensive. But destructive in the extreme.

MSA: So you find the Middle Eastern traditions, particularly those influenced by Islam, destructive in a very significant sense. They are not constructive but destructive.

AS: Yes. And I mention that because I think there are four premises underlying all these (Semitic) traditions, that Truth is One; it has been revealed to one person; he has given it in one Book; that Book is very difficult to understand; you need an intermediary for it; it is the task of that intermediary to offer his services; if you still do not accept it, he must convince you; if you are still not convinced, then you are coming in the way of Jehovah, of Allah, of history; therefore, the intermediary must be allowed to put you out of harm's way.

Then, there is the Eastern tradition. The truth has not been revealed by one particular person. Many persons have thought about it. They have left marks, milestones, carvings on the walls, maps. So that if you choose to tread the path they will be of some help to you. Which of them is yours, you will determine by introspection, by a search for, as the Gita would say, *svadharma*. A test of the right path would not be whether I am conforming to the party line or that it conforms to some book, but my inner perception.

MSA: You were born a Hindu but are deeply attracted to the Buddhist faith. You are a Buddhist by ideology but follow Hindu rites. Supposing you had been born a Muslim, would you have converted yourself either to Buddhism or to Hinduism?

AS: I would have had a great problem, because I would have had to turn to the basic structures and texts—as I did in my own circumstances—and the basic structures would have dealt exclusively with externals and they would not have gone into the cure ...

MSA: So, you would have converted from Islam to some other religion?

AS: I do not know. I do not know.

MSA: Why should there be any doubt? As a Hindu, you were ready to be attracted to a non-Hindu faith. As a Muslim, would you not have wanted to be attracted to a non-Muslim faith?

AS: I would have been attracted, but the conditions are such that it would have made for great trauma and difficulty ...

MSA: So, does that mean being a Muslim makes it more difficult to be an Indian than being a Hindu makes it to be an Indian?

AS: Adhering to Islam in purity would make it impossible to live in a multicultural, multi-religious society and still abide by the tenets (of Islam). But for a Hindu ...

MSA: So you're saying you have to be a bad Muslim in order to be able to live like a good Indian?

AS: Er ... I think that's putting it in strong words, but certainly he would have to depart from the edicts of Islam as enshrined in the Koran and the Hadith.

MSA: The obverse of that is if you're faithful to the edicts of Islam as enshrined in the Koran and the shariat, you would have difficulty in being a good Indian.

AS: I think so.

MSA: So, there is a fundamental antithesis between being a good Muslim and being a good Indian?

AS: What do you mean by a 'good Indian'? For instance, Maulana Azad was a good Muslim—

MSA: Before we get into that—

AS: I don't want to let your observation pass. Being a good Muslim, Maulana Azad would say, is only devotion to God and righteous living. That's his thesis. No difficulty in that, okay?

The difficulty came in defining what devotion to God was and righteous living. The difficulty also came in defining a 'good Muslim'. If 'good Muslim' means brotherhood of man and so on, then there is no difficulty. But if it means, as 1000 verses in the Koran say, 'Spread Islam, have nothing to do with these kafirs, kill them, they are untrustworthy, they are unclean', then? The Hadith is full of this. There are rewards for killing the kafir. If this is a good Muslim then a multi-religious society in India would become impossible.

MSA: Therefore, if one is a good Muslim, in the very broad sense of this word, as defined by Maulana Azad, then it is reconcilable with being a 'good Indian'. But if you are even tending towards faith in the totality of Islam, then it's not possible to be a good Indian?

AS: Or a good Britisher, or a good citizen of any place where Islam is not in full control.

MSA: But supposing you are a faithful Muslim in a Muslim country, then it is not possible to be a good man. Is that what you're saying?

AS: Yes, but then again, it depends what you mean by being a good man. If you mean a good man addressed by the Koran, then there is no difficulty. But if you mean a good man to be one who is compassionate to everybody, you will have great difficulty.

MSA: Anyone, in that case, who is a good man in the eyes of the ulema is necessarily not a good man in your eyes.

AS: I think so. I'll give you an instance. The Prophet's mother died when he was six. The revelations started much later. And in the Hadith, he goes to pray but starts weeping. Everybody says, 'Why are you crying?' He says, 'Because Allah has forbidden me from praying for her soul.' Why? Because, technically, she died a non-believer. Now for me, for there to be such an Allah who would not allow a son to grieve for his mother is not the image of a good man.

MSA: So, if a Muslim is a believer in Islam in a total sense, it renders it impossible for him to be either a good Indian or a good man.

AS: I think you're putting it too narrowly. I do not want to go on subscribing to this view of his not being a good Indian. Then you will say: 'Oh, oh, see this is the RSS view of the Muslims,' etc. That is not my point. My point is much more fundamental. I would like the ulema to answer this question. And it is not specific to (Muslims in) India. Why not ask the question of other countries? Can you be a good Frenchman if you are a purist in Islam?

MSA: Which means you cannot be a good Frenchman, you cannot be a Saudi—

AS: No, Saudi you can be, because Islam is completely in control there. In fact, you can especially be a good Saudi because the Hadith is always wanting the primacy of the Arabs. You can't be a good Iranian.

MSA: So, you can be a good Arab without being a good man?

AS: A good man in the Buddha's sense of compassion and so on? Yes.

MSA: Yes or no? I don't understand your answer. My question is: Are you saying that a good Muslim can be a good Arab, but by definition cannot be a good Iranian, and therefore, cannot be a good man?

AS: It is a much wider concept...That is true. He cannot be...a good person as I would understand it, in the sense of universal responsibility and universal compassion.

MSA: But you're saying that universal responsibility and universal compassion are not part of Islam ...

AS: ... unless the universe has been converted to, and has subscribed to, and shown its subservience to Islam.

MSA: So, until the whole universe becomes Islamic, a good Muslim cannot be a good man in your opinion.

AS: Right. He cannot rest content.

MSA: Then is it possible, in your view, to be a Muslim without believing in the ideology of Islam?

AS: *(Long silence)* Um...For instance, I would think that the Sufis would regard themselves as Muslims, devout Muslims—

MSA: I don't think the Sufis regarded themselves as great believers of Islamic ideas—they had their view of the Islamic idea.

AS: That is a very good distinction. They regarded themselves as believers in true Islam. And the ulema always set upon them.

MSA: So, you are calibrating the goodness of a Muslim to the extent to which he distances himself from Islam?

AS: From...from the tradition, er...from the teaching of Islam in its pure form in the Koran and the Hadith ...

MSA: The more impure his Islam, the purer he is in your eyes as a man and a Muslim.

AS: I—

MSA: All right, let's get on to the next question. Is it possible for a Muslim to be one while denying the shariat?

AS: Most certainly.

MSA: To sum up then, a good Muslim is one who most certainly rejects the shariat, most certainly rejects the ulema, and distances himself as far as possible from the purity of the Islamic ideology?

AS: Yes, that part of the Islamic ideology which decides the attitude one must adopt towards the non-believers.

MSA: You have called your book *The World of Fatwas*. Is this world—the world of fatwas—coterminous with Islam?

AS: *(Pause)* No.

MSA: So, in your book, you're not concerned with the world of Islam, you're concerned with the world of the ulema.

AS: Naipaul's book was called *Among the Believers*. It is the central nerve going through, the core.

MSA: So, the diversity of the Muslims bears a certain resemblance to the diversity of the Hindus?

AS: Yes.

MSA: In which case, our attempting to categorize Indians by religion as Indian Muslims, Indian Hindus and so forth for purposes of sociological understanding is not very legitimate?

AS: Yes and no—because the self-definition, especially the definition by the leaders of a group, becomes the cutting edge of society.

MSA: So, you regard the ulema as the cutting edge of the Indian Muslims.

AS: That is one of the great disabilities of the Muslims.

MSA: Between the Dar-ul-Uloom and other schools of ulema, together they have issued several lakh fatwas. Some have been collected and codified. The bulk of them are papers floating in the air. How do you think this differs from crores of Hindus going to sages, even godmen, and asking them questions about themselves, about their lives? Why does it disturb you so fundamentally that believing Muslims in their lakhs go to religious leaders when it doesn't seem to disturb you in the same way that there are crores of Hindus who seek out their spiritual superiors for advice in exactly the same way?

AS: There are several situations. A Hindu could be as good a Hindu as anyone else even if he followed no spiritual advice. Gandhiji is a classical case. In Islam, that is not possible, because there is a reference point to which you can go back, to which the authority would go back.

Dr A.R. Bedar, the director of the Khuda Baksh Library in Patna, when he was declared a 'kafir' by a campaign carried out by your own colleagues' paper in the Congress, had to run from pillar to post to get another fatwa which said: 'No, we've listened to what he's said and it doesn't amount to *kufr.*'

Second, the advice that the sages would give to the Hindus would be like the advice given to Arjun by Krishna, internally directed, rather than externally directed. This is a major difference.

MSA: But in your book, there are several instances when leading theologians have differed among themselves in interpreting fatwas. They are not always internally consistent. So, the Muslims have a choice of going to another spiritual guru they might prefer if they feel a matter has not been settled.

AS: You've misunderstood the point of law. First, I can't convert from being a Shiite to a Sunnite; I cannot be a Barelvi today and a Deobandi tomorrow.

Second, the shariat itself is the product of such persons who often disagree with one another. A bogey has been created about it. How can you say it can never be touched when it is a product of people who fight about its interpretation?

Third, and most important, is the attitude to the Islamic state and the attitude to non-believers. On these, they (the ulema) are certainly of one mind.

MSA: So, your position is, since all maulanas return to the Koran, the Hadith and the Sunna as sources of knowledge, tradition and direction that in itself makes them people who cannot adjust to the modern world or to a non-Islamic society.

AS: That is a very good summing up.

MSA: In which case what you're saying is, anybody who is regarded as a good Muslim in the eyes of the ulema cannot be a good Indian or a good person in the modern world. Does that not make you an anti-Islamic fanatic?

AS: I knew that from the beginning you were just trying to lead up to these three, four, five words. Maulana Azad, Humayun Kabir, Dr Zakir Hussain and others…They were good Muslims, good men and great patriots. But when you view them from the eyes of the ulema they become deviants.

MSA: But they were part of the ulema.

AS: No, no…Dr Zakir Hussain faced the wrath of the ulema for a long time. Many of them were set upon by the ulema. But some of them were such great scholars.

MSA: The distinction between the ulema who were progressive, and those who were backward in their views doesn't come through because in your introduction (to the book) when you say 'the ulema', you refer to them as 'closed, medieval, antediluvian'. But from what you're saying, there are some members of the ulema who are 'closed, medieval and antediluvian' but others who are not. Yet, would this not be true of the priestly order of any religion? You are saying that the Muslim is in thrall of the ulema, and therefore, the best kind of Muslim is one who is not Islamic.

AS: That is a caricature of what I have said.

—*Sunday*, Kolkata,
September 1995

1

Secularism: An Overview

No word has been more bandied about in relation to the building of our modern nationhood than the word 'secularism'. It is a word of non-Indian origin with non-Indian connotations that has no precise equivalent in any Indian language and is yet central to our identity as a people. The resultant confusion has been ruthlessly exploited by those with an alternative concept of our nationhood, who view India in majoritarian terms as a Hindu nation (Hindu Rashtra) on account of our being a nation of approximately 85 per cent Hindus. They see post-independence India as a nation free from not only 200 years of British rule but also from the previous 700 years of rule by Muslim potentates. Thus, for the proponents of Hindu nationalism, independent India is not about independence from colonial rule but liberation from non-Hindu rule.

Curiously, this ideological construct does not take into account the period of nearly a thousand years of non-Hindu rule from Emperor Ashoka's conversion to Buddhism in the third century BC to the last great Buddhist monarch,

Harshavardhana of Kannauj, in the seventh century AD, interrupted only by three centuries of the revivalist Hindu empire of the Guptas. Neither does it account for the Jain and Buddhist kings and queens of southern India. By equating non-Hindu rule with rule by only Christians and Muslims, Hindu nationalism stigmatizes Christianity as a foreign creed propagated by missionaries; it is even harsher on the Muslim community, its beliefs and traditions, its history and heritage, and its contribution to the composite culture of contemporary India. Indeed, this composite character of our culture and civilization is seen as the bastardization of a pure Hindu flow; thus, 'cultural nationalism' becomes the preferred self-description of Hindu nationalists.

The origins of the making of contemporary India might be dated to the rise of national consciousness in the decades following the brutal suppression of the uprising in 1857, which the imperial authority described as the Sepoy Mutiny and which Indian nationalists of all hues call the First War of Independence. The clash between the exclusivist nationalist camps of the Hindus and Muslims, on the one hand, and the inclusivism of the secular nationalist camp (which included both Hindus and Muslims), on the other, is virtually as long as the making of the modern Indian nation. However, at no stage in the political evolution of contemporary India over the last century and a half have the rival conceptions of India's nationhood been the preserve of either a particular religious community or of rival political formations. Both perceptions, however incompatible, have uneasily coexisted in all religious communities and all political parties. And far from resolving the conflict over nationhood between alternative schools of Indian thought, the partition of India has added an external dimension to the issues in dispute, complicating further its domestic aspects.

The partition of India was as sudden as it was total. Through the whole of 1946, the Congress and the Muslim

League manoeuvred around each other like Sumo wrestlers, clinching, separating, retreating, to tactically determine what grip to spring next. It was not till early 1947 that the Quaid-e-Azam (Great Leader), Muhammad Ali Jinnah, was able to finally worst his political rivals in the Muslim-majority areas, particularly Khizr Hayat Khan of the Unionists in Punjab, and bring the Muslim League anywhere near realizing its distant goal of Pakistan—a goal so distant that till the spring of 1947 it seemed but a mere chimera. For, the Muslim League was quintessentially a party of the Muslim-minority areas of undivided India; its base in the Muslim-majority areas of the country was weak, opportunistic and uncertain. Yet, Pakistan could be realized only in such Muslim-majority areas. Thus, it was only by a cobbling together of disparate elements (much in the manner of our successive Janata Party/Dal experiments) that Pakistan came into existence. In March 1947, the All-India Congress Committee (AICC) accepted the inevitability of partition as the price for independence. Thereafter, in about half the time it takes for a child to be born, Pakistan was born.

From partition and independence in 1947 to the first general elections of 1952, the nature of our nationhood was the dominant political issue. But with Jawaharlal Nehru vanquishing the soft-Hindu school within the Congress by September–October 1951 and then going on to overwhelmingly win the first general elections in February 1952 on a hard secular platform (a platform I would describe as 'secular fundamentalism'), the secular basis of our nationhood remained virtually unchallenged for the next thirty-four years. This was largely because the first general elections of 1952 were also the first-ever elections held in India on the basis of universal adult suffrage. The results, therefore, established beyond argument that public opinion favoured a composite Indian nationhood. Moreover, although the electorate was overwhelmingly Hindu and every adult voter had a searing personal memory of the vicious communal massacres which accompanied partition, the vote was as decisive an endorsement of secular nationalism as it was a rejection of an alternative religion- or community-based majoritarian Hindu nationhood.

That national consensus on the nature of our nationhood was challenged significantly in the aftermath of the opening of the locks on the gates of the makeshift Ram Lalla temple within the precincts of the Babri Masjid complex at Ayodhya on the orders of the Faizabad district and sessions court in February 1986.

Since then, the debate between secularism and communalism has been restored to centre stage in the making of the modern Indian nation. The arguments which had been stilled or marginalized by the influence Nehru exerted have been resurrected, detaching us from the comforting anchor of the parameters on which our nationhood was being built, including the crucial anchor of secularism. The resumption of the dispute has been accentuated by the transition the country and the world have gone through in the last decade of the last millennium and which continues into the first decade of the twenty-first century.

In this turbulent revival of the maelstrom of rival ideologies, reminiscent of the rise of Muslim and Hindu communalism in the 1920s and 1930s, it becomes necessary to revisit every dimension of our secularism. Hence these confessions of a secular fundamentalist. I wear my secularism on my sleeve. But that is not enough. For every communal thrust, there must be a secular parry; for every communal sword, we must fashion a secular shield. The overall goal must be to restore secularism to the core of our nationhood as unambiguously and decisively as Jawaharlal Nehru succeeded in doing in 1951–52.

Let me begin by stating the obvious. In every village of India, in every basti and every mohalla, there are people of different faiths, languages and cultures, who live together as neighbours. While we are a multi-religious, multilingual, multicultural society, we are emphatically not a multinational society. We are one nation, one people. Furthermore, secularism and our nationhood are inseparable. Secularism is the bedrock of our nationhood. It is the sine qua non of our existence. A secular India alone is an India that can survive. And perhaps an India that is not secular does not deserve to survive.

Most civilizations posit nationhood and diversity as antithetical. The single greatest contribution of India to world civilization is to demonstrate that there is nothing antithetical between diversity and nationhood. Indeed, the celebration of diversity strengthens our unity, even as the imposition of uniformity gravely undermines national unity. No other civilization has as long a record as ours in evolving a composite culture. No other country has as long a record as ours of a polity based on secularism. Yet, the history of India is not the story of secularism vanquishing communalism. It is more the history of a kind of dialectic between the forces of secularism, tolerance and compassion, on the one hand, and the forces of communalism, fundamentalism and fanaticism, on the other. It is this never-ceasing battle that we are now called upon once again to fight.

So, what should we understand as secularism?

First, Indian secularism cannot be anti-religious or irreligious, for the bulk of our people are deeply religious. There is a rich vein of spirituality that runs through our culture, history and civilization. It is the source of most of our moral values. Therefore, unlike in Christendom, where the word originated, secularism in India is not about pitting the state against the religious authority but about keeping matters of faith in the personal realm and matters of state in the public realm.

Second, in a nation of many faiths, where people take their faith seriously, secularism must be based on the principle of equal respect for all religions (and for those who choose not to follow any religion). As Nehru once said, '[Secularism] means freedom of religion and conscience, including freedom of those who may have no religion. It means free play of all religions, subject only to their not interfering with each other or with basic conceptions of our state.'

However, in regard to affairs of state, secularism translates not into equal involvement of the state in matters pertaining to each religion but rather the separation of the state from all religions. In secular India, the state must have no religion. For the state, whatever religion an Indian professes or propagates must remain a private and personal matter of the citizen. The state should concern itself not with religion but with protection for all, equal opportunity for all, equitable benefits for all. No religious community should be singled out for favours; no religious community should be subjected to any disability or disadvantage.

Third, these two principles are reconciled in the Indian Constitution by making criminal law, and much of civil law, uniform for all citizens, but leaving personal law in the domain of each religious community. In the Directive Principles of State Policy, there is inscribed a direction to move towards a 'uniform civil code' but it is recognized that this can be done only with the consent of all the communities concerned. As the customs and usages, rites and rituals, traditions and practices of different communities are the very basis on which religious communities distinguish themselves from each other, the prospect of actually securing a uniform civil code is distant. The state has, therefore, provided through legislation such as the Special Marriage Act of 1954 and other such legislation the option of a personal law not based on religion, for any Indian who wishes to take advantage of it. The citizen who does so is not required to sacrifice his or her religion to come within the ambit of the civil personal law; so it is a law that is secular without being anti-religious.

Yet, the Hindu communalist is not satisfied.

It is not as if only the minorities have a personal law and

the majority does not. Indeed, Hindu personal law was codified after, not before, the civil legislation was enacted. Moreover, even fiscal law provides for a Hindu Undivided Family (HUF) without a similar provision for a joint family for any other religious community although most other communities do, in fact, have joint families. Significantly, no minority community has opposed either a personal law for the Hindus or the provisions pertaining to the HUF in our fiscal law; it is only Hindu extremists who, in the name of enacting a uniform civil code, insist on amending the personal laws of other communities without the consent of that community. The insulting argument, sometimes left unsaid but often loudly asserted, is that Muslim personal law tramples on fundamental freedoms and basic human rights, and as Muslims are incapable of humane treatment of their own kind, others have to do it for them. As this is a surrogate way of asserting the superiority of the majority way of life, Hindu communalists have made the question of a uniform civil code the centrepiece of their agenda.

Communalism thrives on denigration of the Other. We have seen this already in the Prologue. Secularism, on the other hand, thrives on respect for the Other. The only religion-based social practices that Mahatma Gandhi criticized and reformed were his own. He left it to the good sense of other communities to reform what was obsolescent or offensive in theirs. He was not concerned with asserting the superiority of his religion over those of others, but of learning, with respect, from the spiritual and moral traditions of the Other with a view to building on his own. Majoritarianism treats such an approach as 'appeasement' or *tushtikaran*. Tushtikaran means, in essence, a Hindu reading the Koran, as Gandhi did, without insisting that a Muslim reciprocally read the Gita. But, tushtikaran is alleged every time a privilege or protection is extended to a minority in the interests of preserving its identity. So, tushtikaran has become the favourite hate word of the communalist.

Integral to the question of secularism is that of nationhood. What is Indian nationalism? I would first like to share with my readers a summary of an analysis made by an Indian Muslim scholar before I share with them my own view.

I was impressed with Professor Rasheeduddin Khan's *Bewildered India*. Professor Khan posits two alternative visions of nationalism that confront the nation: 'segmentary nationalism' and 'integrated nationalism', underlining that the struggle between the two lies at the very heart of the emergence of modern India and the contemporary building of our post-independence (and post-partition) nationhood. He has no difficulty with, indeed applauds, even passionately, the need to assert 'sub-national and segmentary identities'.[1] At the same time, he sees that if such assertion stops at that, if it does not move on to the 'slow and painful development of a syncretic pattern of coexistence', the assertion of sub-identities degenerates into 'segmentary nationalism', disrupting the evolution of an 'integrated nationalism'.[2] It is this thesis that he elaborates with respect to the Hindu–Muslim relationship.

Professor Khan acknowledges that although the politically dominant Muslim elite of medieval India threw up 'persons of wide vision…in practically every century', the 'gravest lacuna in Muslim religious thought in India' was that even the 'liberal, rational and constructive' members of the ulema (theologians) never really succeeded in 'building a powerful trend or school of thought' that would transform the segmentary nationalism of the medieval Muslim ruling class into an integral nationalism.[3] This, however, could not prevent the persistence of a kind of subaltern integral nationalism, thanks to the traditional panchayat system 'at lower levels of civic life and local grass-root administration in the vast rural hinterland' which brought together persons belonging to diverse religious persuasions in running the life of the village community.[4]

Also, overshadowing the political and military dominance of the Muslim ruling class through all these centuries was

India's 'well-entrenched resilient Hindu civilization', the only one in a thousand years of world history neither to submit spiritually or as a civilization to an Islamic takeover, nor to insist on a fight to the end for a political and spiritual triumph over Islam. Professor Khan reminds the reader that 'the triumph of Islam, both as a religious movement and as a political power, was complete' in 'Zoroastrian Iran, Coptic Egypt, Berber pagan Maghrib (North Africa), Christian Sham (Syria) and Turkey (the Eastern Roman Empire), Buddhist Afghanistan, Buddhist–Shamanic Central Asia, and migrant, elementary, distorted Hinduism in Indonesia'.[5] In India, and India alone, did Islam come up against a civilization and a spirituality that stubbornly refused to be subordinated by an outside culture and an alien religion. Nor did India attempt to eliminate Islam, unlike what happened in Iberia after the collapse of the Muslim Andalusian empire.

If, however, the Indian experience was unique for Islam, so was the encounter with Islam unique for Hinduism. Other religions had been assimilated or marginalized; Islam alone could neither be swallowed whole nor be swept into a corner. 'The Hindus were shaken out of their insular mould and faced a phenomenon that had a trans-regional and transcontinental reach. The world's oldest belief system, the *sanatana dharma* [the eternal religion], secure and complacent in its continental enclosure...faced in Islam a growing tornado of alternative and, in many ways, contrary principles of law, social ethics and state-craft'.[6] Had this alternative paradigm been imposed on the people by the sword alone, either Hindu civilization would have perished or Islam would have been driven out, as it was from Europe at the Battle of Tours and at the gates of Vienna. In India, however, although Islam might have secured political and military dominance by the sword, the eminence it achieved as a civilization had little to do with force. Indeed, in Kerala and the Coromandel Coast of Tamil Nadu, where Islam made its appearance long before Mohammad Ghori, or even Mahmud of Ghazni, appeared at the Khyber Pass, there was no sword involved at all. For centuries, Islam in these areas was spread by seafaring merchants from Arabia who brought with them the fascinating new beliefs that had sprung up, suddenly but full-blown, in the deserts of Arabia. In other parts of India, the vast majority of the Muslims were indigenous people drawn from the community of 'artisans, craftsmen and exploited peasant *jaati*', who embraced Islam not because they were compelled to do so at the point of the sword but because 'Islam appeared' to them 'as a liberating and humanizing process for emancipation from a heritage of bondage'. In consequence, 'there is no prototype Muslim in India';[7] the community exhibits all the pluralism inherent in the pluralism of India.

Part of the confusion in the Hindu communal mind over the role of the Muslim in our nation and polity springs from three overlapping concepts that come 'historically' from the 'Arab awakening' in seventh-century West Asia (Mashriq): *qaum* (nation), *watan* (state) and *umma* (religious community). 'The Egyptians would say, as part of *qaumiya* we are Arabs, as a domiciliary reality Egypt is our *watan*, and as Muslims we are part of the Islamic *umma*.'[8] (This recalls the Frontier Gandhi Khan Abdul Ghaffar Khan's famous remark: 'I am a Pakistani for the last 40 years, a Muslim for the last 1400 years and a Pathan for the last 5000 years!')

The Hindu communalists seized (and still seize) on these three categories of identity—which do not have a counterpart in the vocabulary of Hindu India—to portray the Muslim of the subcontinent as an outsider, an invader, an alien whose *punyabhoomi* (sacred land) has never been his *pitrubhoomi* (Fatherland). It was V.D. 'Veer' Savarkar who started this charade. It is one of history's delicious ironies that in recent decades the Sangh Parivar has come to be almost wholly financed by Hindu zealots who have removed themselves from their pitrubhoomi, and who think of themselves as belonging to the Indian qaum even if their watan happens to be Britain or the United States, Hong Kong or Nigeria, and the whole of whose political ideology centres on the concerns of the Hindu umma!

Whatever might have been the thought categories of Islam in West Asia or North Africa, Islam in India has always been an Indian Islam. It interacted with the India that already was and, in consequence, evolved 'a mosaic of synthesis manifested in arts, craft, handlooms, music, architecture, miniature painting, poetry, the humanist literatures of the Bhakti school and the Sufis, culinary arts, sartorial fashions, jewellery etc'. The result is that 'India today, in all the glory of its medieval past, is as much a contribution of the Muslims as the Hindus'.[9]

This Composite Culture (his capitals!), says Rasheed Sahib, is composed of the following eight elements—the Vedantic vision; the Bhagawad Gita; the traditions of the Bhakti Marg; the central concepts of Islam—brotherhood, justice, charity, the rejection of a priesthood, the simplicity of dogma, monotheism, and mercy and beneficence towards the creatures of God in fulfilment of their 'obligations towards humanity' (*haq-il-ibad*); the message of the Sufi *silsilas* (orders); the elegance and the ethos of syncretic Indo-Muslim cultural values; the cosmopolitanism of modern urban development; and the heritage of the Indian national movement.[10] To his eight elements I would add: the Upanishads and the Advaita of Adi Sankaracharya; the teachings of the Buddha and Mahavir Jain; the seminal influence of the Syrian Christian Church and, subsequently, several different versions of the Christian faith, in particular the Jesuits and the Baptists; the Hebrew and Zoroastrian traditions; the best of renascent Europe as brought to us from the eighteenth century onwards through the best elements of the British connection; and now, of course, American coca-colonization!

Professor Khan adduces scores of examples of Indo-Muslim syncretism, drawn from a deep and profound understanding of Indian history, concentrating primarily on the Muslim contribution to this process of syncretization (the denial of which is at the bottom of Hindu communalism), citing examples of great Muslim divines, scholars, theologians, poets, savants and sultans, who have made the composite culture of India a living reality, and of the many, many Muslims for whom India has been pitrubhoomi and punyabhoomi more than it is for the NRIs whom the Sangh Parivar has roped into its cause.

For anyone who thinks of Muslims as dour zealots with closed minds (see the Prologue to this book), Chapter VIII of *Bewildered India*, 'Towards Understanding Hinduism: Reflections of Some Eminent Muslims' is distilled revelation. And for those who still think that history is about sultans and badshahs, Rasheeduddin Khan serves up a potted list of both the good (Zainul Abedin of Kashmir, Ibrahim Adil Shah of Bijapur, Quli Qutab Shah of Golconda) and the bad (Ghazni, Khilji, Aurangzeb) among Indian Muslim rulers. He fascinatingly juxtaposes 'two prototypes of Muslims in each epoch, those with a narrow approach and those with broader sympathies: Ghazni v/s Alberuni; Khilji v/s Amir Khusrau; Aurangzeb v/s Dara Shikoh; Jinnah v/s Azad'![11] The only point to remember is that Muslim kings, like kings and queens everywhere and at all times, were good and bad. Only the very naïve or the blinkered would think of all medieval monarchs as Aurangzebs or of all Hindu kings as Ramas.

The conclusions of Rasheeduddin's tour de force are primarily two in number. One I agree with. The other I don't. The first—the one I agree with—is that statehood based on religion will not work. Rasheed rests his case on the struggle for nationhood in Pakistan and Bangladesh. The effect is devastating:

> In India, triumphant nationalism, with overtones of secularism, continues to battle against irrepressible communalism—Hindu, Muslim and Sikh; in Pakistan, triumphant communalism has choked the prospects of

secular nationalism. In India, dominant secular nationalism is besieged by unreconciled communal forces; in Pakistan, entrenched Muslim communalism subverts sporadic assertions of democratic secular aspirations.[12]

He goes on:

India opted for socio-cultural pluralism, while Pakistan foreclosed its options by emphasizing religion as the major and determinate operative principle of its nation-building. Not only did this lead to the alienation of the non-Muslim population...even in the life of the majority it projected a conflict of loyalties of identity, between demands of modernized social change and adherence to a given dogma.[13]

This is the fate that will overtake us if our saffron Jinnahs were ever to overrun our secular nationhood.

It is Rasheed's second conclusion—that India is a 'bewildered nation' which has lost its way—I have difficulty accepting. Drawing parallels between the rise of communal violence and the rise of the Jana Sangh/BJP since the elections of 1967,[14] his mood of 'despondency, despair, anguish and anger'[15] reflects the national mood in the immediate wake of the destruction of the Babri Masjid, which was the period in which he put his book together. I draw quite the opposite conclusion in reading the national reaction, over the last decade, to the demolition of the Babri Masjid.

First, the BJP itself has had to downplay its role in the events leading up to the demolition of the masjid. And those who raised the slogan '*Ek dhakka aur do, Babri Masjid tode do*' (make one last effort, bring the masjid down) now deny that what they brought down was a masjid at all—the preferred expression is '*vivadit dhaancha*', a 'disputed structure'. The fact is that even as the place of worship was being brought down—

albeit a place of worship built by the votaries of another religion—the Hindu reaction was so adverse that the BJP began distancing itself from the issue almost as the bricks were falling. It is significant for the purpose of reassuring Rasheeduddin Khan and the millions who share his despair that the BJP now insists that it did not want to bring down the 'disputed structure'. For, it was a disgrace—and is widely perceived as such. India is not about to slough off its heritage of secular synthesis. We remain the only example in world history of a civilization that combines millennial antiquity and unbroken continuity with the celebration of heterogeneity. It is this civilizational genius of India that is now finding imitators in the globalized world of multicultural, multi-ethnic, multi-religious societies. As the world becomes more like India, India is not about to regress into a Hindu Rashtra.

Moreover, while the decade after the destruction of the Babri Masjid has seen the BJP emerge centre stage in the nation's polity, it has not been able to do so on its own. The largest number of seats it has ever won in the Lok Sabha was in the 1999 elections—a grand total of 179 in a House of 543, and that too when it was in alliance and, therefore, its vote was not divided by competing anti-Congress parties. It is this inability to come to power on its own that brought about the National Democratic Alliance (NDA), formed under the leadership of the BJP. The NDA partners, however, compelled the BJP to put on the back burner every element of its own programme relating to the crucial divide on the nature of our nationhood. The BJP Gulliver was thus entrapped by the NDA Lilliputians. The NDA could neither be formed nor sustained nor strengthened on the basis of a divisive agenda. And it was only by keeping Hindutva on the back burner that the NDA could hold together to fight—and win—the 1999 elections. They held on to the Treasury benches only by eschewing the quintessence of what the BJP stands for and providing an ersatz secular agenda for the governance of the nation. That is more than a ray of hope. For, it means that the BJP cannot win the heart of India on its agenda of an alternative nationhood for the country. Secular India is not about to give way to a Hindu Rashtra, which remains a private fantasy of the Sangh Parivar rather than the unstoppable demand of the majority community.[16]

This was also amply evidenced in the BJP eschewing, as best as it could, the contentious issues of a religion-based nationhood to concentrate on issues of misgovernment in the assembly elections in three crucial states of the Hindi belt—Rajasthan, Madhya Pradesh and Chhattisgarh—in December 2003. Or in the drubbing the incumbent BJP government received in the assembly elections in Himachal Pradesh in February 2003, which showed that the Hindutva agenda was not decisive even in a state with virtually no non-Hindu voters. Even its much-touted victory in the Gujarat elections in December 2002, after the assembly was prematurely dissolved in the midst of the worst state-sponsored pogrom that India has ever known, owed itself to the fact that in a virtually one-on-one fight, the Congress did not convincingly offer a clear secular alternative. A huge gap opened in the public perception between Congress rhetoric and Congress practice, a gaping abyss of credibility that gave rise to the currently fashionable expression 'soft Hindutva'. Had the alternative of hard secularism been on offer, the outcome might have been different.

There is, however, no cause for complacence. Three of the most communal faces of the BJP's second-line leadership are, in 2004, in key positions of influence in central India: Narendra Modi as chief minister of Gujarat; Uma Bharti as chief minister of Madhya Pradesh; and Dilip Singh Judeo, who runs a contemporary *shuddhi* (purification) movement through which he claims to have converted thousands of tribals from Christianity to Hinduism, is the power behind the throne in Chhattisgarh. And the first announcement the victorious BJP government in Madhya Pradesh made pertained to the installation of an idol in a place of worship common to Hindus and Muslims, while the Rajasthan government has decided to make the singing of *Vande Mataram* compulsory in schools.

Therefore, what has to be guarded against is not so much an outright victory for the BJP—for that will not happen short of an economic disaster or political cataclysm such as the Great Depression that brought Hitler to power—as the insidious spread of an ideology aimed at undermining the secular nature of our nationhood. That, of course, requires a hard secular response of the Nehru variety, or secular fundamentalism, as I prefer to term it. For, as Professor Bipan Chandra has stressed, secularism, in the Indian context, must 'mean, above all, opposition to communalism. It is not enough to be secular; one must also be actively anti-communal'.[17]

I put forward to Rasheedbhai and all Indians that India is not bewildered, the battle for secularism is not lost; it is not even being lost. But those who are bewildered must be shown the way out. And that requires the reiteration and propagation of the secular rationale of our modern nationhood. Those who wish to shatter this nationhood to bits to remould it nearer their heart's Hindutva desire are relentlessly at it. The secularist mistake has been to assume that the communalist has won. He has not. The ideological advance of the Sangh Parivar and the political advance of the BJP constitute a challenge which has to be met anew.

2

The Ideological Dimension

In the first half of the twentieth century, India's secular future was challenged largely by Muslim separatism. Since independence, India's secularism has been primarily—but not exclusively—challenged by 'Hindutva', whose ideological founders were Vinayak Damodar 'Veer' Savarkar (who invented the word 'Hindutva') and Madhavrao Sadasivrao Golwalkar, aka 'Guruji'.

Savarkar, say his admiring biographers Dhananjay Kheer and Jyoti Trehan, 'interpreted Indian history with a view to throwing light on the incomparable achievements of Hindus in different areas of life'. Savarkar's monumental work *Hindutva*, giving ideas of the principles of Hindu nationalism and Hindu state, was written in Marathi in Ratnagiri Jail in 1922 after his repatriation to the mainland from the Cellular Jail in Port Blair. Copies were made by hand and distributed. It was eventually published in Marathi under a pseudonym in 1925. In essence, Savarkar's thesis was: 'Every person is a Hindu who regards and owns this Bharat Bhoomi—this land from the Indus to the seas as his Fatherland (*pitrabhu*) and Holy land (*punyabhu*)—the land of origin of his religion and cradle of his faith.'[1] Savarkar's thesis thus excludes from the Fatherland, Muslims and Christians, besides Jews and Zoroastrians, the land of origin of whose religion and the cradle of whose faith necessarily lie outside 'the land from the Indus to the seas'. Savarkar added, 'We Hindus are not only a Rashtra, a Jati, but as a consequence of being both, own a common Sanskriti, expressed, preserved chiefly and originally through Sanskrit, the real mother tongue of our race.'[2] Thus, any Indian who traces his mother tongue to Turkish or Arabic or Persian or to Hebrew or Greek or Latin is denied a sense of belonging to the 'Rashtra'.

In a speech to the Hindu Mahasabha in Nagpur in 1938, he further said, 'We are Indians because we are Hindus and vice versa...India must be a Hindu land, reserved for the Hindus.' It is also important to note that Savarkar did not equate Hindutva, a political ideology, with Hinduism, the religion. According to him, 'Hindutva is not meant to be a definition of Hindu Dharma or Hindu religion...Hindutva is a new term for a new ideology, the ideology of "Hindu Rashtra"...These are the essentials of Hindutva: a common nation (Rashtra), a common race (Jati) and a common civilization (Sanskriti).'[3] He clarified in his presidential address to the Hindu Mahasabha in 1937: 'The concept of the term "Hindutva"—Hinduness—is more comprehensive than the word "Hinduism". It was to draw a pointed attention to this distinction that I had coined the words "Hindutva", "pan-Hindu" and "Hindudom" when I framed the definition of the word "Hindu".'

Savarkar's thesis of Hindutva so inspired Dr K.B. Hedgewar that 'before starting the volunteer organization known as the Rashtriya Swayamsevak Sangh [RSS], Dr Hedgewar had a long discussion with Savarkar over the faith, form and future of the organization'.[4] Thus, from the beginning, the RSS philosophy got interwoven with Savarkar's 'Hindutva'—which Savarkar regarded as 'Hindudom' rather than 'Hinduism' since he himself was an atheist—and became the cornerstone of the BJP's political philosophy and programme of action.

Apart from articulating that Hindus and Muslims were two antagonistic nations living side by side in India, Savarkar insisted that 'the Muslims cherish secret designs to disintegrate the Indian state and to brand the Fatherland of the Hindus with the stamp of self-humiliation and Muslim domination'. According to him, the theological politics of Islam divided the human world into two groups—the Muslim land and the enemy land, with the Muslim capable of loyalty only to the former, inhabited entirely by Muslims or ruled over by Muslims.[5] At his trenchant worst, he came up with the hysterical ultimatum: 'I warn the Hindus that the Muhammadans are likely to prove dangerous to our Hindu Nation...Let us not be stone blind to the fact that they as a community continue to cherish fanatical designs to establish a Muslim rule in India.'[6]

Savarkar was unfazed that neither during the freedom movement nor for the twenty years that he lived in independent India did the Hindu community take his ranting seriously. He was, therefore, obliged to leave this final will and testament: 'If you wish, O Hindus, to prosper as a great and glorious Hindu Nation under the sun...that State must be established under the Hindu Flag.'[7]

Jyotirmay Sharma, whose *Hindutva* is the most recent authoritative work on Savarkar and Hindutva, concludes (and frankly I cannot better him): 'Savarkar was both a daydreamer and a prophet. He was an angry, resentful, vengeful, violent and intolerant prophet. The RSS, VHP, BJP and Bajrang Dal continue to further his legacy of Hindu *jihad*.'[8]

It is this votary of communal prejudice that Vajpayee and Advani have honoured by hanging his portrait in the Central Hall of Parliament immediately opposite Mahatma Gandhi's.

The irony is inescapable—but it does reveal the true intent of the BJP and its Sangh Parivar.

Golwalkar's ideology is most clearly expounded in two works. First, *We, or Our Nationhood Defined*, a work so offensive to post-Hitler sensibilities that its authenticity is denied even by the Sangh Parivar. The RSS line is that this was an English translation by Golwalkar of a monograph by G.D. Savarkar (elder brother of V.D. Savarkar). This apparently exempts Golwalkar from responsibility for the views expressed. However that may be, Golwalkar was sufficiently enamoured of G.D. Savarkar to bring the man's world-view to the attention of the world. That is significant enough. The second book is undeniably by Golwalkar himself—*A Bunch of Thoughts*, whose provenance cannot be covered up even by the sophistry of the RSS.

The following sampling from pages 12 to 47 of *We, or Our Nationhood Defined* (in which diverse sentences have been run together to provide a coherent exposition of the G.D. Savarkar/ M.S. Golwalkar thesis) needs no further explanation or exegesis:

> Ever since the evil day when Muslims first landed in Hindustan...the Hindu Nation has been gallantly fighting on to shake off the despoilers. The Race Spirit has been awakening...National consciousness blazes forth and we Hindus rally to the Hindu standard, the Bhagwa Dhwaja [which the RSS still raises in preference to the national flag], set our teeth in grim determination to wipe out the opposing forces. We Hindus are at war with the Muslims, on the one hand, and with the British, on the other.

Holding Nazi Germany as a shining example of the highest manifestation of 'national pride', Golwalkar/Savarkar affirm that 'Germany has also shown how well-nigh impossible it is for Races and Cultures, having differences going to the root, being assimilated into one united whole. A good lesson for us in Hindustan to learn and profit by'.[9] And in an argument that is chilling in its stridently intolerant overtones, G.D. Savarkar says through the Guruji:

> ...as far as the Nation is concerned, all those who fall outside the five-fold limits (earlier defined as geographical, racial, religious, cultural and linguistic) can have no place in the National life unless they abandon their differences and adopt the religion, culture and language of the Nation and completely merge themselves in the National Race...There are only two courses open to the foreign elements, either to merge themselves in the National Race and adopt its culture, or to live at its mercy so long as the National Race may allow them to do so, and to quit the country at the sweet will of the National Race...the foreign races in Hindustan must either adopt the Hindu culture and language, must learn to respect and hold to reverence (the) Hindu religion, must entertain no idea but those of (the) glorification of the Hindu race and culture, that is, of the Hindu Nation, and must lose their separate existence to merge in the Hindu race; or may stay in the country wholly subordinated to the Hindu Nation, claiming nothing, deserving no privileges, far less any preferential treatment, not even citizens' rights.[10]

A Bunch of Thoughts reflects the post-independence, post-partition thinking of the Guruji. It might, therefore, be taken as a more accurate, certainly more contemporary progenitor of the philosophy of the Sangh Parivar and the ideology of the BJP. By the time he wrote *A Bunch of Thoughts*, the Guruji appears to have mellowed somewhat. Yet, when asked about Hitler and the difference between his organization and those of the Nazis, Golwalkar does not refer to Hitler's vicious racism, the Final Solution or the Holocaust, or the bloody orgy of his drive for world domination. Instead, Golwalkar limits himself to saying: 'Hitler's movement centred around politics. We try to build life without being wedded to politics'![11]

Golwalkar's brand of race and nation, stridently reflected off the pages of *Mein Kampf*, rings through *A Bunch of Thoughts*. While singing paeans of praise to the tolerance of Hinduism—much of it quite justified—Golwalkar relentlessly targets other religions: 'Buddhist fanatics invited and helped the foreign aggressors who wore the mask of Buddhism. The Buddhist sect had turned traitor to the mother society and the mother religion.'[12] He goes on to deprecate 'those Semitic religions—Judaism, Christianity and Islam' on the grounds that they prescribe a single way of worship for all: 'These creeds have but one prophet, one scripture and one God other than whom there is no path of salvation for the human soul. It requires no great intelligence to see the absurdity of such a proposition.'[13]

From denigration of other religions, it is but one step to the denigration of our minority communities, particularly the Muslims and Christians. Golwalkar says: 'Hindus, whatever the denominations of caste or sect, form a single society, and the Muslims and Christians belong to an alien and often hostile camp.'[14]

It is this dangerous combination of uncritical adoration of the Hindu heritage and contempt for the Other which is the hallmark of the 'Hindutva' way of life as propagated by Savarkar and Golwalkar. It has nothing in common with the 'Hindu way of life'. It is a repudiation of all that is great and good in the Hindu heritage and is based on a paranoid invention of the past and a future filled with hatred and revenge. It is this weltanschauung (a suitably Nazi word for 'world-view') that underlies the Sangh Parivar/BJP's philosophy of our nationhood. And, therefore, it must be fought.

This philosophy rests on the central principle that it is not enough for an Indian to describe himself by the attribute of his citizenship, that is, as 'Indian' or 'Bhartiya'. He must perforce also consider himself a 'Hindu'. The argument is that the word 'Hindu' does not appertain to a religion—the correct name of the religion being 'sanatana dharma'—but to a cultural identity, the specific cultural identity of the inhabitants of Hindustan.

I would have no trouble with 'Hindu' being the adjective for Hindustan if propagandists for the 'saffron cause' were to define 'Hindu' in cultural terms, as the composite of all the cultural influences that have permeated our existence as a nation, whatever its religious provenance. That would mean the assimilation into the 'Hindu' cultural identity of the values and ethos of not only Jainism, Buddhism and Sikhism (the three other religions which arose on the soil of India) but also of the numerous religions that arose elsewhere but secured adherents here. This, of course, is unacceptable to the Hindu nationalist. The 'culture' in 'cultural nationalism' refers to what they decree is 'Hindu culture', not the composite culture of Hindustan.

Dealing with precisely this etymological view of the words 'Hindu' and 'Hinduism', Swami Vivekananda had this to say in a famous speech at Madras on his return from the Chicago Parliament of Religions in 1897:

> The word Hindu was the name the ancient Persians used to apply to the river Sindhu. Whenever in Sanskrit there is an 's', it changes into 'h' in ancient Persian, that is how 'Sindhu' became 'Hindu'; and you are all aware how the Greeks found it hard to pronounce 'h' and dropped it altogether, so that we became Indians. Now this word 'Hindu'—whatever might have been its meaning in ancient times—has lost all its force in modern times; for all the people that live on this side of the Indus no longer belong to one religion. There are the Hindus proper, the Mohammedans, the Parsees,

the Christians, the Buddhists, and Jains. The word 'Hindu' in its literal sense ought to include all these; but, as signifying the religion, it would not be proper to call all these Hindus.[15]

Yet, the BJP/RSS, under the lead given by Lal Krishna Advani, insists that all those who live in this land call themselves 'Hindu'. Proffering Swami Vivekananda as a votary of Hindutva, they cite the above quote in justification of their view that all Indians are 'Hindus', the exact opposite of what Swami Vivekananda said! Vajpayee himself stated quite bogusly on 27 March 2002 and 6 May 2002 in exculpation and justification of the anti-Muslim pogrom in Gujarat that 'Swami Vivekananda spoke of Hindutva' and 'I accept the Hindutva of Swami Vivekananda'.[16]

This cannot possibly be true because Swami Vivekananda died twenty years before Savarkar coined the word 'Hindutva'. The progenitor of Hindutva is Savarkar and Savarkar alone. Therefore, any believer in Hindutva, such as Vajpayee and Advani, is an acolyte of Savarkar, not a follower of Vivekananda.

In an interview to the *Telegraph* in 1989 (and many times before and after that) Advani said that he wants to give our *Hindus* 'a consciousness of being Bhartiya'. This is an excellent objective which we can all heartily endorse. But he is clearly not content with giving our *minorities* 'a consciousness of being Bhartiya'. He insists that our minorities be imbued with the consciousness of being 'Hindu Muslims', 'Hindu Christians', 'Hindu Parsis', 'Hindu Sikhs', 'Hindu Jews' and, presumably, 'Hindu atheists'! This was exactly what Murli Manohar Joshi, as president of the BJP during his Ekta Yatra in 1991, told the *Sunday Observer*: 'All Indian Muslims are Mohammadiya Hindus; all Indian Christians are Christi Hindus.'[17] (Logically, then, a Hindu living in Pakistan should be an Islamic Hindu and Advani's many relatives in the Sindhi diaspora should be Christian Hindus in Canada and Confucian Hindus in Hong

Kong. And the Tamils of Sri Lanka should proclaim with pride, '*Garv se kaho hum Baudh Hindu hain*! [With pride we proclaim we are Buddhist Hindus!]')

In fact, going by a quote in the *Organiser* of 7 April 1991, Advani went a step further by saying that he would like the words Hindu, Bhartiya and Indian to be synonymous. How can they be, unless a Muslim or Christian citizen of India accepts that he is not Muslim or Christian but Hindu?

Even as he prepared for his Rath Yatra, Advani declaimed at Himachal Bhawan, New Delhi, on 13 August 1990, 'The Ram Janmabhoomi movement is the biggest cultural movement in history to unite crores of Indian hearts [note the subtle equation of 'Indian' with 'Hindu'] and assert the emancipation of *Hindu* [my emphasis] culture against the onslaught of medieval vandals and pseudo-secular and pseudo-intellectual elements.'[18] As Bipan Chandra points out, 'The term pseudo-secularism implies that those who profess to be secular are really not so but are really anti-Hindu or pro-Muslim.'[19] In Advani we have the authentic voice of 'positive secularism'— a shrill litany of complaints by an overwhelming majority against a cowering minority. The BJP is not impressed with the fact that the insurmountable majority of Indians—around 85 per cent—are Hindus. They will not rest till they have brought the remaining 15 per cent—particularly the Muslims and Christians—into conformity with their version of the 'Hindu way of life'. The Ram Janmabhoomi movement's loud and clear message, according to Advani, was that Hindu sentiment could no more be trifled with in this country. Who was trifling with this sentiment, he did not say, but nevertheless went on to assert to a gathering of BJP acolytes in Brent Council, London, in June 1990: 'Secularism has come to be equated with allergy to Hinduism.' He followed it with the outrageous parody: 'The practitioners of pseudo-secularism have to believe that though all Indians may be equal yet non-Hindus are more equal than Hindus!' (Note the parallel with Golwalkar's, 'But unfortunately, secularism in India has, in practice, meant anti-Hinduism for people at the helm of affairs.')[20]

The BJP just does not understand the desperate need of the minorities to adhere to and assert their identity. Instead, they see every act of sensitivity to minority concerns as 'appeasement' and every assertion by the minorities of their respective ways of life as a denial of 'justice' to the majority. Why a Muslim turning to Mecca to pray harms a Hindu is not explained, but nationalism is equated with religion and patriotism with majority communalism. The BJP has no confidence in the fact of the Hindu majority. They have no patience with the minorities' need of an identity. They cannot abide the colourful diversity of our society. Theirs is a catatonic obsession with the fear of being overrun.

What Advani's Rath Yatra did was to unleash across the country the lumpen elements of organized communalism into mainstream politics. It brought out the visceral viciousness of the anti-Muslim sentiment which fuels Sangh Parivar communalism, as illustrated by the following quote: 'Our problem is not Muslims but Islam...Islam is not a religion; it is a political ideology. In it, humanity faces a backward and undeveloped spirituality.'[21] And it was not some little-known fringe character but one of the BJP's top ideologues, Jay Dubashi (who has since had the wisdom of distancing himself from this lot) who wrote in the *Organiser* in all seriousness, even as the Advani Rath rolled towards Ayodhya: 'When a temple comes up at Ayodhya, the Punjab problem will be licked. When a temple comes up at Mathura, the Kashmir problem will disappear. And when a temple comes up at Varanasi, Pakistan will beat a retreat.'

It was not only contributors to the *Organiser* but demagogues of the worst description who were given a field day by the Rath Yatra and its aftermath. Sadhvi Rithambara was typical of this breed: 'Hindus, if you don't awaken, cows will be slaughtered everywhere. In the retreats of our sages will be heard the chants of "Allah-hu-Akbar". You will be responsible for this catastrophe, for history will say you were cowards.'[22]

These and other similar priceless oratorical gems reveal more about the true mindset of the Hindu nationalist than the careful evasions of the more sophisticated practitioners of communalism who lead the movement, politically and intellectually.

At the same time, Advani's Rath Yatra also gave a fresh impetus to cerebral communalism, best represented, I think, by two renowned journalists; one, the veteran Girilal Jain, long-time editor of the *Times of India* and, after his retirement, columnist for the *Sunday Mail*; the other, Swapan Dasgupta, till recently editor of *India Today* and now an official BJP media maven.

Throughout the turbulent year of 1990, as Advani advanced the Hindutva cause, Girilal Jain took to enlightening all and sundry on the glories of the Hindu Rashtra in the *Sunday Mail*, week after provocative week, right there on the editorial page, bang next to the lead article. Welcoming the Rath Yatra as 'a stroke of genius',[23] he proclaimed that it showed that the 're-Hinduisation of the country's political domain has begun';[24] that 'with Advani in the ascendant'[25] the Hindus, 'stirred as they have not been stirred before'[26] now 'possess an elite capable of rising to the occasion'.[27] The central issue of the nature of India's true nationhood, said Jain, is out of the 'private places' and into the 'public domain', because 'a body of disciplined cadres, which is available in the shape of the RSS' and 'a political organization, which too is available in the Bharatiya Janata Party', is leading us to 'a Hindu Government in New Delhi'.[28]

Girilal Jain is no longer with us, but the arguments he raised are the staple of secularism baiters, and provide as good an introduction as any to the issues involved. Secularism, said Giri, is the ersatz philosophy of those like me who he damned for their 'alienness, rootlessness and contempt for the land's

unique cultural past'.[29] As Giri saw it, secularism was a Nehru–
Gandhi aberration, consigned by the Advani Yatra to the
throes of a well-deserved rigor mortis. The 'natural inheritors'
of our country, said he, are not, as I had thought, all those who
live in this land—whatever their religion, or, indeed, lack of
it—but the 'Hindus' who 'for the first time in a thousand years
got in 1947 an opportunity to resolve the civilizational issue'.[30]
And what, pray, is the civilizational issue? The fact that, as Giri
himself put it, 'India has been a battleground between two
civilizations—Hindu and Islamic—for well over a thousand
years'.[31]

Swapan Dasgupta set out the stand of the saffron chic—
I call them 'the Hindus of Hampstead Heath'—in a review of
Religion, Religiosity and Communalism (edited by three
prominent cerebral secularists, Praful Bidwai, Harbans Mukhia
and Achin Vanaik) in *Biblio*.

Dasgupta began by asking: 'What is behind the secularist
intellectual's deep contempt of indigenous traditions?' The
answer quite simply is that the secularist intellectual has no
contempt for indigenous traditions. He only thinks there
exists, in addition to the indigenous traditions of Aryavrata
genesis, a large number of non-sanatani traditions, including,
in particular, Muslim indigenous traditions. Why 'in particular'?
Because the Hindutva mindset particularly insists on treating
India's Muslim traditions as non-indigenous. If *all* our
traditions, whether of 'Hindu' origin or not, are indigenous,
why 'Hindutva' in preference to 'Bhartiyata' or plain and
simple 'Indianness'?

Next, asked Swapan: 'Why are westernized Hindus so
prone to self-flagellation?' I am a westernized Hindu. So,
incidentally, is Swapan Dasgupta. I have never flagellated
myself on having been born into a Hindu home. My mother
spent the last twenty years of her life in the Sivananda Ashram
near Rishikesh. She never seemed to have any difficulty in
reconciling her pious religiosity with her secular outlook. She

certainly never imagined that it was incumbent on her to go around Ayodhya, chanting *Ek dhakka aur do* swathed in saffron scarves. The only jam sessions I attended on Saturday evenings as a teenager were bhajan *mandalis*. I enjoy a beer in a Hampstead pub quite as much as Swapan, but my composite being has as much place for bhajans as for beer. I believe it is the antithesis of the Hindu tradition to reserve a distinct and, worse, superior place for so-called 'Hindu' traditions over the other traditions of India. I know my pious Hindu mother would have been scandalized at the suggestion that any one Indian tradition was more 'indigenous' than another. She was, after all, a good Hindu. Swapan Dasgupta—and those of his inclination—are political Hindus.

Swapan's third question is: 'Is secularism a badge of commitment or an employment opportunity?' Well, going by the number of passed-over officers in the foreign office, former accountants-general, superannuated chief secretaries, retired generals and directors-general of police the BJP has taken on, I would guess Hindu fundamentalism is, indeed, a post-retirement employment opportunity, and that the Shyama Prasad Mookerjee Foundation is not a bad perch for those who flunked the IAS exam. The secularist NGO collecting his wad from the welfare ministry can at least comfort himself with the thought that his loot has come from an indigenous taxpayer, not some Hampstead *crorepati* whose corner of some foreign Heath is forever Hindu.

Let us take then Swapan's next problem. 'Is there,' he asks, 'a link between anti-Hindutva and upward social mobility?' Oh, yes, there is a link between anti-Hindutva and upward moral mobility; possibly, even between anti-Hindutva and upward social sensibility. But given the saffron chic that is overtaking our establishment, as radical chic overtook the West in the 1960s and 1970s, I would imagine that good old-fashioned secularism at, say, St Stephen's College, is passé compared to the neo-liberalism of Swapan's Young Fogie Right.

All the preceding questions are, by the way, more designed to show how incisive Swapan is than to address the crux of the whole debate. Which lies in Swapan Dasgupta's last rhetorical question: 'Is there a correspondence between those who despise Hindu nationalism and those who see India as an ethnic menagerie?' In a word, the answer to that is: Yes! What is narrow-minded and wrong-headed about Hindu nationalism is that it reduces the glorious diversity of India into the dull uniformity of its majority religion's alleged cultural profile. The very expression Swapan uses—'ethnic menagerie'—shows the contempt in which he holds the 15 per cent segment of Indians who, by definition, are excluded from embracing Hindutva. It is really this distinction—between those like me, who are 100 per cent Indian, and those like Swapan, who are at best 85 per cent Indian—that lies at the root of the argument over whether it is the secularist view or the Hindutva weltanschauung that is the right one for India. I have resorted to the German expression because 'ethnic menageries' were very much the concern of a man whom Swapan's political guru, Guruji Golwalkar, greatly admired: one Adolf Hitler!

Swapan sees this. Unlike many less intelligent of his cohorts in the Sangh Parivar, Swapan understands that Hindu nationalism is an alternative vision of the nature of India's nationhood. That is why it must be fought tooth and nail. And victory will go not to the party which co-opts the moneybags of Hampstead Heath but to those who mirror the Indian and, therefore necessarily, the Hindu view of India. That view prefers Indian nationalism to Hindu nationalism.

Pamphleteers of Swapan's persuasion believe that the Hindu in modern India sees Indian nationalism as coterminus with Hindu nationalism. The Hindu, they believe, is confused at the suggestion that there might be other strands too to the nation's identity. Yet, ever since 1952, when Indians first went to the polls on the basis of adult franchise and returned only two saffron supporters to the first Lok Sabha, the propagandists of the saffron brigade have failed to explain why Hindu nationalism has held such little appeal to the Hindu majority. The answer, of course, lies in the oft-repeated obiter dicta of the Sangh Parivar: that India is a secular country because Hinduism is a secular religion.

Precisely. That is precisely why the majority of Hindus reject the view that India is exclusively—or even primarily—for its Hindus; or that the nationhood of modern India should be based on a reading of the past which declares as apostate a thousand years of Indian history. It is the ordinary, non-English-speaking resident Indian who sees this most clearly. Whatever the provocations of the NRI-funded Sangh Parivar, the Indian who has chosen India as his pitrubhoomi and punyabhoomi, in preference to Hampstead, wants to see India belonging to all its inhabitants, who do, in fact, constitute an 'ethnic menagerie', even if there are less pejorative descriptions possible of our unity in diversity.

Swapan seems to think he is on the winning side because the Hindi-speaking Hindu of Hindustan is now being liberated from the thrall of *angrezi/mlechcha* secularism. What he does not understand is that westernized secularists like me are only articulating in a non-Indian tongue the spirit of goodwill and brotherhood which we have learned from our own people, our own parents, our own culture and our own traditions.

In contrast, the BJP and the Sangh Parivar make brotherhood and goodwill contingent on the acceptance of their terms of nationhood. As articulated by Satyadeo Singh—among the most eloquent of BJP back-benchers during my first term in Parliament in the tenth Lok Sabha—during a debate on 29 November 1993 on the proclamation of President's Rule in Uttar Pradesh, 'When we talk of Ram, it is of our nationhood that we speak.' Moreover, he went on, when we talk of the Ram Mandir, it is a question of 'strengthening the country'; one's mind then runs to countering conspiracies and terrorism.

Consider the almost Joycean stream of thought. Note the

free association of Ram with nationhood, and the seamless connection of this with conspiracies and terrorism that weaken the nation. Anyone who does not believe in Ram becomes an enemy of the nation, a terrorist, a spy. The litmus test of patriotism becomes adherence to Ram and to a nationhood built on fidelity to the majority religion. It is this mentality, this mindset that is at the root of Hindutva. Whatever siren songs Atal Behari Vajpayee sings to the Muslims (e.g. his '*Bismillah*' at the start of the Kashmir debate), when it comes to the crunch it is the verities of Satyadeo Singh, not the archness of Vajpayee, that determine the BJP's course. That is why the Babri Masjid fell. The BJP leadership lost control. The Satyadeo Singhs and Vinay Katiars took over. If you want a glimpse of what will happen after the 'saffron revolution' comes, you should listen not so much to the sweet but irrelevant reasonableness of the Vajpayee position or the opportunistic sophistry of Advani, but the authentic Hindutva accent of the Sadhvi Rithambaras and Pravin Togadias. Then alone will the full horror of Hindustan under Hindutva dawn on you.

These voices—Girilal Jain's, Swapan Dasgupta's, Satyadeo Singh's—are among the most articulate of those who have an alternative vision of the meaning and purposes of India as a nation, India as a civilization. But, unfortunately for them, the BJP is up against the bedrock of Hindu secularism which, even at the height of the worst incitement to religious sentiment, instinctively opts for a clear distinction between religion and politics. As history has repeatedly shown, to mix religion with politics is *not*—emphatically *not*—the Hindu way of life. The BJP's problem in attempting to articulate a Hindu way of life is that it resorts to the utterly un-Hindu way of mixing religion with politics.

The one reason I view our unique cultural past with pride is that I do not see the story of our civilization as, to use Girilal Jain's word, a 'battleground' in which the majority community has always been worsted. I see our civilization as the unique example in world history of an unbroken civilization that has survived millennia of turbulence and disruption—spiritual and intellectual as much as economic and political—only because of its utterly unique capacity to synthesize and move forward. Ours is the only major civilization in the world to combine antiquity and continuity with heterogeneity, the only one whose unity derives not from uniformity but diversity.

In India I see a civilization whose majority religion had the incredible genius to take 4500 years (at least) to evolve from the Vedas to the Vedanta. For that is how long it took from the first recitation of the opening lines of the *Rig Veda* in the lost mists of antiquity to Adi Sankaracharya's delineation of the Advaita in the ninth century AD. The Hindu religion, perhaps the only one among the major religions of the world, had the strength and the self-confidence to know that Truth is not revealed in an instant or in a flash but evolves through a long process of absorption, assimilation and synthesis. Thus it is that our civilization has incorporated in it all new thought and new ethical values it found of excellence, whatever the ethnic or racial source they came from—the Dravidians, the Greeks, the Scythians, the Huns (Mongols), the Persians, the Turks, the Arabs—and from whatever religion they emanated— be it Buddhism, Jainism or Sikhism (all three of which the Sangh Parivar loves to club with Hinduism) or Christianity and Islam.

It is this profoundly eclectic, humble, inclusive and quintessentially Gandhian recognition that no religion taken in its traditional sense could serve as the basis of a universal faith or religion which the Hindutva brigade transgress when they make the superficial and deeply offensive claim that India is secular only because Hinduism is secular.

There is nothing 'unique' to our history if it is viewed only through the prism of a string of conflicts, a succession of wars, a pendulum oscillating between victory and defeat as one feudal fought another and one king trampled on another's domain. That is the history of all humankind all over the world. What makes our civilization unique is its capacity to incorporate other influences. Remarkably, many of the greatest virtues of our civilization—non-violence, compassion, tolerance, equality—owe at least as much to non-Hindu sources (Buddhism, Jainism, Christianity and Islam) as they do to the Vedas, the Puranas and the Upanishads. For, ours is a legacy of an Indian civilization and not, as our VHP/RSS/BJP friends would have it, a civilization to which Hinduism alone has made a worthwhile contribution.

In contrast to the BJP–RSS tradition, which looks back in anger seeking to set right the imagined wrongs perpetrated on India more than a thousand years ago when, they say, Bharat was stolen from the true Bharatvasis, the Gandhi–Nehru tradition exults in our composite culture. It not merely accepts but celebrates the immense variety of India. It does not just come to terms with diversity; it treats diversity as the cornerstone of our unity. It is a tradition that holds that if India is not a palimpsest of every major—and several minor—religions of the world, it would not be the Bharatvarsha we have known for 5000 years and more.

The choice for the secularist is not, as is often mischievously or maliciously projected, between secularism and soft Hindutva, but between soft and hard secularism. In terms of principle, the secularist has no difficulty in projecting a clear secularism easily differentiated from the idiom and concerns of the Hindutva brigade. But when it comes to the application of secular principles (over which there is no dispute) to specific issues (over which there is dispute), confusion does arise between the hard line and the soft line. Soft secularism is to be commended for its sensitivity to communitarian concerns, majority and minority. Hard secularism has the disadvantage of being easily portrayed as anti-religious in a country that is deeply religious.

Communal forces raise issues which are communitarian in origin and communal in expression. The classic example is the Ram temple at Ayodhya. The communitarian desire for a temple at the Ram Janmabhoomi is perfectly understandable. A secularist need have no difficulty with the demand. But when this communitarian demand is projected not as '*mandir banayenge*' but as '*mandir* wahin *banayenge*', and that too as '*Ram ki saugandh hum khaatey hain, mandir wahin banayenge*', the communitarian demand becomes communal, for 'wahin' does not refer to the location in general but to the *garbha griha* of the temple being built at the exact location of the *mirab* (the niche in a mosque's *qibla* or wall which points to Mecca) of the masjid, entailing the dismantling of a minority place of worship for the construction of a majority place of worship. That is when a communitarian demand becomes a communal demand.

That is also when a secular response becomes imperative. But that, alas, is usually when secular forces in politics (as distinct from secular forces not in politics) tend to shy away from or inordinately delay a response. This applies perhaps most of all to the Congress, which is, after all, the most pervasive and widespread political challenge to the BJP. What the Congress must realize is that an imitative response makes no ideological or even political sense—for the issue has been chosen by the Other, it is being played out by the Other on a field of its choosing and if, by omission or commission, we yield ground to the Other, it will always and invariably be advantage BJP. Therefore, on issues raised by the BJP and its Sangh Parivar, a rapid-action, hard, secular response is the only valid response possible. When, however, the Congress projects secularism on its terms, on issues raised by it as distinct from responding to issues raised by the Other, the party must combine, as Mahatma Gandhi particularly did, an unyielding secularism with sensitivity to religious sentiment and communitarian considerations.

What secular political forces must avoid is a vacuous 'middle path' of the kind that led the P.V. Narasimha Rao government to the disaster at Ayodhya. For, there are times when 'those on the middle path are knocked down by traffic from both ends'. I owe the felicitous phrase to K. Natwar Singh on Atal Behari Vajpayee: it applies also to the choice the Congress must make to re-emerge as the standard-bearer of secularism as Nehru did half a century ago. Soft secularism of the V.N. Gadgil–K.M. Munshi kind (Bharatiya Vidya Bhavan secularism, I call it) will not make the Congress the champion of the secular cause. In the face of today's challenge, a hard secular line of the 1949–51 variety à la Jawaharlal Nehru is the only way of corking the communal genie for the foreseeable future. I am confident the strong secular line will prevail. India is secular because its people are secular. They will not acquiesce to the building of our contemporary nationhood at the behest of sadhus or mullahs or padres; it is a secular India at peace and harmony with itself that they want.

There is an unbridgeable gap between what I call 'secularism' and what the BJP calls 'Hindutva'. My vision is cradled in what Mahatma Gandhi taught us: that India's unity rests in its diversity; that everything which celebrates our diversity strengthens our unity; and that every attempt at forging unity through uniformity imperils our unity. This approach to national integration incorporates, of course, the dimension of religion and religious community. A profound believer himself in the religion we call Hinduism, Gandhi warned against basing our nationhood on the culture or beliefs of the major religious community. Our nationhood, if it were to be moral and if it were to last, had to recognize, he said, that India was both the largest Hindu congregation in the world and one of the largest Islamic congregations in the world, not to mention home to virtually every religion, major or minor, that humankind has embraced. For the passion and persistence with which he held to this vision, even as India went through the trauma of partition, Gandhi was assassinated by a madman who espoused an alternative view of India as a nation. Nathuram Godse, the assassin, was the editor of a journal called *Hindu Rashtra*. A Hindu Rashtra is, of course, the rationale and raison d'être of the Sangh Parivar, of which the BJP is the most prominent member.

The real danger before the country is not a BJP electoral victory. The real danger lies in the rest of us seeking to thwart the rise in electoral support to the BJP by becoming pale imitations of the original. We are faced with a replay of the challenge that Nehru faced between 1949 and 1951. The BJP phenomenon was born in a blaze of communal frenzy in 1951. It appears to have reached its apotheosis now, fifty years later. Nehru proved that unalloyed secularism was not only the right moral response, but it was also the politically winning response. Those who wished then to mimic Shyama Prasad Mookerjee, either out of conviction or with an eye to electoral gain, lost out—both morally and politically. It is a lesson of history that might well be learnt by all those in secular politics today—whether outside or inside the Congress.

The Congress and other secular forces would, therefore, do well to heed the warning given by Professor Bipan Chandra: 'Concessions do not lead to the recession of communalism; they lead to the popularisation and spread of communal ideology; they make communalism more respectable.'[32]

3

The Historical Dimension

The origins of our secularism lie in the encounter between the Aryans and the Dravidians at the commencement of our recorded history as a civilization. It is well illustrated in the contrast between the treatment meted out to Ekalavya at the start of the Mahabharata and the reverence to Siva (Dakshinamurti—God of the south) expressed later in the same epic over Siva teaching the Pandavas the mysteries of the Brahmastra. Ekalavya, the non-Aryan, is excoriated for learning the Aryan art of archery so effectively that he outshines even the disciples of Dronacharya. An infuriated Dronacharya, Teacher of Teachers, enquires from whom Ekalavya learned his skills. Ekalavya leads him to a statue he has built of Dronacharya as the source of his inspiration. At this, Dronacharya demands his gurudakshina, which Ekalavya willingly offers to tender. Dronacharya demands Ekalavya's right thumb as his recompense. And Ekalavya immediately slices it off, ending his career as an ace archer and thus saving Aryan honour. Such was the contempt in which the lesser breed was held.

But when the Pandavas are exiled to the forest, the

Dravidian god, Siva, appears before them in the guise of a tribal chieftain, thus underlining his non-Aryan identity. He then imparts to Arjuna, paragon of the Aryan order, the secret knowledge that eventually enables good to triumph over evil and injustice to be worsted by justice.

Inexorably, it was such assimilation leading to eventual synthesis that progressively, over centuries, converted Aryavarta into Bharatvarsha.

Between the *Rig Veda* (completed in 1500 BC) and Adi Sankaracharya (AD 788–820) was a history of several thousand years during which a host of home-grown schools of philosophy interacted with spiritual influences from outside, imparting a rich diversity of spirituality to our civilization and influencing its unique symbiosis of the many different strands which have gone into the making of our culture. Thus, the special genius of Hinduism lies not in instant revelation but continuous evolution.

One sees this in the unfolding of Buddhism and Jainism in the country. They rose as rebel religions out of the womb of Hindu society, spread till they ousted Hinduism as the state religion, but so influenced the further evolution of Hinduism itself that Hinduism acquired its final shape only with the Advaita of Adi Sankaracharya in the early ninth century. And it was only after Adi Sankaracharya that the political revival of Hinduism under the Guptas (fourth to sixth centuries AD) acquired the spiritual momentum to restore Hinduism as the first religion of the country.

As Dr Sarvepalli Radhakrishnan put it in his renowned Oxford lectures on *The Hindu View of Life*:

> Throughout the history of Hinduism the leaders of thought and practice have been continually busy experimenting with new forms, developing new ideals to suit new conditions. The first impulse came when the Vedic tribes came into contact with the native

tribes. A similar impulse contributed to the protestant movements of Jainism and Buddhism when the Aryans moved into the Gangetic valley. Contact with the highly civilised Dravidians led to the transformation of Vedism into a theistic religion.[1]

Contrast this interpretation with the twist given to the tale by Guruji Golwalkar:

> Who was it that came up as the redeemer of our dharma and our society? Sri Sankaracharya! Buddhism, as a distinct sect, was erased from the mother soil, though, of course, the Buddha remained as an incarnation.[2]

The Sangh Parivar likes to call the religion not 'Hinduism' but the sanatana dharma. It is a misnomer. Adi Sankaracharya came two centuries after Prophet Mohammad. Hinduism is thus both the most ancient and the most recent of the great religions of the world. The sanatana dharma of the Sangh Parivar has little to do with the evolutionary traditions of Hinduism. It is a stultified version of the Vedic dharma, stultified and, therefore, perverted. In this significant sense, it is doubtful whether the practitioners of Hindutva would qualify as Hindus at all!

Apart from Buddhism and Jainism, two other significant forces entered the subcontinent before the Hindu revival. The first were the Greek through the satrapy of Seleucus Nikater and the Kushan empire of the Scythians. It is a tribute to the inherent power of synthesis in our civilization that whereas all the Romano–Greek ruins from Volubilis in Morocco to Persepolis in Iran are clones of the original, in the belt from Bamiyan in Afghanistan to the images recovered at the site of the Taxila University between Peshawar and Rawalpindi, the technique might be heavily Greek but the theme is Indian and Buddhist.

The second powerful influence was Christianity. It overwhelmed much of the existing civilizational and spiritual order wherever it spread and took root elsewhere in the world but arrived in India peaceably with one of the apostles, St Thomas, as early as AD 52, to coexist with extant religious and spiritual beliefs with little backlash or controversy. Thus the Syrian Christian Church in India pre-dates the establishment of the Catholic Church. Nearly a millennium and a half later, the Jesuits arrived with the Portuguese and Spaniards. There is little in the story of the spread of Christianity in India to suggest that the Christian advance took the form of armed conquest, except for the wresting of Goa from Adil Shah of Bijapur in the early sixteenth century. That significant aberration apart, the spread of Christianity in India is a story of spiritual suasion, not of conversion at the point of the sword. The contrast with the manner in which the same Iberians Christianized Latin America is striking.

Contemporary north-east India, of course, contains at least three states which are largely, indeed almost entirely, Christian: Meghalaya, Nagaland and Mizoram. All three states took to Christianity through intrepid Baptist and other missionaries who went where virtually no Hindu had dared to venture and, over a period of about fifty years between the last quarter of the nineteenth century and the first quarter of the twentieth, harvested the hill men's souls for Christ. The Jesuits, Presbyterians and others were also active in this period, establishing tribal Christian communities in central India, from Orissa across the belly of India to the Dangs district of Gujarat and the union territory of Dadra and Nagar Haveli and into Diu, the former Portuguese enclave on the Saurashtra coast. They profited from the protection of the Union Jack (and other forms of colonial occupation), but it was by and large through good deeds that they propagated the church's mission.

Mention may also be made at this point, before we move

to the defining symbiosis of Hinduism and Islam, of a part of the Jewish diaspora finding a haven in and around Kochi (Cochin) in Kerala, and the Zoroastrians (Parsis) driven from Persia who found refuge in coastal Gujarat. Both communities were left unmolested and flourished over centuries, losing nothing of their religious identity but synthesizing their language, culture and way of life with those around them. The Jewish community gave us Nissim Ezekiel, perhaps our most outstanding English-language poet, and Brigadier J.F.R. Jacob, later general and governor of Goa and Punjab, who organized the surrender of the Pakistani armed forces at Dhaka. The Zoroastrians gave us the great early nationalists, Dadabhai Naoroji and Pherozeshah Mehta; the pioneering industrialist, Jamsetji Jeejeebhoy Tata; the founding father of Indian nuclear science, Homi Bhabha; and the field marshal who worsted the Pakistanis in the Bangladesh war, the inimitable Sam 'Bahadur' Manekshaw. If by being kind to a minority of a few lakh we get so much in return, how much more do we stand to benefit from common humanity towards 150 million of our fellow citizens of the Muslim minority community?

The aim of this potted history of our tradition of synthesis, which has made us heir to the only ancient civilization maintaining its unity through heterogeneity rather than homogeneity, is really to set the stage for an understanding of India's encounter with Islam. This began in south India in the century of the Prophet but reached north India nearly a hundred years later in AD 712 with the transgression of Mohammad bin Qassim who sailed up the Indus and defeated the local ruler, Raja Dehar. He returned to Damascus a few months later (with two of Raja Dehar's daughters in tow), only to be put to the sword by the Caliph who thought the young man had insulted him with the manner of 'gifts' he had brought back from Sind. Activists of the Sangh Parivar who wish to avenge themselves on Mohammad bin Qassim might be advised that their thirst for vengeance was sated by none less than the Caliph himself 1300 years ago!

It is pertinent to mention here that for all his misdemeanours, Mohammad bin Qassim took the utmost care to not give needless offence to local religious belief. This is evident from the following plaque placed by a Pakistani civil servant and chief of the local administration at the site of the mosque constructed by Qassim on the ruins of Raja Dehar's fort at Alore (Alrur) on the left bank of the Indus opposite modern-day Sukkur:

> Biladuri, speaking of Mohammad bin Qassim's march northwards, after the fall of Brahmanabad, says: 'At last he reached Alrur, one of the cities of Sind. It is situated on a hill.' Muhammad bin Qassim seems not to have interfered with the temples 'for the temples,' he said, 'shall be unto us like the churches of the Christians, the synagogues of the Jews and the fire temples of the Magians'.

The plaque is dated 23 March 1977, the thirty-seventh anniversary of the adoption of the Pakistan resolution at Lahore by the Muslim League in 1940 with 'repainting on 11.3.94, Ramzan-ul-Mubarak day' by the assistant commissioner, Rohri, followed by the stern admonition: 'The curse of God's wrath upon him who would try to destroy this stone!'

The late Bishambar Nath Pande, in his justly celebrated 1985 Khuda Baksh Memorial Lectures on 'Islam and Indian Culture', published by the Khuda Baksh Library, recalled that:

> Al-Hajjaj, governor of Iraq, uncle of Qassim and his immediate superior, wrote to him as follows: As they [the Hindus] have made submission and agreed to pay taxes to the Khalifa, nothing more can be properly required from them. . .Permission is given to them to worship their gods. No one should be forbidden or prevented from following his religion. . .[Accordingly]

> Qassim directed his nobles, the principal inhabitants, and the Brahmans to build their temples, traffic with the Muhammadans, live without fear and to strive to better themselves.

There was no further Islamic incursion from outside over the next 285 years. But Islam spread through the gentle Sufi saints, which gave Islam in Sind its definitive eclectic stamp. It was not till AD 997—nearly three centuries after Qassim—that Subuktgin forced his passage through the Khyber Pass. This opened the route for his son, the notorious Mahmud of Ghazni, who invaded India seventeen times over the next twenty-six years, plundering, among many other shrines and temples, the great temple at Somanatha, the ransacking of which has become the symbol of Muslim vandalism to not only the Sangh Parivar but many other Hindus too. Although historian Romila Thapar has conclusively established that the treasures of the Somanatha temple were always a target for Hindu rulers fighting each other (which is how Ghazni learned of the rich rewards for looting it) and that Somanatha's riches contributed significantly to Mahmud of Ghazni's subsequent efforts to establish renowned centres of learning and scholarship in Central Asia,[3] there can be no disputing that the raids of Mahmud of Ghazni exposed the vulnerability of India (now returned to Hindu from Buddhist rule) and the weakness of its defences.

It is astonishing, therefore, that after Mahmud of Ghazni a further two centuries were to elapse—195 years to be exact—before the Delhi sultanate came to be established in AD 1192, at the invitation, as it were, of Raja Jaichand who begged Mohammad Ghori to assist him in a family quarrel with his son-in-law, Prithviraj Chauhan. (Raja Jaichand's descendant, V.P. Singh, later compensated for his ancestor's mistake by clambering on to the prime minister's gaddi in 1989, kind courtesy the BJP. This, of course, opened the way to Hindu communalism, ousting V.P. Singh before the year was out. History, as T.S. Eliot once said, is full of 'cunning passages': the Lord clearly has a keen eye for irony and a wicked sense of humour!)

The two centuries between Ghazni and Ghori were notable for the spread of the message of the Prophet through large swathes of north India. Again, it was not the sword but the appeal of Islam that promoted its propagation through the five centuries from Qassim to Ghori when, for the most part, the state was not Islamic. Islam spread because it carried a revolutionary message—the message of equality between human beings at least in the eyes of god, if not in the eyes of badshahs and nawabs. Hindu India watched in astonishment and disbelief as slave and sultan washed in the same pool and bowed together before the mirab with no priestly intermediary between the petitioner and his Lord. Allah could be approached directly in the language of the petitioner and His blessings were for all, high or low.

This was a severe challenge to the entire Hindu philosophical and social construct. The fact is that the world is a very unjust place and much of its pervasive inequality is grounded in the accident of birth. Those born poor remain, with rare exception, poor; those born with a silver spoon in their mouth more often than not have the option of turning it to gold. The only explanation for the manifest injustice of the human condition is either to eschew a metaphysical explanation altogether or resort to the only satisfactory metaphysical answer ever given, in my view, to the conundrum of a just Creator and His unjust Creation: the Hindu theory of karma, the singular belief which unites all Hindu and related schools of thought, and distances Hinduism from all other schools of philosophy and religion. In karmic belief, inequality today is explained by the imperative of expiating the sins of a previous life or lives; but better positioning in one's next life is guaranteed by good works in this. The institutionalization of inequality in the caste system is thus validated—one's place in the hierarchy being the consequence of actions in the past and one's expectation of improvement in the next round being contingent on one's performance in this life.

Islam's message of *musawwat* (equality) presented the prospect of escape from such a relentless cycle of birth and death for those who found themselves subjected in this birth to prejudice and discrimination in the name of a divinely ordained inequality for crimes they could not remember. Many, therefore, converted to the new religion. Yet, Hinduism survived the revolutionary challenge of both the message of Islam and the sword of Islam. After nearly 700 years of Muslim rule from around AD 1200 to the end of the Mughal empire in 1857, the Muslim community remained a minority—about a quarter of the population being Muslim before independence and partition, and about 12 per cent in India as per the latest census figures.

The contrast with much of the rest of the world where Islam penetrated is significant. From North Africa to the Indonesian archipelago and out to the southern Philippines, Islam as a religion, a way of life and a code of statecraft overwhelmed and completely replaced all that went before. The advent of Islam opened not just a new page of history but a new page of civilization in these countries. This is well captured in Iqbal's evocative poem, *Yeh gumabde miani* (*These glass-spangled domes*), written in Granada, the centre of the Andalusian empire established in Spain. On the other hand, where Islam was worsted, as in Andalusia after 500 years of Muslim rule (which is the proximate cause of Iqbal's *Shikwa* [Complaint to God]), Islam has been vanquished without almost a trace. Only in the Indian subcontinent, Islam has neither triumphed totally nor has it been totally repulsed or entirely uprooted. Pre-Islamic Hinduism has flourished even as the subcontinent has become home to by far the largest community of Muslims in the world. There are more Muslims between Peshawar and Chittagong and between Kashmir and

Kerala/Lakshadweep (extending down to the Maldives) than in all of West Asia and North Africa, indeed, than in all of the area stretching from Xinjiang (Sinkiang) in China to the western reaches of the Sahara desert in Mauritania. Islam today is as inconceivable without India as India is inconceivable without Islam. Yet, the Muslims of India, and in South Asia as a whole, are a minority. How did Hinduism remain the majority religion even as Islam acquired its largest concentration of adherents in the same geographic region and the same political space?

The answer lies in our civilization's aptitude for fusion. It was not on the battlefield but in the heart and soul of every Indian that the question of Hindu–Muslim coexistence and Hindu–Muslim symbiosis was resolved.

The story of the Hindu spiritual response to Hindu orthodoxy and, later, its spiritual renaissance as the bhakti movement in synthesis with revolutionary Islam, begins in eleventh-century south India with Acharya Ramanujam, the Martin Luther of the Hindu reformation. Born into the priestly Brahmin caste, and a theologian and religious philosopher of renown, Acharya Ramanujam emerged, in a defining moment of defiance to narrow orthodoxy, out of the sacred precincts of the temple to impart religious instruction to the people. He did so not in Sanskrit—the language of religious discourse known only to a select few—but in the language of the people. Moreover, he spoke his profound spiritual truths not to the twice-born who wore the sacred thread but to anyone and everyone. He went further, dispensing with priests as the necessary intermediary between man and god and encouraging the worshipper to worship the god or goddess of choice or preference (*ishta-devata*) in the seclusion of the home, thus opening the doors to bhakti (devotion) for both men and women, breaking the stranglehold of an exclusivist caste and a mysterious sacrosanct tongue.

While Ramanujam launched the bhakti movement primarily

in response to the philosophical challenge of the Vaishnavite alvars who questioned the orthodoxies of the Shaivite nayanars,[4] over the next several centuries bhakti became the vehicle for synthesizing the ancient beliefs of the sanatana dharma with the social and cultural mores that came with the message of the Islamic Prophet. This movement reached the pinnacle of its achievement in the Sikh faith of Guru Nanak in the sixteenth century and took its final shape under Guru Gobind Singh (died AD 1708) whose span of life broadly corresponded to that of the last notable Mughal emperor, Aurangzeb. Through the teachings of Ramanujam and Ramanand in south India, Tukaram and Namdev in the west, Krishna Chaitanya and Sankardev in the east, Kabir and Mira in the north, and a host of others, the Hindu religion was rejuvenated, not in opposition to or in confrontation with the tenets of Islam (although sometimes with Muslim rulers) but by incorporating the lessons of Islam in terms of human rights, social customs and cultural practices, while retaining, indeed renewing, the spiritual springs of this ancient but ever-evolving faith. To cite Dr Radhakrishnan again: 'The reform movements of Ramananda, Chaitanya, Kabir and Nanak show the stimulus of Islam.'[5]

Hence the miracle of a three-fourths Hindu majority even after a millennium's encounter with Islam.

The communal challenge to secular India comes from those who understand nothing of our civilization's gift for fusion and who concentrate on historical instances of Muslim atrocities. That such atrocities were the currency of feudal power politics, as true of the atrocities which Muslim rulers inflicted on Hindu rivals as of the treatment meted out by Hindu rulers to each other and Muslim rulers to one another, is something they are unable to comprehend.

Hindu–Muslim relations entered a new phase with the crushing of the War of Independence in 1857, the extinction of the remains of the Mughal dynasty, and the embedding of imperial rule, which remained without effective challenge for about half a century till the early 1900s. It was the reaction to British rule and the aspiration to freedom that spawned the great historical forces which took us to both independence and partition. We need now to consider why and how the 'end of empire' also signalled a division of the spoils.

Mughal rule was the symbol of non-British rule even in 1857. And the mostly Hindu upper-caste mutinous sepoys from Meerut marched to Delhi not to establish a Hindu India but to restore Bahadur Shah Zafar, the last Mughal emperor, to the throne. The British initially concentrated on destroying the remnants of Muslim power. Moreover, while a section of the emerging Hindu elite had taken to modern education and the social reforms with which Raja Rammohan Roy is associated, the Muslim elite, by and large, remained sullen and resentful, nursing their nostalgia for a lost glory. While Roy showed the way to progress for the Hindus, it was left to Sir Sayyid Ahmed Khan to rejuvenate the Muslims who were still caught in the past. Sir Sayyid represented the new generation of post-Mughal Muslim gentry who realized that it was not in the interest of the community to nurture resentment against the British or be confrontational with them. Recognizing that for Muslims the way to development lay in cooperating with the British, he led the resentful community to the realization that 'British sovereignty cannot be eliminated from India', holding, as Rajmohan Gandhi puts it, that 'rebellion was folly and loyalty rewarding'.[6]

When, however, Lord Ripon introduced a limited one man–one vote democracy through elections to local bodies, Sir Sayyid, in a submission to Lord Ripon as early as 1883, articulated a minority perspective on democracy for India which eventually resulted in partition being the precondition for independence:

> But, my Lord, in a country like India, where caste distinctions still flourish, where there is no fusion of

various races, where religious distinctions are still violent, where education in a modern sense has still not made an equal or proportionate progress among all sections of the population, I am convinced that the introduction of the principle of election, pure and simple...would be attended with evils of great significance... [T]he larger community would totally override the interests of the smaller community.[7]

Here was the dilemma put bluntly and squarely. Should the one man–one vote principle override other considerations, or should democracy in India be weighted by community considerations to make it more acceptable to the minorities?

While Sir Sayyid was concerned with the Muslim community in elections even under British sovereignty, virtually the same concerns manifested themselves later in the freedom movement when it came to the Hindu and Sikh minorities in the Muslim-majority provinces of Punjab and Bengal and in the instructive story of the separation of Sind from Bombay province. There are, therefore, Hindu origins of partition too.

Contemporary communalism in India concentrates on Muslim separatism to the virtual exclusion of parallel concerns expressed by non-Muslims where they were in a minority. Therefore, before we take up the thread of the better-known story of Muslim separatism beyond the time of Sir Sayyid, who died in 1898, it would be appropriate to consider the lesser-known, less-told story of the Hindu origins of partition.

The Hindu Origins of Partition

The Story of Sind

The story behind the communal overtones imparted to the discourse relating to the separation of Sind from Bombay impinges least on contemporary India's understanding of the origins of partition. This is perhaps because Sind now falls entirely in Pakistan, in contrast to Punjab and Bengal which were divided between India and Pakistan with the Muslim-minority provinces remaining in India. Therefore, rather than recounting the causes of partition in all-India terms, as is usually done, or narrating events in more populous parts of India, let me begin with Sind where the minority Hindu population displayed exactly the same (unfounded) fears of subordination to the Muslim majority which the Muslim minority, in many other parts of British India, displayed in regard to domination by a Hindu majority. After Sind, I shall turn to other manifestations of the Hindu contribution to the partition of India.

For an Indian, the most riveting part of the Cambridge- and Oxford-educated Pakistani historian Dr Hamida Khuhro's biography of her father Ayub Khuhro is the story of the separation of Sind from the Bombay Presidency, effected eventually in 1936 but preceded by an agonizing struggle through the turbulent 1920s and tempestuous 1930s. Young Ayub Khuhro (born on 14 August 1901, forty-six years to the day before Pakistan came into existence!) was, through these years, in the vanguard of the struggle for the separation of Sind from Bombay in the teeth of opposition from the Hindu community which feared becoming a minority in Muslim-majority Sind instead of remaining in a decisive majority in Hindu-majority Bombay. It was the refusal of Hindu Sind to get swamped in a Muslim-majority province that got replicated through the following decade in the Muslim League's stand vis-à-vis the Muslim community in India as a whole getting overwhelmed in a Hindu-majority independent India.

The nationalist politics of the region till the decade of the 1920s was dominated by Rais Ghulam Mohammed Bhurgri and his Hindu comrade-in-arms, Harchandrai Vishindas. Communal harmony was the baseline of nationalist politics. Communal politics in Sind, as elsewhere in the subcontinent,

came into play only after the collapse of the Non-cooperation
Movement in 1921–22. Mahatma Gandhi had launched the
movement in 1919, with the restoration of the Islamic Khilafat
as the major objective, to bring Muslims on to the bandwagon
of the all-India independence movement. Muhammad Ali
Jinnah resigned from the Congress, protesting against this
injection of religion into politics. When the movement failed
to usher in freedom from colonial rule within six months, as
widely promised and implicitly anticipated, and Kemal Ataturk's
Turkey rejected the restoration of the Khilafat in its own
traditional seat of Istanbul, nationalist politics in India started
its historical split into competing religious nationalisms—the
Hindu Mahasabha on the one hand, and the Muslim League
on the other, with the Congress and Gandhi left holding the
banner of a secular India.

It was in this era of communal politics that young Ayub
Khuhro had his blooding. He had participated in a Khilafat
conference organized in his home town of Larkana in 1920 but
eventually got disenchanted, says his daughter, with 'Gandhi's
terms for self-rule and ideal government, couched in Hindu
religious language'. Ironically, instead of adopting a secular
idiom to promote his anti-Gandhian view of politics, Ayub
Khuhro comfortably slipped into the vocabulary of Muslim
communalism, thus aggravating, instead of sensibly bridging,
the Hindu–Muslim divide. Where he should have articulated
a composite Sindhi identity and a secular Sind as the alternative
to Hindu communalism, he wasted a great deal of his energies
fighting off Hindu opposition which would have been much
better spent fighting British obduracy in separating Sind from
Bombay.

It is, however, difficult to reprove the views of twenty-one-
year-old Ayub Khuhro when his elders and betters were talking
in the same tone. By the mid-1920s, and especially after the
passing away of the veteran Bhurgri in 1924, Vishindas led the
Hindus in determined opposition to autonomy for Sind because

such autonomy would render the Hindus, who made up the overwhelming majority in the Bombay Presidency, an insignificant minority in separate Sind. Thus ended the joint Hindu–Muslim, all-Sind campaign for a separate Sind whose leaders were as much Bhurgri and Shaikh Abdul Majid as Vishindas and Diwan Gidumal. The arguments these leaders had so far put forth for looking at Sind as a self-contained territorial unit were based on its distinctive geographical and ethnological features and did not have communal connotations. (After all, Bombay was nearly a thousand kilometres from Karachi by sea at a time when there were no air or rail links and land crossings were possible only on camelback!) Now, instead of looking at the issue from an administrative point of view, so as to improve the lot of ordinary people, the argument began to be increasingly addressed in communal terms.

The battle was joined before the Simon Commission which held its sittings in Karachi from 12 November 1928. The case for separation was put by the Sind Muslim Association led by Khuhro and assisted by Ali Mohammad Rashdi. The case against separation was argued by Professor H.L. Chablani of Delhi University on behalf of the All-Sind Hindu Association. While articulating the fears of being swamped by the Muslim majority, the Hindus argued against the separation mainly on the grounds of Sind's alleged inability to pay for itself. This was despite the Secretary of State for India, Sir Edwin Montagu, having concluded as far back as 1917 that Sind contributed more to Bombay than Bombay did to Sind. The essentially communal argument thus came to be couched in terms of Sind's financial viability or otherwise. The first round went to the Hindus. The Simon Commission rejected Sind's claim to autonomy, with Muhammad Ali Jinnah endorsing this view, although he advised his colleague, Syed Miran Mohammad Shah (also assisting the Commission), to put in a note of dissent.

Quick to recognize that the case for a separate Sind would be won or lost not so much in terms of communal mobilization as in persuading the British that they would not have to pay a price in terms of heavy government subsidies for separating Sind from Bombay, Khuhro hit back with his 1930 masterpiece, *Sufferings of Sind*. This took on the anti-separatists on the terrain they had made their own, detailing with facts and figures the inherent financial strength that Sind had to stand fiscally on its own. Professor Chablani issued a rejoinder titled *Separation of Sind from Bombay Presidency* with the subtitle 'A Story of the Sufferings of Sind', but Khuhro had made his point.

The First Round Table Conference, which opened in November 1930, set up Sub-Committee IX to look into the question of Sind. The anti-separation Hindu lobby was led by the diehard Hindu communalist of the Hindu Mahasabha, B.S. Moonje, while Jinnah and others, notably two Sindhi Muslim grandees, Ghulam Hussain Hidayatullah and Shahnawaz Bhutto (father of the future prime minister of Pakistan, Zulfiqar Ali Bhutto) steered the discussion into more rational channels. As a consequence, an expert body, the Financial Enquiry Committee, under Sir Miles Irving, was established to address the central question of whether autonomy for Sind could be granted on financially viable terms. When the Financial Enquiry Committee sat in Karachi from July to September 1931, Khuhro led evidence before it. The wisdom of talking out the issue in financial terms became apparent when the communal divide was broken and a number of Hindus argued the case for separation. Of course, the bulk of the Sindhi Hindus, including the aforementioned Professor Chablani, who tendered evidence before the Irving Committee were dead opposed to the separation.

While Khuhro had succeeded in focusing Muslim advocacy on the financial question, thus diluting the advantage which the Hindus had secured in doing the same before the Simon Commission, the Irving Committee concluded that Sind would have a deficit of nearly eleven lakh rupees. Therefore, British

Prime Minister Ramsay MacDonald, announcing his otherwise notorious Communal Award of 16 August 1931 after the conclusion of the Second Round Table Conference, agreed to the separation of Sind but subject to satisfactory means of financing it being found. Khuhro had won his first battle in securing British endorsement, in principle, for a separate Sind, but he was still to carry conviction that this was financially feasible. But from Simon to MacDonald, he had indeed come a long way. He was only thirty-one years old and without a degree (Ayub's father had died before Ayub could complete his degree, and, as the eldest son, he had to abandon his studies to look into the affairs of the ancestral estate). His opponents were professors of economics.

The British prime minister's statement led to the Sind Conference of April–May 1932 under the chairmanship of the Punjab ICS officer, A.F.L. Brayne. The chief antagonists were the selfsame Chablani and Khuhro. The Hindus made a mess of their case. The Brayne report noted that the Hindu members of the conference, who opposed the separation, contributed little to the debate while the majority who advocated separation demonstrated that the problems associated with the separation could be overcome. Khuhro had stolen the Hindu thunder by appropriating the Hindus' financial garments. An autonomous province of Sind was on its way. But there were still the final skirmishes to be fought.

In tandem with the Third and final Round Table Conference which convened in London at the end of 1932, the House of Commons established a Joint Parliamentary Committee (JPC) to examine the draft legislation which was to become the Government of India Act, 1935. In April 1933, the JPC decided to ask witnesses from Sind to depose before it on the question of the separation of Sind from Bombay. Khuhro and his friends felt it imperative that he present his evidence to the JPC. The problem was finances. Although Khuhro was one of the richest and largest landlords in the region, it is quite astonishing to learn from his biography of the immense difficulty he had in raising the apparently modest sum of money needed for the passage. (Of course, this was before the Sukkur Barrage became operational and transformed the Khuhros and the Bhuttos into millionaires many times over.)

The journey to London proved well worth the expense and the effort. For, by the conclusion of the Third Round Table Conference, those who advocated separation had made a good case and the political atmosphere overwhelmingly favoured separation. Simultaneous with the passing of the Government of India Act, 1935, the decision was made to separate Sind from Bombay. Sind became a province on 1 April 1936. Khuhro was not quite thirty-five. His biographer-daughter was yet to be born.

The Lucknow Pact, 1916:
The Congress Capitulation to Separate Electorates

Viceroy Lord Minto's proposals of 1906, eventually embodied as the Morley–Minto reforms in the Act of 1909, instituted separate electorates as the touchstone of community-based politics in India. This was the immediate provocation for the establishment of both the Muslim League (in 1906) and the Hindu Sabha in Punjab (in 1907) as the counterpoint to the Punjab Muslim League founded the same year—progenitors of the communal pincer movement which, in 1947, crushed the secular and nationalist aspiration for an independent, undivided India.

In the demonology of partition, as popularly understood in India, the villain of the piece is Muhammad Ali Jinnah, the 'Quaid-e-Azam' in the vocabulary of the Muslim League and Pakistan. It is the selfsame Jinnah who joined the Muslim League 'on condition that it did not imply any disloyalty to the idea and cause of a united India'.[8] As a nationalist, but also a Muslim, Jinnah was instrumental in bringing to fruition the

Congress–League dialogue between 1909 and 1915 which climaxed in the Lucknow Pact of December 1916, based on acceptance by the Congress of the concept of separate electorates for Hindus and Muslims.

It was Jinnah's comrade-in-arms, Mohammed Ali (destined to be subsequently Mahatma Gandhi's chief Muslim partner in the first Civil Disobedience Movement before turning into the Mahatma's most vicious and vociferous critic), who summed up the problem of the interface between national interest and community interest when he defined the purpose of the Muslim League as 'recognition of all the legitimate claims of India as a whole' but—and this was the crux of the matter—*including* 'the legitimate rights and interests of the Muslim community'.[9] This was a rebuff not only to the views of the founders of the Punjab Muslim League—the Baghabanpura Mians, father Mian Shah Din and son Mian (later, Sir) Muhammad Shafi—that the Muslims 'constitute a distinct community…separate from and often antagonistic to the majority'[10] but also of the Punjab-based Hindu Sabha which held that 'the Hindus have organized themselves into a separate body in the belief that by such separate organizations alone can they safeguard the interests of their community'.[11]

Till the Lucknow Pact, the Congress had adamantly opposed separate electorates on the fundamental principle that separate electorates would sow the seeds of the communal divide and thus forestall the emergence of an indivisible Indian nationhood and an undivided independent India. This fundamental principle was given the go-by, with Gopal Krishna Gokhale and the 1912 Congress president, R.N. Mudholkar, arguing that 'separate electorates would minimize friction and ensure the representation of minorities'.[12] Bal Gangadhar Tilak smashed the last vestiges of Hindu opposition to separate electorates when he threw in his lot with Gokhale. That brought around Madan Mohan Malaviya, the tallest leader of the Hindu right within the Congress, who urged:

There is a feeling among Hindus that too much has been given to the Muslims. As a Hindu I have no objection to making this concession...We cannot rise from our intolerable position without the aid of the Muslims. So, in order to gain the desired objective there is no objection to giving a percentage, a greater percentage, to the Muslims.[13]

It was a triumph of pragmatism over principle in a spirit of compromise intended to yoke together the two great communities of India to the common cause of freedom. And for a while it worked, notwithstanding constant sniping on communal representation, particularly in Punjab and Bengal, where the two communities were substantially balanced, as also in the United Provinces where the Muslims received a higher weightage than their share of the population. For six glorious years from 1916 to 1922, when the first Non-cooperation-cum-Khilafat Movement was called off by Gandhi in the wake of the killing of policemen at Chauri Chaura, communal harmony prevailed, communal considerations were marginalized and a united front held centre stage.

So much so that the lieutenant governor of the United Provinces, James Meston, writing 'sorrowfully', says Mushirul Hasan, to the viceroy in February 1917 of 'the strength of Nationalist feeling in India' being 'greater than it has ever been in our time' lamented:

Extremists and Moderates have united after years of misunderstanding; and, greatest marvel of all, the Mahomedans also have come into the fold. A few moderates may grumble here and there; and a few conservative Mahomedans may urge that the League does not represent their community. But they do nothing. They are voiceless in public...the resultant union of all voices has filled educated India with a pride and a feeling of nationality which is impossible to ignore.[14]

Yet, it was precisely the playing out of reservations and separate electorates at the local level, in the provinces and the local bodies, after dyarchy came through the Government of India Act, 1919, that led to the 'Terrible Twenties', the decade in which India was handed over to the devilries of communalism.

In Bengal, the Congress minister of local government, the same Surendranath Banerjea who had proposed the abolition of separate electorates in 1921, conceded separate electorates to the Muslims in the 1923 Calcutta Municipal Bill, accepting the argument advanced by Maulvi Abdul Karim that 'in India, which is a land of many communities, many creeds, many cultures and many traditions, it is not possible to have a thorough national fusion, completely separating the religious and socio-religious concerns of life from the economic and political interests (of the communities)'.[15]

After the Banerjea group was routed in the elections later that year by C.R. Das of the Swarajists, the latter proposed implementing the Lucknow Pact which provided for 40 per cent representation for Muslims in the local bodies. At this point, Surendranath Banerjea literally lit the funeral pyre of the Lucknow Pact in Bengal, burning copies of the Das-brokered accord in Krishnagar, in cohorts with totally communal elements like Khuda Baksh who sought to wreak political vengeance on his rivals by joining hands with All-India Hindu Mahasabha activists M.R. Jayakar, B.S. Moonje and N.C. Kelkar, not to mention Lala Lajpat Rai and Madan Mohan Malaviya (and, a little later, vice chancellor of Calcutta University, Sir Ashutosh Mookerjee, father of the Jana Sangh founder, Shyama Prasad Mookerjee).[16]

In Punjab, the Unionist government formed by Sir Fazli Husain, who had worsted the bigoted Baghabanpura Mians, father and son, to win the elections on a secular platform—or, at any rate, a joint Hindu–Muslim–Sikh platform—was soon thwarted by a combination of Sikhs demanding a separate electorate for themselves, and Hindu communal forces mobilized by the Punjab-based Arya Samaj, Shuddhi Sabha and Sanatana Dharma Sabhas, backed by the All-India Hindu Mahasabha, and led from the front by none less than the 'Lion of the Punjab', Lala Lajpat Rai. Such was the communal tenor of their demands that Nehru's *Autobiography* reserves some of its harshest language for the 'Lion of the Punjab'. It was this atmosphere that not only pushed Fazli Husain into the waiting arms of the vicious Islamic counterpart to the Hindu Mahasabha, the All-India Muslim Conference, but, worse and much more tragically, transformed the Iqbal of *Saare jahan se achcha Hindustan hamara* into the 'ideological father' of Pakistan. Mushirul Hasan quotes Iqbal as lamenting in 1923: 'It is a pity that in the Punjab the jealousy, no, rather enmity of Hindus and Muslims is growing. If it remains like that, then life will become difficult for both communities during the next thirty years.'[17]

Partition came, in fact, within the next twenty-five! Such was the legacy in Punjab of the 1916 Lucknow compromise on the principle of separate electorates. Professor Mushirul Hasan assesses the surrender of principle to pragmatism in the Lucknow Pact in the following terms:

By negotiating the Lucknow Pact on the questionable terms of communal representation, the Congress legitimized what were later derided as 'separatist' and 'communal' demands. By allowing itself to be dictated by narrow regional and sectarian causes, the Congress created a space within which such concerns had to be accommodated even at the risk of destroying the democratic and secular structures it was striving to build. Instead of curbing divisive tendencies through a concerted ideological campaign, the Congress settled for hastily concluded agreements for immediate political benefits. Consequently, it lost the moral authority and the political conviction to challenge the assumptions that went into the making of the Montagu–Chelmsford reforms.[18]

Mushirul Hasan's assessment echoes Professor Bipan Chandra's:

> In 1916, the Congress–League pact was signed on separate electorates and it was declared by no less great men than Tilak and Jinnah, who were the architects of this plan, that the communal problem was solved forever. In fact, it was the beginning of the communal problem in serious form.[19]

Hindu/Sikh Minorities and the Delhi Proposals

The 1916 Lucknow Pact and the Congress's abject surrender on the issue of separate electorates, far from spreading the light of communal harmony, stoked the fires of communal disharmony as never before. Further evidence of the Hindu and Congress complicity in furthering the communal divide is provided by the sad story of how Muhammad Ali Jinnah's acceptance of joint electorates, through his interpretation of the Delhi Proposals of 1927, was rejected by the Congress. In a complete turnaround from their position on the Lucknow Pact, Jinnah had persuaded the All-India Muslim League to accept the Delhi Proposals. The Congress was, however, unable to free itself from the clutches of communal passions and communal suspicions raised by Hindu and Sikh leaders, most from within the Congress fold, in provinces where the Muslims were in the majority—Punjab, Bengal and Sind. No doubt the Muslim side did not lack in communal passions, communal suspicions or communal leaders, but the fact is that the Delhi Proposals did offer joint electorates, the AICC did endorse the Proposals, and it was expected that Motilal Nehru and Tej Bahadur Sapru would incorporate the Delhi Proposals substantially in the Nehru Report on constitutional reforms. But eventually, not even Mahatma Gandhi was able to persuade the Congress to insist on the incorporation of the AICC-endorsed version of the Delhi Proposals in the Nehru Report. Thus was lost the last real opportunity for a united India. Jawaharlal Nehru admits as much:

> Success seemed almost within grasp. Only two or three points remained to settle, and of these the really important one was the Punjab, where there was the Hindu–Muslim–Sikh triangle…But all this was in vain. Fear and mistrust remained on either side, and the little step to cross the short distance that remained was not taken.[20]

What a tragedy! There was no problem in the Congress over the bottom line—joint electorates. The devil lay in the detail. The Nehru Report came towards the end of the worst decade of communal violence the country had ever known. Bloody and widespread riots had not only engulfed almost all parts of Punjab and the United Provinces, but even places like Delhi which till then had had an impressive record of communal amity.[21]

It was not only the rival *tabligh/tanzeem* (preaching/ discipline) and *shuddhi/sangathan* (purification/organization) movements of the Muslims and Hindus respectively which stoked the fires; there was endless trouble in the United Provinces and Bihar over routes for religious processions, the playing of music before mosques, and cow protection. Labour conflicts and agrarian tensions, rooted, one would have thought, in class distinctions and economic causes and consequences, took on a communal hue. And the Moplah uprising of 1921 in Kerala, which had its origins in landlord–tenant disputes, cast its long shadow over the entire decade. It was this charged atmosphere which emboldened B.S. Moonje of the Hindu Mahasabha to write that it would be his mission in life to ensure that Gandhi's philosophy of love and ahimsa did not take root at least in Maharashtra, because these, he was convinced, would lead to the elimination of Hindus.[22]

This disillusionment with secular nationalism had the backing of Congress leaders associated with the Hindu Mahasabha, including, most importantly, Lala Lajpat Rai in Punjab and Pandit Madan Mohan Malaviya in the United Provinces, both of whom were instrumental in getting shuddhi inscribed on the programme of the All-India Hindu Mahasabha.

Mohammed Ali, president of the Congress in 1923–24, urged Gandhi to rein in Malaviya, but the Mahatma responded: 'I cannot accept that Malaviyaji and others are enemies of Muslims.' It was little comfort to Mohammed Ali that Gandhi added: 'Nor can I agree to calling Mohammed Ali an enemy of Hindus.'[23]

Thus exempted from Gandhi's censure, both Malaviya and Mohammed Ali mirrored each other in driving India down the 'rift valley' of the communal divide. Malaviya's success lay in taking on Motilal Nehru on the Nehrus' home ground of Allahabad, in particular, and the United Provinces in general. So relentlessly did he espouse the cause of the Prayag Hindu Samaj, the Sanatana Dharma Mahasammelan and the United Provinces Hindu Sabha that in the council entry elections of 1926, the Swarajists led by Motilal Nehru and Sapru lost half their seats—dwindling from thirty-one in 1923 to sixteen in 1926.

It was against this background that, following a private talk between Jinnah and Motilal Nehru in January 1927, the Delhi Proposals were formulated by thirty leading lights of the Muslim League in March 1927.[24] Alarmed, perhaps by the violence and communal hatred that separate electorates had unleashed in the decade following the Montagu–Chelmsford reforms, Jinnah persuaded a majority of the Muslim League (a minority under Sir Muhammad Shafi walked out in fury) to eschew its long-standing commitment to separate electorates and accept joint electorates as the way forward. For the first time the Muslims agreed to have joint electorates.[25]

Perhaps Jinnah saw this as a way of returning to the

nationalist mainstream from which he had excluded himself since the stormy August 1920 session of the Nagpur Congress. Whatever might have been Jinnah's mix of principled and personal reasons, he got the demand for separate electorates replaced by the offer of joint electorates, but subject to four conditions which ultimately wrecked the initiative. On the face of it, and in the light of subsequent developments, which in 1947 reached a horrific climax, the four conditions attached to the offer of joint electorates should not have posed any insuperable difficulty:

- Muslim representation in the legislative councils in proportion to their population in Punjab and Bengal;
- One-third reserved seats for Muslims in the Central legislature;
- The separation of Sind from Bombay to constitute it into a separate province; and
- The upgrading of the 'North West Frontier Province (NWFP) into a full-fledged province.

But the trio of Malaviya, Lajpat Rai and Jairamdas Daulatram (of Sind), abetted by Punjab's Sikh leaders who pitched for 30 per cent representation although they constituted 14 per cent of the population, launched such a concerted assault on the four subsidiary proposals that the All-Parties Conference, called in February 1928 to inter alia endorse the Delhi offer, ended in chaos. After a subsequent meeting of the Conference in May, it was decided to leave it to a committee comprising Motilal Nehru, Tej Bahadur Sapru, M.S. Aney and Mangat Singh to draw up a draft constitution as India's alternative proposals to whatever might emanate from the all-British Simon Commission, which the Congress had decided to boycott at its Madras session, presided over by Dr M.A. Ansari, in December 1927.

It is often forgotten that Jinnah overcame objections in his camp to make common cause with the Congress in boycotting the Simon Commission, thus opting for an all-India solution through the Nehru–Sapru report, ignoring the British altogether. Also brought on to the anti-Simon Commission bandwagon by the time of the Madras Congress session were the All-India Khilafat Conference and the Jami'at ul-Ulema, besides the All-India Nationalist Muslim Party to which many Congressmen simultaneously belonged.[26] By September 1928, the Punjab Khilafatists led by Saifuddin Kitchlew and the Bengal Provincial Muslim League were persuaded by Jinnah and his colleagues to endorse the Nehru Report broadly.[27] Here was the opportunity to harness the bulk of Muslim opinion to the nationalist cause or, at any rate, to divide the Muslim communalists from the Muslim nationalists so that 'the great bulk of the Mussalmans'[28] remained with the Congress-led anti-colonial movement.

But if Muslim opinion was being dragged by Jinnah in the direction of joint electorates, hardliners in the Hindu and Sikh communities were unwilling to dilute their positions, and the publication of the Nehru Committee report on 15 August 1928 effectively killed the Delhi Proposals and the last hope of joint electorates. For, the Nehru Committee's arguments against proportionate representation for the Muslims in Punjab and Bengal, and the reduction of reserved seats for the Muslims in the Central legislature to 25 per cent as against Jinnah's figure of 33 per cent, became the bone of much contention between Hindu and Muslim hardliners. Till the last minute and beyond, Jinnah pinned his hopes on Gandhi. After presiding over the December 1924 Belgaum session of the Congress, Gandhi had withdrawn to Sabarmati Ashram to concentrate on his other concerns. This, of course, left a vacuum in secular, nationalist Congress politics that gave space to communal concerns at the expense of the national interest. The Calcutta session of the Congress in December 1928 signalled Gandhi's return to the Congress. He came at the behest of Motilal Nehru who needed Gandhi's support to counter his son Jawaharlal's rebellion over the Nehru Report settling for Dominion status,[29] and thus avoid the embarrassing possibility of the report bearing his name being rejected at the very session over which he was to preside.[30]

Jinnah, meanwhile, had prevailed on the Muslim League and other sister organizations to hold a convention in Calcutta at the same time as the Congress session. At the convention, Jinnah suggested three amendments to the Nehru Report:

- Reservation of one-third seats (as against 25 per cent, later raised to 27 per cent, proposed in the Nehru Report) for Muslims in the Central legislature;
- Reservations for Muslims for ten years in Punjab and Bengal, if adult suffrage were to come into effect; and
- Residuary powers vesting not in the Centre but in the provinces.

He reinforced his specific proposals with this impassioned general plea:

> We are all sons of this land. We have to live together...Believe me there is no progress of India until the Mussalmans and Hindus are united, and let no logic, philosophy or squabble stand in the way of coming to a compromise and nothing will make me more happy than to see a Hindu–Muslim union.[31]

Jinnah believed Gandhi could be won over to the amendments in the Nehru Report which could bring it broadly in line with the Delhi Proposals, as endorsed by the All-India Congress Committee, burying once and for all the pernicious consequences of separate electorates. (This, in fact, was the strategy Gandhi resorted to in 1932 to negate Ramsay MacDonald's Communal Award of separate electorates for the scheduled castes [SC] by providing, through the Yeravada pact with Dr Ambedkar, for generous SC reservations, raising the number of reserved SC seats in the provincial legislatures from seventy-one to 147 and in the Central legislature to 18 per cent of the total.) But at this crucial juncture in Hindu–Muslim relations, Gandhi blinked. His grandson, Rajmohan, says Gandhi 'personally' approved of the Delhi Proposals but baulked at the objections raised by Lajpat Rai and Madan Mohan Malaviya.[32] Historian B.R. Nanda (who, incidentally, takes no note of Jinnah's acceptance of joint electorates in his otherwise very revealing *The Nehrus*) has this sagacious assessment to offer of where matters stood at the end of 1928 in regard to the unresolved demands of the Muslim League:

> These were modest demands—compared with those of ten years later. It is, however, difficult to say whether their acceptance would have halted the crescendo of communal claims which culminated in the demand for Pakistan. The narrowness and rigidity of the Hindu and Sikh politicians in these negotiations was bad enough, but the fluidity of Muslim demands was worse.[33]

Only one Muslim could have staunched the fluidity of those Muslim demands: Muhammad Ali Jinnah. But his stand was not accepted. And only one Hindu could have brought off the coup that might have kept India united and all Indian communities on the same side: Mahatma Gandhi. But he did not press his 'personal view'. I suspect that this was because of two factors. First, in 1927–28, the influence of the Muslim League over the Muslims was declining, and that of Jinnah within the League no longer overwhelming; there were doubts, therefore, about the sustainability of any deal with Jinnah. Second, Gandhi also believed that 'we have lost our hold upon the masses'.[34]

Jinnah argued that minorities always dread the possibility of a tyrannical majority and as such their interests and rights needed to be safeguarded through clear statutory provisions. In saying this, Jinnah was echoing the precise argument that Lajpat Rai and the Sikh leaders in Punjab, Jairamdas Daulatram in Sind, and a host of Hindu Congress leaders in Bengal were making. But Jinnah's plea for compromise was rejected not only by the Muhammad Shafi faction of the Muslim League; it was also rejected by the Congress.

The stage was thus reoccupied by the extremists. In the All-India Khilafat Conference, Mohammed Ali thundered at the Congress, with his usual lack of circumspection: '...25 per cent is our proportion of the population and yet you will not give us 33 per cent in the assembly. You are a Jew, a bania.'[35]

Choudhary Khaliquzzaman, the Muslim League leader from the United Provinces, put it a little more circumspectly:

> The heavens would not have fallen if a few amendments that were proposed had been generously accepted and the sad chapter of communal bickering and disharmony closed. The short-sightedness of Hindu politicians on this occasion could not be surpassed.[36]

'It is a fact,' concludes Rajmohan ruefully, 'that after Calcutta no Muslim outside the Congress spoke of joint electorates.'[37] Dr Ansari himself wrote to Gandhi to say that had the Congress stuck to the Delhi Proposals, with the modifications outlined by Jinnah, the opposition of the Hindu Mahasabha could have been overcome and Hindu–Muslim unity would have been accomplished.[38] Instead, Malaviya went to London to argue the Hindu Mahasabha case before the 1931 Round Table Conference and returned in time to be elected president of the Congress in 1932.

Yet, notwithstanding the severe setback he had suffered in Calcutta in 1928, Jinnah conferred twice with Gandhi in 1929. Nothing came of it. As recounted by M.C. Chagla, his colleague at that time, there were no takers for Jinnah's argument that the Hindu–Muslim question be tackled as a 'national problem' and not a 'communal dispute'. Jinnah added in a letter to Tej Bahadur Sapru on 14 December 1929—his last as an Indian nationalist:

It is the duty of every Nationalist who wants self-government for India to take with him seventy million Mussalmans and other communities, and [accept] any reasonable concessions, though not logical, that can secure the whole-hearted support and co-operation of such a large body of people in our country.[39]

Jinnah went to London for the First Round Table Conference in 1930, where he decided that, rejected as he had been by both the Congress and the Muslim League, he would give up politics and settle for a flourishing and remunerative practice at the Privy Council. His parting words, uttered privately to a student at Oxford, stung both the Hindu community and his erstwhile Muslim League colleagues and almost rivalled Mohammed Ali's in waspishness: 'The Hindus are short-sighted and I think incorrigible. The Muslim camp is full of spineless people.'[40]

The explanation for the indifference shown by the secular elements to the Delhi Proposals perhaps lies in the precipitous decline which had by then overtaken the Muslim League. By 1927, membership of the League had dwindled to just 1330. The Bombay branch, which included several of the most distinguished nationalist members of the Congress, was down to a mere seventy-one members. At its annual meeting in Bombay in 1929, the League could not even gather together a quorum of the minuscule seventy-five members from all over India required to commence proceedings. So, the League had to shift the venue to Allahabad, change its quorum rule, and rope in Allama Iqbal as its president even to hold a formal session. Ironically, that session, with less than seventy-five members present to applaud the Allama, lay at the genesis of the movement for Pakistan.[41]

The Congress shifted focus from the communal question to Jawaharlal Nehru's call for Poorna Swaraj, and Gandhi returned centre stage to politics in March 1931 with the Dandi

March. However, it is sad but significant that of the seventy-two persons who set out from the Sabarmati Ashram for Dandi, only two were Muslims.

Jinnah returned to India in 1934. He was no longer a communitarian–nationalist but a communalist–separatist. From then till 1947, the story is more a struggle between the Congress and the Muslim League than a Hindu–Muslim story. Yet, before we turn to the Muslim origins of partition, perhaps we should cast a glance at the pernicious role of the Hindu Mahasabha once the restrictions on V.D. Savarkar were removed in 1937 to enable him to become president of the Hindu Mahasabha.

He notoriously said in his presidential address: 'We are Indians because we are Hindus, not vice versa.' Holding 'nationalism' to be a 'perverse conception' and the 'Indian nation' to be a 'mirage', Savarkar denounced the whole of the Muslim community as 'communal' and urged: 'Sirs, Congressmen, you are Indian nationalists but I am a Hindu and this is a Hindu electorate.'[42]

That is, of course, where he got it wrong and why even up to the sixth decade of our independence this hugely Hindu-majority country has not given the Hindutva brigade anywhere near a majority ever. But in its illusions and misconceptions, the two-nation theory advocated by the Hindu Mahasabha mirrored the two-nation theory espoused by the Muslim League. The history of post-partition Pakistan, including the second partition which brought about Bangladesh, only goes to show that the Muslim League under Jinnah, post-1934, was a Muslim League in saffron, as was the Hindu Mahasabha under Savarkar the Hindu Mahasabha in a Jinnah cap!

The Muslim Origins of Partition

I have deliberately set out the Hindu origins of partition first in order to highlight the fact that the concerns of the Muslim minorities in Hindu-majority areas of the country were reflected, almost as in a mirror, by the non-Muslim minorities in Muslim-majority parts of the country. Leaders of both the Muslim League and the Congress were also not equally alive to the concerns of the other side. So, partition, when it came, was less the desired outcome of either side than the consequence of failing to accommodate each other's views on time, thus allowing the imperial power to bring matters to a snap conclusion through what Sir Winston Churchill cruelly but accurately described as the British 'scuttle' of its Indian empire.

Notwithstanding the first major communal riots of the freedom struggle in Bombay in 1893, controversy over the partition of Bengal in 1905 and the revocation of the partition in 1911, the formation of the All-India Muslim League at the instance of the Aga Khan in 1906, and the announcement of separate electorates through the Morley–Minto reforms of 1909, Muhammad Ali Jinnah, who, like many other Muslims, was a member of both the Congress and the Muslim League (which were not seen as incompatible), declared that his ambition was to be 'the Muslim Gokhale'. The mood was generally upbeat, Hindu–Muslim unity being regarded as entirely feasible if certain key constitutional questions were set at rest. This expectation was validated by the Lucknow Pact of 1916, negotiated during the separate but simultaneous sessions of the League and the Congress in the same city. Jinnah was the architect of the agreement. Its terms are admirably summed up by Rajmohan Gandhi:

> Under [the terms of the pact] Hindus and Sikhs had agreed to separate Muslim electorates and to weightage for Muslims in Hindu-majority provinces; in return the Muslims had agreed to equality between Muslims and non-Muslims in the council of Punjab, which had a Muslim majority, and something like a minority status [for Muslims] in Bengal, which too had a Muslim majority.[43]

In the opinion of Khaliquzzaman, the seeds of the partition of India were duly laid in Lucknow when the Muslims, due to their inexperience, agreed to have equality in the Punjab and a minority status in Bengal.

That separate electorates engendered rather than ended communalism has already been stated. The Lucknow spirit evaporated by the 1920s and Jinnah's constitutionalism was overtaken by Mahatma Gandhi's head-on confrontation with the Raj after the passage of the Rowlatt Act and the Jalianwala Bagh massacre.

In taking on the British through a mass movement, the Ali brothers, Mohammed and Shaukat (and their remarkable mother, Bi Amman), were Gandhi's principal comrades-in-arms. The first Jinnah–Gandhi clash in September 1920 was over Gandhi renaming Annie Besant's Home Rule League as the Swaraj Sabha and substituting the expression 'within the empire' (with reference to 'self-rule') with a straightforward demand for swaraj. The end came within months at the Nagpur session of the Congress in December 1920, where, after the crowd booed and jeered Jinnah, Mohammed Ali ridiculed him for his self-righteousness in full view and hearing of the public. Jinnah 'sat down with a hurt look on his face',[44] then took an early train to Bombay before the session was over, thus bringing to an end his fourteen-year-old association with the Congress. He secured his vengeance twenty-seven years later when Pakistan was born.

When Gandhi hitched the wagon of the Khilafat Movement to the Non-cooperation Movement, Hindu–Muslim unity reached its zenith. But when Mustafa Kemal rejected the Caliphate (Khilafat) and Gandhi withdrew the non-cooperation satyagraha after Chauri Chaura, Gandhi and the Ali brothers began drawing apart.

Symbolically, the Gandhi–Mohammed Ali association ended when Mohammed Ali, president of the Congress in 1923–24, handed over the baton to Gandhi at the Belgaum session in December 1924, at which Gandhi agreed for the first and last time to serve as president of the Congress. Meanwhile, the Moplah insurrection in Malabar and the competing communal rivalries of the sangathan and shuddhi movements of the Hindus versus the tabligh and tanzeem movements of the Muslims were wrenching the two communities emotionally apart. 'Communal riots,' notes Rajmohan Gandhi, 'were growing in frequency. There had been 11 in 1923, 18 in 1924, 35 in 1926, and 31 by November 1927.'[45] The riots in Kohat in NWFP, over which Gandhi embarked on a twenty-one-day fast, led to a joint visit to the region by Gandhi and Shaukat Ali but ended in disagreement over what they had seen and concluded. The breaking point came in the deadlock over the Delhi Proposals.

From the time of Jinnah's return to India in 1934, the nationalist discourse came increasingly under challenge from the two-nation theory. The idea of Pakistan has been traced back to Chaudhry Rahmat Ali, a student at Cambridge in the early 1930s, and even earlier, but it remained in the realm of crank ideas until Jinnah gave it political advocacy, starting with the May 1937 conference of the Muslim League at Lucknow. He wrote to Gandhi that the time had come for everyone to recognize the Muslim League as the one authoritative and representative organization of the Muslims of India.

This was absurd as the elections just held showed that the Muslim League commanded under 5 per cent of the vote of Muslims even under separate electorates for reserved Muslim seats and had won a mere 109 of the 482 seats allotted to Muslims, largely in Muslim-minority provinces. In Muslim-majority provinces, it was leaders like Sikandar Hayat Khan of Punjab, Fazlul Haq of Bengal and Khan Abdul Ghaffar Khan of NWFP (and a slew of Sind Muslim leaders) who represented Muslim opinion rather more than Jinnah and his League.

Jinnah added that Gandhi and the Congress represented the Hindus throughout the country. This too was absurd, but

Jinnah insisted that it was possible to proceed further only on this basis. From his 1938 presidential address to the Muslim League, Jinnah began taking extreme postures, alleging that the Congress high command was determined to crush all other communities and cultures and establish Hindu raj.

In 1940, Jinnah proclaimed at Lahore that Hindus and Muslims could 'never evolve a common nationality'; in his 1941 address he claimed that in a united India, Muslims would be absolutely wiped out; and in 1942, he succinctly summed up his two-nation theory in an interview to a British newspaper:

> The difference between Hindus and Muslims is deep-rooted and ineradicable. We are a nation with our own distinctive culture and civilization, language and culture, art and architecture, names and nomenclature, sense of value and proportion, legal laws and moral codes, customs and calendar, history and traditions, attitudes and ambitions.[46]

This again was specious. Maulana Abul Kalam Azad articulated the alternative nationalist Muslim view in his presidential address at the 1940 session of the Congress at Ramgarh:

> Muslims in India are a vast concourse spreading out all over the country...It is true they number only one-fourth of the total population but the question is not one of ratio, but of large numbers and the strength behind them...If we view [the future of India] with fear and suspicion, then, undoubtedly, we will have to follow a different path. No present declaration, no promise for the future, no constitutional safeguards can be a remedy for our doubts and fears...I am a Mussalman and proud of the fact. Islam's splendid traditions of thirteen hundred years are my inheritance. I am unwilling to lose even the smallest part of this

inheritance. In addition, I am proud of being an Indian. I am part of the indivisible unity that is India's nationality. I am indispensable to its noble edifice. Without me this splendid structure of India is incomplete. I am an essential element which has gone into the building of India...Islam has now as great a claim on the soil of India as has Hinduism...Our languages were different but we grew to use a common language. Our manners and customs were dissimilar, but they produced a new synthesis.[47]

And so the Muslims of the subcontinent were offered these two diametrically opposite views of the place of Islam and of Muslims in India. The Indian Muslim today would have no difficulty accepting the Azad view, as would indeed that majority of Indians who are secular. But faced with the choice between the Quaid-e-Azam's view, and the view of the Maulana whom Jinnah dismissed as a Congress 'show-boy', did the Muslims of pre-independence India opt for Jinnah or for Azad?

Elections 1945–46: Did the Muslims Opt for Pakistan?

In the elections of 1945–46 held under the separate electorates system, the Muslim League, which had done so badly in 1937, secured all thirty Muslim seats in the central assembly and 427 of the 507 Muslim seats in the provincial legislatures, while non-Muslim League Muslims ('nationalist Muslims' as they were called) won only twenty-two seats, in contrast to the 382 constituencies in which they had worsted Muslim League candidates in 1937. From this it seems obvious that the pre-independence Muslim community rejected Azad and plumped for Jinnah, thus paving the pathway to Pakistan. But is that the whole story? Who wanted Pakistan: the Muslims or the Muslim Leaguers?

By the time I reached Karachi in 1978 to serve as India's first consul general in the city, Ayub Khuhro had been away from the limelight for twenty years. He was, therefore, delighted to give me all the time in the world. We spent hours on his graceful lawns, chatting about Sind, Pakistan and his own turbulent political career in the tumultuous times that had led to Pakistan and its aftermath. And it was from him that I learned the curious little fact, which, to the best of my knowledge, has not yet found its way into history books, viz., that the British deputy commissioner of Karachi was such an enthusiastic supporter of Pakistan that he gleefully stuffed the ballot boxes with bogus Muslim League votes. When one of the great founding fathers of Pakistan tells me that is how Pakistan came into being, who am I to disbelieve him?

Perhaps Pakistan would have come into being anyway, with or without the benevolent helping hand of the ICS, because between 1937 and 1946, in less than ten years, Pakistan and the Muslim League became synonymous with the thousand-year-old connection between India and Islam. There were a host of reasons for this, among which I would underline what I regard as three of the most important. One, the Congress unwittingly left the field entirely to its opponents when all its leaders went behind bars in the Quit India Movement. Nehru himself emerged from a three-year incarceration only months before the elections that commenced in December 1945 and continued into 1946. Second, the transformation of the Muslim League under Jinnah from a party merely pleading for protection and privileges for the Muslim minority in Hindu-majority India into a party demanding an independent and sovereign homeland for the Muslims of the subcontinent. And, third, the unbending will, the inflexible determination and ineffable charisma of one man: the Quaid-e-Azam.

It is the overwhelming showing of the Muslim League in 1946 that constitutes the basis of the joint Muslim League–Sangh Parivar thesis that the Muslims of India brought about the partition. But let us look at the facts a little more closely.

The British Indian province in which the Muslims had the most overwhelming majority was NWFP. The 1941 Census of India tells us that of the total population of 3.3 million in the province, only 300,000 were Hindus. Yet, the Muslim League secured only seventeen of the thirty-six Muslim seats. Accordingly, the Congress, not the Muslim League, formed the ministry. Which accounts for why NWFP continued to be such a restive province in Pakistan and why their fellow Pakhtoons across the border in Afghanistan so loathe Pakistan and adore India and that, apart from the brief interregnum of the Taliban, India's relations with Afghanistan have always been much closer, warmer and friendlier than Pakistan's.

The second-largest Muslim province was Baluchistan, containing four million Muslims out of a total population of five million. The Government of India Act, 1935, did not give the Baluchi the right to vote. So no one ever found out what they really wanted. And going by the continuous state of revolt in which Baluchistan remained for decades after the creation of Pakistan, it would be reasonable to assume that whatever else they might have wanted, they certainly were not part of the faction in favour of Pakistan.

Which brings us to Sind—three million Muslims out of a population of 4.5 million. With a little bit of help from sundry ICS mandarins, 47 per cent of the electorate did vote for the Muslim League, but not without conceding three of the thirty-four Muslim seats to the Congress and denying the Muslim League victory in three other Muslim seats.

In Punjab, the Muslim League tally shot up from one in 1937 to seventy-five in 1946, but not without so many seats going to other parties, including the Congress, that the government was formed not by the Muslim League but, with Congress support, by Sir Khizr Hayat Khan of the Unionist Party in coalition with miscellaneous others.

Moreover, the elections of 1946 were confined to British India and so Muslims in princely states with large Muslim populations, such as Kashmir and Hyderabad, never got around to saying what they wanted. To go by what Sheikh Abdullah did, it would be reasonable to assume that Muslim opinion in Kashmir wished to have little to do with Pakistan. And the wrapping up of the Nizam's rule in a few days of police action in September 1948 indicates that the sentiment to remain in India was probably at least as strong among the Muslims of Hyderabad as was the Razakar sentiment to merge Hyderabad with faraway Pakistan.

Where then was the demand for Pakistan voiced unambiguously? Well, Bengal, of course, where the Muslim League swept the Muslim seats, claiming 113 out of 114 seats, and winning virtually every Muslim seat in every province where the Muslims were in a minority.

Thus, while a substantial chunk of the Muslim vote in the areas where the Muslims were in a majority did not favour Pakistan even in the fevered atmosphere of 1946, it was where the Muslims were in a minority that the Muslim vote went overwhelmingly to the Muslim League.

So, does that not prove that it was the Muslims who created Pakistan? Not quite, because no one really asked 'the Muslims' what they wanted.

I do not merely mean that Muslims were denied the opportunity of voting for non-Muslim candidates or even against Muslim candidates, as they have frequently done in independent India. More importantly—and this is the crux of my argument—no one asked the Muslims at large in 1946 whether or not they wanted the Muslim League and all its works. The Muslim League may have won 75 per cent of the votes in Muslim seats but the total votes cast in all Muslim seats, all over India, was six million (of which 4.5 million went to the League and 1.5 million to others). The total Muslim population of India, on the other hand, was seventy-nine million.[48] If we assume that half the Muslim population were adults, it would mean that the 1946 elections ascertained the views of merely 16 per cent of the adult Muslim population on whether or not they wanted Pakistan. At least 84 per cent of the subcontinent's Muslims were disenfranchised. Their opinion was never sought.

It was the Sixth Schedule to the Government of India Act, 1935, that determined who was enfranchised and who was not. There were different qualifications prescribed for different provinces—but all uniformly make for hilarious reading today. In the Madras province, for instance, only those adults were entitled to vote who had paid taxes under the Madras Motor Vehicles Act, 1931, and profession tax for both halves of the year, not to mention property tax, house tax and income tax or were 'the sole tenant of a house' on which property or house tax had been paid. In rural Madras province, the vote could be exercised only by a 'landowner, ryotwari pattadar, kanamdar, or kuzhikanamdar' or, most generously, by 'a holder of a kudiyiruppu or verumpattamdar' provided he be 'a mortgagee with possession or levy throughout the entire previous fasli year'. And if you weren't one of these, the British were not going to ask you what you wanted.

In Bengal, in addition to much of the above gobbledygook, you could get to vote—if you were a man but not if you were a woman (unless you happened to be the widow or mother of a soldier who had laid down his life for King and Country, provided even then 'she is shown in the manner prescribed to be literate')—if you happened, in the municipal limits of Calcutta (but not, alas, elsewhere), to be the owner or occupier of 'any land or building separately numbered and valued at not less than Rs 150 per annum'. Outside Calcutta, you could get to vote by paying no less than Rs 42 per annum as house tax or even 'cantonment fees of not less than eight annas' or chaukidari tax 'of not less than six annas'.

The consequence of all this guff was that only 13 per cent of India's adults were deemed entitled to exercise their franchise in the elections of 1946. And they had to be rich and well heeled to vote.

So, those Muslims who voted for Pakistan were the rich and the well-to-do. When Nehru had launched his Muslim Mass Contact campaign in the late 1930s, he made the gross error of sneering that he knew more about the Muslim masses, their hunger and poverty and misery, than most members of the Muslim League whose only concerns, he alleged, seemed to be the number and percentage of seats in councils.[49]

Jinnah, knew better. He knew that, under the imperial dispensation, Pakistan was going to be secured not through the support of the unwashed millions but from the solid backing of the carpetbaggers who would be able to achieve—through promotions, postings and profits—in a few years in Pakistan what would take them decades, if ever, to get in the normal course in undivided India. So, he concentrated on them. His meteoric rise in the esteem of the Muslim elite got him Pakistan. Nehru had to be content with the support of the Muslim masses who, when they were at long last given the right to vote in 1952, overwhelmingly voted for the Congress.

Whether or not they wanted Pakistan, Muslims who lived in north-west India and east Bengal became Pakistanis. Muslims who lived elsewhere and wanted Pakistan migrated to the Promised Land. They amounted to a minute fraction of independent India's Muslim population. An overwhelming number of Muslims who had not voted for Pakistan—and many who in the excitement of the moment had—stayed on in India.

It was not the Muslims but the Muslim Leaguers who wanted, and won, Pakistan. The Muslim elite may have voted with their hands for Pakistan. But the Muslim masses voted with their feet to stay on in India. That is the true measure of their loyalty to this land.

My analysis is that of an observer born into the majority community. What really lends authenticity to the cold statistics of the question of whether the Muslims at the time of independence wanted Pakistan is the cry from the heart of a profoundly reflective Indian Muslim, Mushtaq Naqvi. Naqvi experienced the pain of partition as a thirteen-year-old adolescent and spent his adulthood suffering the consequences to his community and country of that tragedy.

Naqvi dubs partition as a wholly avoidable tragedy, 'a surgical operation performed in the dark on a pavement with a butcher's knife'.[50] He details all those elements of the Muslim community who positively opposed partition, beginning with such fundamentalist groups as Maulana Maudoodi's Jama'at-e-Islami and the Ahrars who dubbed Jinnah as the 'Kafir-e-Azam' (The Great Infidel) and going on to such sectarian groupings as the Jami'at-ul-Ulema-e-Hind of Deoband and the All-India Shia Conference, besides the Khaksars and the Momins. He cites the renowned poet revolutionary Hasrat Mohani denouncing the notion of Pakistan as 'Jahannamistan' or hell[51] and the Tiger of Bengal, Fazlul Haq, as saying that those who divided the country were traitors.[52] He also quotes Hussain Suhrawardy, Jinnah's lieutenant who delivered Bengal to the Muslim League in the 1945–46 elections, as bemoaning that the partition of Bengal was a calamity.[53] Naqvi adds that a number of Muslims who held high offices were all opposed to the idea of Pakistan and had expressed their grave doubts. Of Allama Iqbal, who is credited with being the founder of the idea of Pakistan, Naqvi says that he only sought 'a Muslim India within India' and quotes Iqbal's letter to the British historian, Edward Thompson: 'Pakistan is not my scheme. [What] I suggested in my address is the creation of a Muslim province as part of the proposed Indian Federation.'[54]

Naqvi also analyses in depth the elections of 1945–46, pointing out significant anomalies in interpreting the results as an endorsement of Pakistan and nailing the lie of the Muslim League's 'remarkable' performance. He points out that since the elections were based on limited franchise, the 'percentage of qualifying Muslims was less than ten per cent'.[55] Considering that only 52.3 per cent of the electorate exercised their right to vote, he further reasons that only 5 per cent of the Muslim population of undivided India actually voted. Of these, Naqvi states, '30 per cent did not vote for the Muslim League'.

In the United Provinces, the bastion of the Muslim League, less than half a million out of a total Muslim population of nine million voted for the League. Even if every vote is taken as a vote for Pakistan (which definitely was not the case), only 3.7 per cent were in favour of Pakistan. Despite separate electorates in which Muslims alone could vote for Muslims and only Muslims, candidates other than Muslim League candidates won in several heavily Muslim-dominated districts, including Saharanpur, Muzaffarnagar, Moradabad, Amroha, Meerut, Bijnore and Bahraich. In the eight other constituencies, including Khurja, Lucknow and Basti, the Muslim League managed a bare majority by a mere five percentage points or less. Further, out of a total of seventy constituencies that were reserved for the Muslims, it was only in twenty-two that the Muslim League won more than three-quarters of the Muslim vote.[56]

Hence, Naqvi's almost Churchillian peroration:

> Never before in history have such a small number of people played such a colossal fraud on such a great number of people...Hindus and Muslims alike, who were never consulted nor even remotely had anything to do with the game a few were playing in New Delhi were put at the mercy of the consequences, not knowing the what and the why of what was happening around them.[57]

Cross-communal Alliances

We now come to a curious chapter in inter-communal relations which marked the period between the resignation of the Congress ministries in 1939, after the British took India into their war without consulting India, and the decisive moves made by the imperial power in 1942–43 in favour of the Muslim League to shore up the empire's response to the Japanese at the gates.

During this phase, a third alternative to both secular nationalism and communal separatism was tried in Punjab, NWFP and Sind, but most strikingly in Bengal, to harness rival Hindu and Muslim communalisms to a common regional cause. After the elections of 1937 revealed that the Muslim League's support base was largely confined to Bombay and the United Provinces where the Muslims were in a minority, the premier of Muslim-majority Punjab, Sir Sikandar Hayat Khan, accommodated a member of the Hindu Mahasabha as minister in his Unionist-led Cabinet. At this, V.D. 'Veer' Savarkar succeeded in smuggling the Hindu Mahasabha into the overtly Muslim communalist Sind government constituted after the fall of the secular Allah Bux Soomro ministry in 1942. He also tried, but did not quite succeed, in effecting a similar cross-communal arrangement in NWFP.

But it was in Bengal that Premier A.K. Fazlul Haq undertook the most significant attempt to forge a cross-communal coalition between Haq's Krishak Proja Party and Shyama Prasad Mookerjee's Hindu Mahasabha. This alternative to both the secular nationalism of the Congress and the communal separatism of the Muslim League must also be examined before we move out of the historical dimension of secularism into contemporary post-partition, post-independence India.

The little-researched story of the Fazlul Haq–Shyama Prasad cross-communal alliance in Bengal has been told nowhere better than in the undergraduate dissertation that won the Alan Coulson prize for the best undergraduate dissertation in imperial history at Cambridge University in June 2003. That the prize went to my daughter, Sana Aiyar,[58] is no reason for keeping her thesis under wraps—although I must confess to having privileged access, as her father, to her as yet unpublished manuscript!

Sana argues that 'while provincial politics was concerned with religious solidarity, it was equally informed by regional loyalty and was thus able to form inter-communal political alliances without falling back on secular claims'. She says that in offering 'a reconciliation of the twin identities of region and religion within the same political paradigm…Fazlul Haq…best epitomized the pluralistic identities that Bengali Muslims struggled to come to terms with in the 1940s. Neither the Nehruvian claims to secular politics, which prioritized the nation above any other regional or religious identity, nor Jinnah's "communal" nationalist claims that placed religious identity over pre-existing regional or national identity, suited the pluralisms of Bengal'.

Haq also pointed to the differences between policies required for Muslim-majority and Muslim-minority provinces, protesting that if the Muslim leaders of Muslim-minority provinces (i.e. Jinnah) 'meddled too much with the politics of the majority provinces', it would be 'to the peril of the interest of the entire Muslim community of India'. Therefore, Haq emerged as 'the regional Other for Jinnah'.

'Muslim separatism' was thus challenged 'not only by politicians who presented themselves as secular, but also by regional leaders who were part of the Muslim discourse'. Fazlul Haq was the exemplar of a brand of Muslim politics which refused 'to let provincial politics be subsumed by all-India concerns'. He, therefore, 'forged a coalition ministry with the Hindu Mahasabha leader, Shyama Prasad Mookerjee'—whom the renowned Pakistani historian, Ayesha Jalal, has called 'the symbol of Hindu fanaticism'—in an alliance that was 'cross-communal' in that it 'never made any secular claims'.

This apostasy, argues Sana, threatened not only those who espoused the cause of a secular India which separated religion from politics, but also '…those who sought legitimacy on the grounds that religion and region were separate and oppositional identities [which] could not be brought into the same conceptual framework'. Thus, '[w]here the Muslim League privileged religion over the pre-existing region [or nation] and the Congress privileged the pre-existing nation [or region] over religion, for Haq the two were intertwined, and allegiance to one did not exclude the other on ideological grounds'.

It also moderated the Hindu Mahasabha's approach to the Muslim Other during the period of the Haq–Mookerjee alliance, as Mookerjee 'appealed to the religious sentiments of the Hindus, not in terms of an opposition to the communal Other, but as a recognition and reconciliation of different religious identities. He was aware of the dangers of either placating or dominating the other religious community in an irrational manner' and so attempted to 'consolidate Hindu solidarity but not to such an extent that it would exclude cross-communal political alliances'.

At the same time, 'Haq's brand of "communalism",' Sana says, 'offered a kind of identity politics which Jinnah, as the Sole Spokesman, was trying to prove could not exist in India'. Indeed, the 'seemingly religious divide in Bengal' between a largely Muslim peasantry and a majority of Hindu landlords reflected 'in reality' a 'stratification which was more economic than religious'. But Sana does concede that 'the cost of keeping the coalition stable was the alienation of the Krishak Proja Party from Haq'.

The Haq–Mookerjee cross-communal alliance, founded in 'the interplay between religious and regional identity' achieved 'a fine, albeit vulnerable, balance for a short period of time and…foreshadowed the second great partition of the twentieth century in the Indian subcontinent'. She concludes: 'Not all appeals to religion were communal. Moreover, non-communal community building was not necessarily secular.'

Given the transience of the third alternative and its being swept away once the field of battle was given over to the Congress and the Muslim League in the run-up to partition and independence, it is difficult to conclude whether cross-communal accommodation was ever a valid alternative to secular nationalism and communal separatism, but it is important to note that when he smelt power, the founder of the Bharatiya Jana Sangh and father figure of the BJP, S.P. Mookerjee, went in search of cross-communal alliances. It is a tradition of cohabitation across ideological divides that the BJP has persisted with to the present.

4

The Constitutional and Legal Dimensions

When Two Equally Solemn Oaths Clash

In Parliament's monsoon session of 1992, after the Rath Yatra was behind us but before the Babri Masjid was brought down, I put the following proposition to Lal Krishna Advani, then a senior BJP member of Parliament (MP) on the Opposition benches:

> When within the precincts of this House, we take an oath, which we swear in the name of God, or an oath, which we merely solemnly affirm, to uphold the Constitution, if there is a clash between such an oath and a private pledge or private oath, which is the one that will prevail?[1]

I had raised the question specifically because almost all the members of the BJP had entered Parliament after telling the people: '*Ram ki saugandh hum khaatey hain, hum mandir wahin banayenge*! [We swear in the name of Ram, we'll build the temple only there.]' While as an individual I respect and

honour everybody's right to take an oath, what I wanted
L.K. Advani to confirm was, in the event of a contradiction
between an oath to the Constitution, which we take as members
of Parliament, and a personal oath we take outside the House,
which of the two would prevail.

Advani's unequivocal reply no doubt earned him brownie
points:

> I want to say that my and my party's commitment
> [*nishtha*] to the Constitution is without compare
> [*ananya*] and indivisible [*avibhajya*]. There is no 'if' or
> 'but' in this, there is no question of any conflict. I see
> no conflict. Without a shadow of doubt, it is the
> commitment to the Constitution that is supreme.[2]

However, this assertion could be taken at its face value only
with a pinch of salt. Only a year earlier, in 1991, the president
of the BJP, Professor Murli Manohar Joshi, had gone to
Ayodhya with Kalyan Singh, the newly elected BJP chief
minister of Uttar Pradesh (UP), accompanied by the whole
caboodle of the UP Council of ministers, immediately after
they had sworn fidelity to the Constitution (ananya and
avibhajya, no less), and taken a second but rather more
colourful oath (as, mind you, duly sworn-in ministers of the
UP government): '*Ram lalla, hum aaye hain, hum mandir yahin
banayenge!*'[3]

For that is really the core of Advani's problem. The
authentic voice of Hindutva is far gruffer than the dulcet tones
of L.K. Advani in Parliament. Take this statement from one of
the few respectable intellectuals of Hindutva, Professor Gopal
Krishna of that 'think-tank of think-tanks', the Centre for
Developing Societies, New Delhi:

> Our master text, the *Mahabharata*, has for its central
> theme the idea of a just war, *relentlessly pursued*. A dose

of Nietzsche, who extols the virtues of struggle in human pursuit, will do us no harm. [The last guy to say that was Adolf Hitler!] The struggle for Ram Janmabhoomi is an essential part of this larger understanding, and it would, therefore, be a great tragedy if the Hindus were, *for any reason whatsoever*, to compromise their claim to the sacred site in Ayodhya, or for that matter to those in Kashi and Mathura.[4]

Now, if it is no less than a scriptural injunction of Lord Krishna Himself that the war for Ayodhya must be 'relentlessly pursued', even if the courts, under the Constitution, order you to relent, and if nothing, 'for any reason whatsoever', including an explicit order from the courts, is to be allowed to stand in the way of compromising the claim to Ayodhya, 'or for that matter to Kashi and Mathura', of what worth is Advani's assurance in the sacred precincts of Parliament that, in the event of a conflict between *Ram ki saugandh* and the pledge to the Constitution, the latter will 'of course' prevail and that too 'without a shadow of doubt'?

No, I was not sanguine that Advani would prove equal to the challenge. He never got around to explaining that when he says he holds his pledge to the Constitution higher than his pledge to Ram, what he means is that, only if the court says that the masjid is a mandir, will he, in accordance with his constitutional obligation, uphold a mere earthly oath over an oath made in heaven, and subordinate his *Ram ki saugandh* to the legal legerdemain of the founding fathers of the Constitution.

Less than six months after this exchange on the floor of the House, both Advani and Joshi, accompanied by Uma Bharti with Chief Minister Kalyan Singh of UP in tow, were in Ayodhya on that infamous Black Sunday, 6 December 1992. The Babri Masjid came tumbling down, vandalizing not only a sacred place of worship but the entire composite heritage of India. Advani did nothing about it. Had he actually held his pledge to the Constitution higher than the personal pledge he had made to his Lord, he would have stepped under the dome of the first *gumbaz* to be assaulted and proclaimed that the next brick to fall would fall on his head. That is what Gandhi would have done. Advani did not. But then Gandhi was a secular Indian. Advani is not. The Babri Masjid fell because the communalist in Advani proved far stronger than the constitutionalist.

Uniform Civil Code

The Constitution enjoins the state to 'endeavour' to frame a 'uniform civil code' but wisely refrains from prescribing a time limit or from making this Directive Principle of State Policy enforceable through the courts.

The point to be noted is that we already have a voluntary civil code: the Special Marriage Act, 1954 (under which I got married). This Act, read with several other pieces of legislation not based on religion, notably the Indian Succession Act, 1925, provides a comprehensive legal framework for all matters of marriage, divorce, maintenance and succession for any Indian who wishes to eschew religion-based jurisprudence. It is a voluntary civil code unconnected to personal laws of any particular religion.

The first lot of Indians who refused to accept the voluntary civil code as a compulsory civil code were the Hindus. It was after the Special Marriage Act was passed in 1954 (the Act which Jawaharlal Nehru described as the 'forerunner' of the uniform civil code) that the Hindus not only secured for themselves the Hindu Marriage Act of 1955 but also the Hindu Succession Act of 1956. Not content with these two pieces of religion-based legislation, the majority community pushed through Parliament the Hindu Adoption and Maintenance Act of 1956, notwithstanding the maintenance provisions of the Code of Criminal Procedure (CrPC), 1898 (whose 1973 version was the matter in dispute in the Shah Bano case). Indeed, alarmed at the secular provisions of the Guardians and Wards Act of 1890, the Hindu community persuaded Parliament to have a new Hindu Minority and Guardianship law enacted for their benefit in 1956.

The story does not end there. In 1976, Parliament excluded Hindus married under the secular provisions of the Special Marriage Act from the jurisdiction of the secular provisions of the Indian Succession Act, 1925—but did not so exclude Muslims, Christians or Parsis. This has resulted in the extraordinary anomaly that a member of the majority community who accepts the voluntary civil code can escape from its secular rigours whenever he likes, but a member of a religious minority who voluntarily accepts the common civil code is bound to it for life! If this is not appeasement of the majority community, I would like to know what 'appeasement' is.

I do not in the least begrudge a Hindu the right to his religion-based personal law. What I object to is Hindu communalists pretending to be in favour of a uniform civil code while assiduously protecting and promoting their own personal law. Is the 'uniform civil code' a euphemism for the Hindu civil code? If not, what prevented the BJP-led government in power at the Centre from 1998 to 2004 from repealing the application of Hindu personal law in favour of the compulsory application to all Hindus of the Special Marriage Act, 1954, and the Indian Succession Act, 1925, not to mention all the other non-religion-based legislation that is already on our statutes?

None of this can be done as long as our people take their religion and customs seriously. Indian secularism cannot be based on the denial of religion. It has to be based on the affirmation of dharma while recognizing that dharma appears in the form of different religions (or *panth*) to different groups of Indians. Hence, *sarva dharma sambhaava* (all religions are worthy of equal respect) as the first principle of Indian secularism.

But can all religions be treated with equal respect if gender inequalities are condemned in Islamic law but consecrated in Hindu law? Indeed, was not the Indian Succession Act made inapplicable to marriages between Hindus under the Special Marriage Act only because the former gave equal rights to sons and daughters while traditional Hindu law, as embodied in the Hindu Succession Act, not only prevents Hindu daughters from seeking partition of joint family property, it even prohibits daughters from objecting to sons undertaking such partition without their consent? While granting a son a share in his father's property as a matter of his birthright, Hindu law imposes various constraints on the daughter who has to demand and secure these rights within the ambit of such restrictions. Contrast this with the position in Islamic law, where a daughter acquires unfettered and total rights to her share of her father's property the minute the father dies. Or for that matter take the right which a daughter has in Islamic law to remain an integral part of her father's family, with all the legal rights over property pertaining thereto, whether she be a maiden, married or divorced, contrasted with the basic proposition in Hindu law that a daughter leaves her father's family on marriage and becomes a part of her husband's family. Or compare the Hindu rite of marriage which treats the *saptapadi* as an indissoluble sacrament with the nikah, which coldly sets out the terms on which the marriage may be annulled at the very moment it is being contracted.

All religion-based laws, being traditional in nature and originating in an era less enlightened than ours, are infected with the virus of gender discrimination. Codification of personal law through Parliament opens the way to the reform of personal law—but the reforms proposed have necessarily to come from within the community. No Muslim suggested any of the changes that have been effected in Hindu personal law.

Similarly, it is only Muslims who have brought about major reforms in Muslim personal law in every Muslim country from Indonesia to Morocco. Nor is there anything in Islamic jurisprudence that stands in the way of removing social evils such as polygamy and triple talaq. Triple talaq has been banned in most Muslim countries and even bigamy, let alone polygamy, is banned or severely restricted—and in any case, permitted only with the judicial sanction of family courts. (In our great secular country, the Bar has prevented the establishment of family courts even in Delhi merely because family courts require no lawyers!)

Yet, even Ghuman Mal Lodha, a retired high court chief justice and then BJP MP, sneered in a speech delivered in Mumbai, in 1993, that Muslims will never accept a uniform civil code voluntarily, adding quite derogatorily that the 'imams' will never let them. Why will they not let them? If even in Pakistan the 'imams' (whatever Lodha's offensive and communal use of the term 'imam' means) have not been able to stop the emergence of the very progressive Pakistan Family Law, what is it that really stands in the way of the codification (and, therefore, reform) of Muslim personal law in India?

One and only one factor stands in the way of the reform of Muslim personal law and its codification through laws passed by Parliament: the demand for the immediate imposition, by brute majority, of a uniform civil code on the Muslims by a political party which had only one elected Muslim member each in the twelfth and thirteenth Lok Sabha, articulated by people like Lodha whose idiom is full of anti-Muslim communalism (he denounces an optional civil code as 'trickery'!), who are assiduous in protecting and practising gender discrimination within their own community in dereliction of the country's voluntary civil code and who, in the guise of a uniform civil code, wish to impose on the Muslims and the other minorities a basically Hindu civil code. (See how clever they are: Hindu personal law prohibits marriages between not only first cousins but even second cousins; virtually a majority of Muslim marriages are between cousins, usually first cousins; the Special Marriage Act prohibits marriages between first cousins but not between second cousins: so a Hindu wishing to escape the rigours of his personal law's prohibition on marrying a second cousin can seek refuge in the Special Marriage Act, while a Muslim wanting to marry a first cousin is left with no alternative to his personal law!)

The Muslims of India have long accepted a common criminal code. They have also consented to the codification by the legislature of key elements of Islamic jurisprudence, through such pre-independence legislation as the Shariat Application Act, 1937, and the path-breaking Dissolution of Muslim Marriages Act, 1939. The single most significant post-independence attempt at bringing Muslim personal law within the ambit of Parliament—and our civil courts—was Rajiv Gandhi's Muslim Women (Compensation on Divorce) Act, 1986, discussed in greater detail in a later section. In the howl of controversy which enveloped that initiative, further progress in the direction of codifying Muslim personal law through Parliament with the voluntary consent of the Muslim community was halted in its tracks.

We are left with the obiter dicta of Justice Kuldip Singh and the ranting of the BJP. The latter we are used to. But what are we to do about the pronouncements of a sitting judge of the Supreme Court who implies that anyone supporting a personal law for the Muslims subscribes to the 'two-nation theory'? I thought the Constitution rejected the two-nation theory but protected the personal law of all our religious groupings, not only the minorities but also the majority. Do you think any self-respecting Muslim will cheerfully acquiesce to a uniform civil code imposed on him because for him to want to marry his first cousin, as his father did and his father's father before him, makes him a traitor? The two-nation theory said one religion will be supreme in one country. Our

Constitution says all religions will be equal in our country. The Muslims of India have as much right to their personal law as the Hindus. What would be desirable is reform and codification of laws within each community before we move to the far more complex task of culling out elements from the laws of different communities with a view to evolving an acceptable uniform civil code for all.

The only place where codification of Muslim personal law and, subsequently, a uniform civil code can be seriously considered is the Law Commission. L.K. Advani himself has indicated that the BJP would ask the Law Commission to examine the personal laws of the various communities to cull out the modern, progressive and equitable ingredients of these laws and, on that basis, draw up a common civil code. Excellent. But does Advani know that in fifty years of independence, we have had a Muslim as a member of the Law Commission only once—Justice Nasrullah Baig, who died within months of his appointment, and who was never an acknowledged expert in Islamic jurisprudence? What faith will the minorities have in the pronouncements of an all-Hindu Law Commission?

Conversions and the Constitution

The Constitution grants every citizen the fundamental right to propagate one's faith. It does not confer a right to convert. However, it also gives every citizen the right to be converted. One is free to change one's religion—or abandon religion altogether. There are no conditions attached to that right. The citizen is not obliged to explain to any court, or to any self-appointed guardian, why he has changed his religion. He has to explain that only to his conscience.

To tamper with the right to freedom of religion is to tamper with the right to freedom of expression. And the right to propagate religion is inherently both a right to freedom of expression and a right to freedom of religion. Leave alone the Constitution, there is nothing in any law of Hinduism which says a Hindu cannot leave his faith. There is not even a spiritual injunction against apostasy as in several Semitic religions. Indeed, ever since the Charvakas, a Hindu does not even have to be a theist to be a Hindu.

The Sangh Parivar has taken this a step further and declared that you do not even have to be a Hindu to be a Hindu! For, they insist, the Indian Muslim and the Indian Christian are 'Muslim Hindus' and 'Christian Hindus'. To call oneself, and consider oneself, a Hindu has been made the litmus test of not only what is politically correct but of patriotism itself.

This leads to conundrums that are at once both amusing and dangerous. Amusing because if the expression is civilizational rather than denominational, as the Parivar claims, surely we should have not only agnostic Hindus and atheist Hindus, but also Hindu Hindus! Dangerous because those who have no difficulty in calling themselves Hindu are put on a pedestal of nationality higher than those citizens of this country who do not call themselves Hindu for the good reason that they are not Hindu but Muslim, Christian, atheist, or whatever. These latter have no problem with, indeed take pride in, calling and considering themselves Indian Muslims, Indian Christians, Indian atheists and so on. But the entire spectrum of the Sangh Parivar has confused Hindutva with Bhartiyata, thus targeting the minorities as the enemy within.

This is why the demand for a national debate on conversions is about conversions from Hinduism, not converting to Hinduism. If missionaries as a whole, rather than Christian missionaries alone, are to be considered, a good starting point might be the Ramakrishna Mission. The Ramakrishna Mission is probably the most widespread, most influential and most effective of the missions operating in the country—certainly more widespread, more influential and more effective than the

Evangelical Mission of Graham Staines, who was brutally murdered by zealots of the saffron brigade.

The Ramakrishna Mission runs schools, dispensaries and hospitals. It reaches out to people in the remotest and poorest parts of the country, including Arunachal Pradesh where the locals are followers of Donyi-Polo rather than Brahma, Vishnu or Siva. It works among lepers. It comforts the incurable. Its missionaries wear a habit that marks them out. They do their work in the name of their god. They believe in the beliefs of Sri Ramakrishna Paramahamsa. They aspire to the example of Swami Vivekananda. They propagate their faith, as Swamiji did at Chicago. Moreover, they are living exemplars of the best in their faith. And they receive into their fold those who wish to follow their way of life.

Father Graham Staines did exactly the same. He, like all missionaries—Christian, Islamic or other—worked among the afflicted and the deprived. Most of his time and energies were devoted to healing the sick, comforting those in pain, tending to the dying, imparting self-respect to those marginalized by society, educating the illiterate, bringing a ray of hope into the enveloping darkness. Like the missionaries of the Ramakrishna Mission, he did his work in the name of his god. But he never said: '*Isai nahin, toh dawai nahin* [no medicine without Christianity]'—the grim, terrible charge trumpeted by the Bajrang Dal and other harbingers of crime in the name of religion. Yes, he propagated his faith, and received into his religion those who wished to follow his way of life.

To those who will point out that the Ramakrishna Mission is working in its own country, while Staines came out to India to do his dark deeds, I can only say that the Ramakrishna Mission does its good work not only here but also beyond the political frontiers of India, that is, Bharat. It is to be found not only in countries where substantial numbers of Hindus reside like Nepal, Trinidad and Tobago, Fiji, Mauritius or South Africa, but also in Europe and America. The ashrams of the

Ramakrishna Mission—as those of Maharishi Mahesh Yogi or the late Osho or of Swami Sivananda's Divine Life Society—whether abroad or in India, are filled with Hindu followers who were born in a different faith. Those who deem that an accident of birth placed them in a faith other than the one they believe in are welcomed in their thousands into the Hindu fold by Hindu religious organizations both at home and elsewhere.

Staines was doing no more. The numbers he served ran into thousands. The numbers he received into the Christian church added up to a few scores. He neither insisted on conversion as the price to be paid for his assistance, nor did he turn back from the church door those who wished to be received into his faith. The impact of the good works of this Christian missionary is more widespread than his evangelism. It is the same with other Christian missionaries in other parts of the country. That is the reason why the district of Dangs in Gujarat, snatched from obscurity and thrust into notoriety by the Vishwa Hindu Parishad (VHP) and its ilk, has a single-digit percentage of Christian tribals. One estimate I have read places the Christian share of the tribal population of Dangs district at under 2 per cent. Many of these are being brought 'home' to the Hindu fold, i.e. being reconverted, precisely by those who dub all conversions a non-Hindu sleight of hand.

The Constitution and the law, not to mention explicit rulings by the Supreme Court, forbid conversion by force. There are three levels at which conversion by force can be countered and countermanded. First, since there is no right to convert, but a Fundamental Right to be converted, any individual can sue for annulment of his conversion on grounds that he was converted by force, threat, bribery or blandishment, or, indeed, any other reason extraneous to the desire to be converted.

Second, any organization—in this case, the Sangh Parivar or any of its sister outfits—has only to take to a court of law, under public interest litigation, any evidence of compulsion (including '*Isai nahin, toh dawai nahin*'). Foreign missionaries, in particular, would find it practically impossible to stay on in the country if faced with such strictures; foreign donations to their organizations would then come under the heady and disapproving eye of the Foreign Contributions Regulation Act (FCRA).

Third, if the state has any evidence of innocents being threatened or cajoled against their free will into changing their religion, it only has to act under the law. Instead, lawless criminals are being encouraged, supported and backed to trample on our constitutional rights and take the law, as they see it, into their hands.

The latest assault on the constitutional provisions for propagation arose in Tamil Nadu where the legislature, dominated 196 to thirty-four by Chief Minister Jayalalithaa's AIADMK, passed a legislation in 2002 obliging anyone who changes his or her religion to inform the local district authority and swear through an affidavit that the conversion has been undertaken voluntarily and without threat or blandishment.[5] The explanatory statement attached to the legislation claimed: 'Reports have been received by the Government that conversions from one religion to another are made by the use of force or by fraudulent means.'

If this were true, it was the state government's duty to bring the offenders to book. Not one case was prosecuted on the grounds alleged in the explanatory statement, which went on to state: 'Bringing in legislation to prohibit such conversions will act as a deterrent against the anti-social and vested interest groups exploiting the innocent people belonging to the depressed classes. It may also be useful to nip in the bud attempts by certain religious fundamentalist and subversive forces to create communal tension under the garb of religious conversion.'

Note how Christian padres fulfilling their constitutional right to propagate their religion were equated with 'anti-social and vested interest groups' and 'religious fundamentalist and subversive forces'. Note also the equation of 'conversion' with 'exploitation'. And finally, note the Brahmin Jayalalithaa objecting to the 'depressed classes' expressing their resentment at upper-caste discrimination by converting to another religion.

The legislation was wholly unnecessary. The courts would in any case hold as fraudulent any forced conversion, as has been determined by the Supreme Court decades ago. The aim of the Tamil Nadu legislation was clearly to intimidate prospective converts by bringing in the 'awesome majesty' of the state through its bureaucracy into what is surely a private matter between individuals and their conscience.

It is argued that the purpose of the legislation was not to limit conversion out of conviction on the part of individuals but to put an end to the mass conversion of whole habitations of the kind that first caught the public eye at Meenakshipuram in the early 1980s when Harijans converted to Christianity. But the effect of such legislation remains intimidation because the poor and the deprived, especially the 'depressed classes', would want to protect themselves from social censure and ostracism by converting en masse rather than take such a bold step individually, rendering themselves vulnerable to retribution.

The legislation needlessly spread social tension in the state, pitting the Christian organizations of the country against the Tamil Nadu government. The Catholic Bishops' Conference protested that the legislation was 'particularly oppressive of the already oppressed groups like dalits and women', arguing that as 'the church has very clearly stated many times in the past' that 'forced conversion is no conversion', the legislation goes against both the Constitution and the Universal Declaration of Human Rights.

The ideologues of Hindutva are diligently spreading the idea that any faith which has not originated within the boundaries of modern India is alien to our culture. This is what lies behind legislations like the one passed by the Tamil Nadu government, behind the suspicion we harbour against Christian missionaries and, indeed, behind the acrimonious debate on conversions and its often violent repercussions that we have witnessed in the recent past.

Cow Slaughter

The issue of cow slaughter was settled once and for all during the drafting of the Constitution in 1948–49. On 24 November 1948, on a motion moved by Seth Govind Dass and Pandit Thakur Das Bhargava, and after a Muslim representative from the United Provinces, S.H. Lari, had spoken pleading for clarity in the matter to obviate communal clashes over cow slaughter, Dr Ambedkar agreed to incorporate a reference to cow protection in the Directive Principles of State Policy. Later, T.T. Krishnamachari, speaking for the Congress in the Constituent Assembly on 2 September 1949, said that the relevant entry in the state list of legislative powers ensures that state governments 'have ample powers to ban cattle slaughter' but the entry could not refer to cow slaughter as such because that is a 'statement of policy' which is for the state government concerned, not the Central government to take nor for the Constituent Assembly to impose.[6]

The cow is protected in all states not under communist or Christian sway. Fascinatingly, the state with the oldest record of a ban on cow slaughter is Muslim-majority Jammu and Kashmir (J&K). Among the two most prominent states where such legislation is still to be passed are Goa, where the BJP is in office, and Nagaland, where Chief Minister Nephiu Rio is in office as a partner of the BJP. The main point of Rio's first press conference in New Delhi after becoming chief minister in March 2003 was an adamant refusal to change the beef-eating habits of the Nagas. Rather than communalizing the issue, the advocates of a ban on cow slaughter would be better advised to see if this is feasible or desirable in tourism-dependent Goa (where beef is on the menu of almost every restaurant and beach shack) and Nagaland (where beef is the local equivalent of *daal chawal*).

In the run-up to independence, Ramkrishna Dalmia, uncle of the VHP leader, Vishnu Hari Dalmia, launched himself and the newspaper he then owned, the *Times of India*, on a fierce campaign to secure a ban on cow slaughter. He roped into his cause the president of the Constituent Assembly, Dr Rajendra Prasad, who brought to Jawaharlal Nehru's attention a large number of telegrams and other representations urging an outright ban on cow slaughter.

Nehru's reply of 7 August 1947 deserves to be retrieved from the archives.[7] First, Nehru dismissed the campaign as 'slightly spurious': 'Dalmia's money is flowing and Dalmia is not exactly a desirable person.' Nevertheless, Nehru was well aware of the widespread Hindu sentiment on the matter of cow protection and that Hindu sentiment affected the country in many ways. He also conceded that there might be an economic argument for preventing the slaughter of cows although he felt this aspect required deeper study. What he objected to was a ban on cow slaughter 'purely on the grounds of Hindu sentiment'. For him India was a composite country despite its overwhelming Hindu population. As such, any solution to the problem had to originate within the framework of this composite culture. The issue could not be resolved only to the satisfaction of the Hindu majority, ignoring the viewpoint of other groups.

He also made the telling point that even Mahatma Gandhi, in spite of being a strong advocate of cow protection, was opposed to any compulsory stoppage of cow slaughter simply because India could not function as a Hindu state. Gandhi's position on cow protection, as reported by Tendulkar, was bluntly stated on 25 July 1947 in the run-up to partition:

The Hindu religion prohibited cow slaughter for the Hindus, not for the world. The religious prohibition came from within. Any imposition from without meant compulsion. Such compulsion was repugnant to religion. India was the land not only of the Hindus, but also of the Mussalmans, the Sikhs, the Parsis, the Christians and the Jews and all who claimed to be of India and were loyal to the Indian union.[8]

The BJP argument is the diametric opposite of the Gandhi–Nehru line. They say that precisely because Hindus predominate, we must function as a Hindu state. What secularists need to recognize is that the argument is not about gaumata at all, but about whether we are to function as a secular state or a Hindu Rashtra.

Shah Bano Revisited

I too was outraged by the Shah Bano case. That any court in a civilized country should believe Rs 25 a month is adequate to save a woman from becoming a vagrant is, indeed, shocking. Yet, that is all the Indore Sessions Court awarded Shah Bano. And that a high court, in response to an appeal from the indigent woman in question, should munificently raise the sum to Rs 179.20 (nice touch of judicial finesse, that 20 p)— well below the minimum wage for rural labour in the country— is even more shocking. Yet, that is precisely what the Madhya Pradesh High Court did. And that the highest court in the land, in a judgment delivered by its longest-serving (and, doubtless, longest-winded) chief justice should have no comment whatsoever to make on the effrontery of obliging an indigent woman to shell out Rs 10,000 to receive through a court order a measly Rs 179.20 per mensem (which she could have got merely by investing her ten thousand in any fixed deposit) is most shocking of all.

And yet the utter injustice of the vagrancy provisions of our CrPC towards indigent women booted out by their husbands is the one injustice that no one—least of all the crusaders for a uniform civil code led by King Advani the Lion-Heart—has bothered to undo. No one then—or since—has sought to say that the minimum maintenance to be paid by a Hindu husband or a Christian one or an agnostic mate to an indigent wife or ex-wife should at least equal the statutory minimum wage in force in the area where the poor woman lives (which, in a city like Mumbai, should set back the culpable by well over a thousand a month). Neither has anyone said that it is ridiculous to fix the maximum limit payable to stave off vagrancy at Rs 500 per month, however affluent the husband might be. If, says our CrPC, even the wealthiest industrialists and businessmen of this country were to get rid of a meddlesome wife, and she, poor waif, were to be rendered indigent, the businessman in question would be required to cough up, at most, Rs 500 a month—less than the tip he may give the *darwan* who opens his car door outside the five-star hotel he visits—and not a paisa more.

Is this justice?

Well, in a curious way, it perhaps is. Because the vagrancy provisions of our CrPC (Sections 125 and 127)—which is all that was at issue in the Shah Bano case—deal only with the minimum steps to be taken to keep a woman in penury off the streets. They do not—emphatically do *not*—deal with divorce law. Marriage, and its sometimes unfortunate concomitant, divorce, are and remain firmly within the ambit of personal law. And all personal laws—not just Muslim personal laws but the personal laws of all religious communities—need to be repealed and substituted by a mandatory common civil code.

I stress this because I am yet to discover what response, if any, the BJP has to the questions posed as long ago as 9 March 1986 in an interview to the *Sunday Observer* by the man most experts would rate as India's greatest authority on Islamic jurisprudence. Not some bearded maulana pulled out of some wretched madrasa, but the thoroughly contemporary, non-theocratic and indubitably secular academic, Dr Tahir Mahmood, professor of law at the University of Delhi and editor of *Islamic and Comparative Law Quarterly*.

Dr Mahmood pointed out that conversion by a man or

woman into a non-Hindu religion is a ground for divorce under Hindu law. Hindu law also prohibits a Hindu from inheriting from a non-Hindu, and stipulates that a Hindu mother does not remain a guardian of her children on becoming a Muslim. If these are all elements of personal law and so long as there is a Hindu personal law and a Christian personal law, Muslim personal law is bound to claim application and protection.

Until sensitivities such as these simmer down, it would, of course, be best not to get entangled in the thicket of such uncomfortable questions. But, as the BJP insists that the *only* reason it has politicized the Ram Janmabhoomi affair—an issue on which it had no position till 1986—is the Muslim Women's Act, an authoritative answer to Dr Tahir Mahmood's poser is surely in order.

Arguments (especially between husbands and wives but, as often as not, between political parties too) are usually not about what they seem to be. The BJP seized upon the Shah Bano issue not out of great concern for Muslim women but only because it gave them a populist opening to pander to prevalent Hindu misconceptions about the role of women in Islam and to stoke communal passions. That is why no one, least of all the BJP, paid any more attention to the Shah Bano case, as it wound its tortuous way through seven long years from the first class magistrate's court in Indore to the high court in Jabalpur to the Supreme Court in Delhi.

What made everyone sit up was not poor Shah Bano's maintenance requirements but Chief Justice Chandrachud's ex-cathedra pronouncements on Islam and the two questions that this gave rise to: one, whether the vagrancy provisions of the CrPC were in conflict with the shariat. And, if so, would it be the shariat that would prevail or the penal code.

That—and not whether Rs 179.20 would prevent Shah Bano drifting into vagrancy—was the minefield opened not so much by the sentence pronounced by the Supreme Court against Shah Bano's husband but by Justice Chandrachud's lengthy and, in my view, wholly unnecessary disquisition on the true meaning of the shariat, departures from the shariat in present Muslim personal law, and that totally irrelevant hornets' nest: the forcible imposition of a uniform civil code on a minority struggling to preserve its characteristic rites and rituals, customs and usages.

When the CrPC—which dates back to 1898—was thoroughly recast in 1973, Ram Niwas Mirdha, the minister who piloted the bill through Parliament, made it clear that the government did not intend to have any provision of the recast CrPC (specifically, Sections 125 and 127) infringe in any way on any Muslim personal law: 'We would not like to interfere with the personal law of the Muslim through the Criminal Procedure Code.'[9]

Chief Justice Chandrachud went to inordinate lengths in his judgment—quoting chapter and verse from the Koran, the Hadith, the aiyats of the sura and every authority from Marmaduke Pickthall to Mulla's *Principles of Mahomedan Law* (would that he had heeded the poet Alexander Pope: 'A little learning is a dangerous thing/Drink deep or taste not of the Pierian spring'!)—to establish that the vagrancy provisions of the CrPC, far from being an infringement of Muslim personal law, were in fact perfectly compatible with that law.

And Arif Mohammed Khan, the then minister of state for home affairs, took great pains in his personal intervention in the debate on private members' bill to insist that the vagrancy provisions were not in conflict with Muslim personal law.[10] The gravamen of his argument was that it was not the whole of marriage and divorce law for the Muslims that was at issue but only the limited question of how Islam would view a secular law providing for Muslim husbands to save from vagrancy women who have no means of subsistence and who are also not capable of making a living.

Arif expressly regretted Justice Chandrachud's needless

intrusion into controversial realms, insisting that the Supreme Court need not have gone into it at all and that such a big controversy would not have arisen if the Supreme Court had shown some restraint and judicial discretion.

So, everyone who believed Sections 125 and 127 of the CrPC should apply to the Shah Bano case also believed that it did not conflict with Muslim personal law. Therefore, there was no need to tackle, in the Shah Bano context, the related but vital question of whether, in the event of such a conflict, Muslim personal law would or would not have to submit to the dictates of the secular law. Tragically, instead of keeping his mouth shut on an issue which he himself held did not arise in this case, Chief Justice Chandrachud delivered himself of the obiter dicta that, if any conflict arose, Muslim personal law must bow before the secular law of the land. Thus was ignited the bush fire. Quarrels are, indeed, rarely over what they seem to be about.

Article 30: Minority Educational Rights

Article 30 of the Constitution provides that 'all minorities, whether based on religion or language, shall have the right to establish and administer educational institutions of their choice'. Also, that there shall be no discrimination by the state in the matter of aiding an educational institution 'on the ground that it is under the management of a minority'. A subsequent additional clause, brought in by way of an amendment, provided that if the state were to acquire property belonging to a minority educational institution, it should not be done in such a manner as to expunge the right of that minority to continue establishing and administering educational institutions of their choice.

Article 30 has to be read in conjunction with Article 29 which stipulates that 'no citizen shall be denied admission into any educational institution maintained by the state or receiving aid out of state funds on grounds only of religion, race, caste, language or any of them'.

Now, would anyone other than the BJP suggest that Article 30 is either the source of all evil in our society or the root cause of all mischief? Or that the deletion of Article 30 is the magic panacea for our problems? Can it be held that the educational and cultural rights of our minorities, whether religious or linguistic, require no constitutional safeguards?

Article 30 does not stand in the way of anyone, majority or minority, establishing an educational institution. Nor does it prevent anyone from reciting the Gita in a Hindu educational institution even as it assures the Muslims the right to study and recite the Koran in theirs. It is perfect nonsense for Advani to say that Article 30 stands in the way of schoolchildren singing *Vande Mataram* or intoning the Bhagawad Gita. Perhaps they are confusing Article 30 with Article 28 of the Constitution.

Article 28 says that 'no religious instruction shall be provided in any educational institution wholly maintained out of state funds'. Dr B.R. Ambedkar gave three reasons for this provision when replying to the debate on this in the Constituent Assembly:

- Since another Article in the Constitution prohibits the imposition of taxes to bolster any particular religious belief or practice, tax revenues deployed for wholly funding a state educational institution cannot be used for propagating any one religion;
- It would be impossible to provide for religious instruction for all the different religions and indeed the different sects among Hindus represented in a state school;
- Problems would arise if any one religion were to claim that its teachings constitute the only right path for salvation, that all other religions are wrong. The peaceful atmosphere of the institution would in that case be disturbed.

However, Article 28 itself makes it clear that the prohibition on religious instruction (but not moral teaching) applies only to wholly state-funded institutions. It does not apply to institutions which rely but partly on state funding. And if the state is merely administering an educational institution set up by a Trust, whose deed contains specific injunctions with regard to religious instruction, those injunctions will be respected. Finally, Article 28 says that no person attending a state-aided or state-recognized educational institution will be compelled to participate in any religious instruction courses unless the student or his/her guardian agrees to it.

In short, if Advani so wishes, he can hear the *Vande Mataram* sung in any school not covered by Article 30, just as any Muslim can learn the Hadith or the suras in a minority institution established under Article 30. Similarly, Advani and his boys can get the Upanishads taught to students who are willing to be so taught, in any but 100 per cent state-aided schools, even as schools set up under Article 30 are free to teach the Koran and the Bible to those who seek admission to such avowedly minority institutions established by the minority concerned to cater to the cultural and religious requirements of that community.

Does any of this warrant an assault against secularism? There is, of course, scope for improvement and I, for one, would be prepared to expand Article 30 to cover any denomination, especially if that would silence Advani. But not to appease Advani who claims that Article 30 is the source of all 'mischief', and its amendment or deletion an overriding national priority.

The issue came to the fore in the Supreme Court decision in a case relating to my alma mater, St Stephen's College of Delhi University, regarding the quota which could be reserved for the admission of Christian students in a minority institution. St Stephen's has been run by the Cambridge Mission since its establishment in 1881. The details of that case need not detain us, but the views of the eleven-member Supreme Court bench established by Justice B.N. Kirpal do. Among the issues framed for decision were the following:

- Does the minority's right to establish and administer educational institutions of their choice include procedure and methods of admission and selection of students?
- Can the admission of students to minority educational institutions, aided or unaided, be regulated by the state government or by the university to which the institution is affiliated?
- Was the ratio laid down by the court in the St Stephen's case (St Stephen's College versus Delhi University) in 1992 correct? What is meant by religion in Article 30(1)?

The definitive majority Supreme Court judgment, which came in 2002, held that:

- While unaided minority institutions would have unfettered rights, subject to providing qualifications and minimum conditions of eligibility in the interest of academic standards, aided institutions might be subjected to minimal regulatory measures such as ensuring that admission procedures are 'fair and transparent and the selection of students in professional and higher educational colleges should be on the basis of merit'.
- There could be no a priori fixing of percentages for the number of seats that might be reserved for the minority concerned even in an aided minority institution but state governments might fix the percentage according to the type of institution, the nature of the courses offered and general educational needs.

That is, of course, where the catch is. An unbiased state government would not take unfair advantage of this to unjustly reduce the share of reserved seats but a biased government could. Thus giving rise to the dilemma which minority educational institutions targeting the poor and the marginalized are facing, admirably summed up by John Dayal, secretary general of the All-India Christian Council and vice-president of the All-India Catholic Union, as a 'Catch-22 situation': Anyone who wants to run an institution for the poor, in rural and tribal areas, with government aid runs the risk that the state will impose its will. And if they want to forego state aid, these will necessarily have to be high-cost/high-fees institutions and as such be beyond the reach of the poor.

Reservations for Muslims

On 6 November 1996, I penned an open letter to a Muslim Indian I greatly admire—Syed Shahabuddin, my former colleague in both the Indian Foreign Service and in the tenth Lok Sabha, and editor of *Muslim India*, a magazine excoriated as communal by the communal Hindu right but which has always seemed to me to address communitarian concerns without being communal, a distinction of considerable importance.

I had, in a number of articles around that time, advocated reservations for women in the legislatures, and Shahabuddin had posed the question whether I agreed that there should be similar reservations for Muslims in our legislatures since Muslims are woefully under-represented and indubitably constitute a 'backward class' within the meaning of Articles 15 and 16 of the Constitution.

I pointed out that the concept of the 'backward classes' was introduced into our Constitution through the First Amendment in 1951. While great care was taken to use the expression 'class' rather than 'caste', the Mandal Commission, in its wisdom or lack of it, chose to take caste as the basic unit of our society and so based its identification of the 'backward classes' on caste rather than class. The Supreme Court sought to reintroduce the distinguishing element of 'class' rather than 'caste' by ordering the exclusion of the 'creamy layer' from the special measures that are taken in favour of the 'backward castes'. Equally, the talk of introducing economic criteria in the steps taken for the 'backward classes' is designed to extend the benefits of such affirmative action to 'classes' that are backward rather than confine such action only to 'castes' that are backward.

The Muslims, as a community, are without doubt a backward class. As such, they should be included among the beneficiaries of all employment and, above all, educational programmes based on Mandal. However, there should be no objection to the creamy layer of Muslims being excluded from such benefits. At the same time, I argued, if Mandal were extended to backward Muslims, Mandal should also be extended to backward segments of other minority religious communities, and, in fact, the logic could be taken further to include the backward segments of the so-called 'forward castes'.

The Mandal Commission restricted itself to proposing reservations in Central government employment and educational institutions. It did not suggest reservations in the legislatures. Though the 73rd and 74th amendments to the Constitution provide for reservations for backward classes in the local bodies, these local bodies are not legislatures. They are elected institutions of participative, popular governance, primarily concerned with the planning and implementation of programmes of economic development and social justice. They have no legislative functions of their own and are empowered through devolution and decentralization, not through legislative authority. Reservations for the backwards in the local bodies does not of itself legitimize similar reservations for them in the legislatures. That will require a constitutional amendment, and is ultimately fraught with dangers.

My plea for reservations for women was not based on Articles 15 and 16 of the Constitution. Nor does my argument in favour of reservations define or treat women as 'a backward class'. The argument in favour of reservations for women is based on recognizing that women are woefully under-represented in our legislatures and it would be beneficial to the polity as a whole if a larger participation of half our population were to be deliberately promoted in our legislatures. Reservations for women are based on considerations of gender discrimination, not community discrimination. Since there are only two genders, gender-based reservations will apply to only one gender, a gender represented in every community. Community-based reservations cannot, however, be limited to one community; all unrepresented or under-represented communities would, in equity, have to be given the same opportunity. Since India is a congeries of communities, we will end up with a congeries of reservations. In effect, I concluded, proportionate representation for the communities will have the same consequence that separate electorates had under the imperial dispensation.

Looking back at what I wrote eight years ago in the light of what I have since learned from two Muslim Indian scholars—Omar Khalidi of the Massachusetts Institute of Technology, Harvard University, and Rafiq Zakaria—I fear I may have been a little too sanguine and a little too glib in my response to Shahabuddin. Worse, it was perhaps an example of the 'patronizing secularism' which Mukul Kesavan so rightly deplores in *Secular Commonsense*: 'Secularism in independent India soon became patronage when it was practised by the state and gallantry when practised by the self-consciously secular...Secularists see Muslims individually and the Muslim "community" in general as objects of gallantry.'[11]

Khalidi argues that Muslim leaders and journalists, while alleging discrimination as being responsible for the poor representation of Muslims in virtually all spheres of our national life, have not been able to provide conclusive evidence to establish the alleged discrimination. In view of this, I wonder if I have been guilty of what Kesavan terms the 'gallantry of the self-consciously secular' in my adherence to secularism.

Yet, that Muslims are very poorly represented in government services and public sector enterprises, all the way from the highest to the lowest echelons, cannot be denied. There is gross under-representation also in the police and security forces, as well as in the armed forces. Khalidi cites authorities like N.C. Saksena, Vijay Karan, Murali Krishnan and R.K. Raghavan to state that in sensitive and secret services like the Central Bureau of Investigation (CBI), the Intelligence Bureau (IB) and the Research and Analysis Wing (RAW) of the Cabinet Secretariat, Muslim representation appears to be nil or close to nil. The figures speak for themselves:

- Under 2 per cent of officers in the Indian Administrative Service (IAS) are Muslim (1.6 per cent in 1994, just eighty out of a total of 4872, as per a memorandum submitted by K.M. Aarif of the United Economic Forum of Bombay);[12]
- Whereas some 30 to 36 per cent of officers in the British Indian army were Muslims, the percentage dropped to under 2 per cent in the immediate aftermath of independence (as minister of state for defence, Mahavir Tyagi, informed students of Aligarh Muslim University in 1953)[13] and is even now not much higher;
- Under 3 per cent of officers in the Indian Police Service (IPS) were Muslims in 1993; the percentage infinitesimally increased to 3.65 per cent in 2002;[14]
- Neither the National Security Guard (NSG) nor the Special Protection Group (SPG) have any Muslim personnel and the Central Reserve Police Force (CRPF) representation reflects the low overall representation in the IPS;[15] in Assam Rifles, Muslims constitute a tenth of the personnel although Muslims make up almost 30 per cent of the population of Assam;[16] in the Provincial Armed Constabulary (PAC) of Uttar Pradesh, where nearly 20 per cent of the population is Muslim, Muslim representation hovers around 5 to 7 per cent.[17]

Professor Bipan Chandra succinctly sums up the consequences of low minority representation in our security forces when he mentions that the growth of communal violence since 1964 is largely because of the gradual communalization of the police force in many parts of the country. Officials at various levels overtly or covertly encourage communal tendencies. While in Bombay (1992–93) and Gujarat (2002) the police forces actively participated in communal violence against the minorities, in other places like Bhagalpur and Delhi in 1984 and Punjab after 1981, they remained passive spectators to communal atrocities.[18]

He also brings to light the gross under-representation of Muslims in government and non-government employment, and in educational institutions.[19] Only 4.5 per cent of Class I and II employees and 6 per cent of Class III and IV employees in government service are Muslims. Of 310 judges of the high courts in 1980, only fourteen were Muslims. There has been some improvement since then, including the appointment of a Muslim chief justice (Justice Ahmadi), but the percentage of Muslim judges is still way below their share of the population. In the Central Secretariat Service, Muslims account for only 1.43 per cent of the total number of employees; and only 0.72 per cent of the section officers are Muslims. In the educational sector, only 3.41 per cent of engineering students and 3.44 per cent of medical students are Muslims. This unequal representation of Muslims is true of all spheres of everyday life in the country.

Is this because Muslims are inadequately represented in our legislatures? The fact is that Indian democracy has not given Muslims anything like proportionate representation in Parliament or the state assemblies. Muslim membership of the Lok Sabha has varied from 5 to 7 per cent in most Lok Sabhas and reached a peak of 8.5 per cent only in the 1980 elections to the seventh Lok Sabha.[20] What is more disturbing is the decline in the number of Muslims elected to the UP legislature, a state with a proportionately large, much threatened and educationally/economically backward Muslim community: from a high of fifty-two in 1984 to a low of twenty-one in 1991 in a House of 425.[21] The position is no better in the Rajya Sabha, which could have been used to give representation to communities poorly represented in the directly elected lower house. As Zakaria mentions, in the forty-year period from 1952 to 1992, out of a total of 1500 members in the Rajya Sabha, only 154 were Muslims.[22]

While I have no figures for Muslim elected representatives, including elected Muslim women in seats/posts reserved for women in the panchayats and nagarpalikas after the passage of the historic 73rd and 74th amendments to the Constitution in 1992, one guesses that Muslim representation is fairly satisfactory at the village level in villages or wards where there is a Muslim concentration; somewhat less so at the intermediate level; and very unsatisfactory at the district level for the panchayats as well as in most municipalities and metropolitan corporations (but marginally better in Muslim-dominated nagar panchayats).

So, should there be reservations for Muslims in our legislatures and at the panchayat/nagarpalika level? The answer given by Mukul Kesavan, a secularist I rather admire, is: '...affirmative action and state-sponsored community preservation...is not the way to go about it. The way to do it is by institutionalizing the sharing of power: reserved seats, mandatory quotas, separate electorates, etc.'[23]

I have no doubt that unless Muslim representation is substantially increased in all elected bodies, the Muslim community will continue to suffer subtle but real discrimination and fail to effectively avail of facilities for education, employment or economic opportunity extended to the poor in general. However, are reservations the answer? Kesavan offers no answers to the 'huge historical, political and operational difficulties' attendant on institutionalizing power-sharing between the majority and minority communities on the pattern recommended by him. Here, he is as guilty as the other scholars he blames for not solving the attendant difficulties, such as Neera Chandoke whose patronage secularism he has critiqued.[24] Indeed, Kesavan contradicts himself two pages down when he says that 'the secularist manifesto…should be procedural equality, not preferential rights based on minority status'.[25]

Yet, it is precisely preferential rights based on minority status that lies behind his advocacy of reserved seats, mandatory quotas and separate electorates!

As of now, the considerations urged by Sardar Patel, as cited by Khalidi, remain:

> There is no place here for those who claim separate representation…For a community to think that its interests are different from that of the country in which it lives is a great mistake…You will exclude yourself and remain perpetually in a minority…For the future of a minority, it is best to trust the majority. If the majority misbehaves, it will suffer.[26]

For those like me who find the Sardar's argument too sanguine in the light of the experiences over the last half a century, Khalidi serves up the rather more convincing argument put by Sir Ivor Jennings, the British constitutional authority: 'To compromise with communal claims may be the height of statesmanship because it enables the majority to secure the support of the minorities. To recognize communal claims, on the other hand, is to strengthen communalism.'[27]

Moreover, where does one draw the line? The Muslims are not the only community under-represented in our legislatures. One need go no further than the Tamil Brahmin community into which I was born (as was Mukul Kesavan): should there be reservations for grossly under-represented Tam Brams in the Tamil Nadu state assembly? Perish the thought! As for the local bodies, Karnataka and some other states have shown the way: include Muslims in the category of backward communities and the door to reservations immediately gets opened to them. But a similar provision cannot be made in our legislatures unless we have reservations for backward classes in Parliament and the state assemblies. Perish that thought too! In any case, artificial constitutional constructs for community representation, as in Lebanon, usually come a cropper sooner rather than later. Moreover, can it be seriously argued that reservations for scheduled castes (SC) and scheduled tribes (ST) over the last fifty years have rendered the SC/ST communities any better off than the poor in the Muslim community? Less than one per cent of officers and less than 5 per cent of the enlisted ranks in the armed forces belong to the SC/ST communities.[28]

The answer, I believe, lies in education. Virtually the entire Muslim aristocracy and middle class fled as carpetbaggers to Pakistan; it is the Muslim farmer and proletariat that remained in India. Their educational standards neither enable them to secure jobs in the government or private sector nor does it provide the kick-start the community needs in business. That is what the priority should be. As Khalidi argues, education is the key to the transition of the lower classes into the middle class. The middle class will not grow in the absence of universal and vocational education.[29]

This, of course, is true of all educationally backward communities and individuals. And it is as much for government as for civil society, including NGOs, to address themselves to the desperate educational requirements of the Muslims and other educationally backward communities.

It is imperative for Muslims to involve themselves in electoral politics and in nation building as a whole rather than remaining obsessed with communitarian concerns. If the Muslim community withdraws in protest from politics, as some elements among them urge, it would be suicidal. The experience of Muslims who have made it big in Indian democracy (such as my friends Shahabuddin and G.M. Banatwala) shows that

Muslims can secure non-Muslim votes provided they permeate the political scene. The argument is not utopian. I recall the celebrated case in Ambala, 1957, where a Muslim got elected from a constituency that virtually all Muslims had abandoned in the partition exodus only a decade ago. As quoted by Shyam Chand in *Saffron Fascism*, this drove Golwalkar ballistic as he ranted about the 'suicidal and self-oblivious condition of our society'.

That is where 'Guruji' got it dead wrong! If anything, the victory of a Muslim candidate in an all-Hindu constituency only proves the secular essence of our society. Every under-represented community, including the Muslims, must strive to become more active politically, but as Indians rather than as Muslims. The results will show.

The Four Wives of the Apocalypse: Sex, Lies and Tushtikaran

Nothing has aided the anti-Muslim jihad of the Hindu communalist more than the spectre they have conjured up of the Muslim population overtaking the country's Hindu population. With a wink and a nudge, they whisper to every passing Hindu: the Muslims are opposed to a uniform civil code because that would deprive them of at least three of their four wives! Bring the Islamic quota down to the one the rest of us are permitted, says the Sangh Parivar, and this nation will remain Hindu for ever. Otherwise, they warn, while the other lot breed at four times our rate, we will be reduced, sooner than later, to a minority in our own land.

The lie needs to be nailed.

We have the BJP to thank for having introduced a splendid new word which sums up their favourite preoccupation: tushtikaran, meaning appeasement. That is the essence of their charge against what they so disarmingly hold to be the 'minorityism' of the 'pseudo-secularist'. Tushtikaran, in their view, takes many forms but the worst possible form, says the Sangh Parivar, is our aiding and abetting the Muslims in having their own personal law. The single worst feature of this inequity, so we are told, is that whereas the poor deprived majority has to stick to one spouse for ever, the appeased minority is able to have a multiple choice of four at a time— all a Muslim has to do to widen the range of his options is to pronounce 'talaq, talaq, talaq' three times and, hey presto, four becomes eight, eight becomes sixteen, sixteen becomes thirty-two and so on and so forth.

Further, while the blind Hindu allows himself to be propelled into family planning, the mullah urges the faithful to hold that contraception is Satanic and resorting to it will send the circumcised for ever to *jahannam* (perdition). The consequence of this, sternly warns the saffron brigade, is that the Muslim population is going to overtake the Hindu population before you can say 'Jai Shri Ram' 108 times—and there goes the Hindu Rashtra! The Christians say it is the arrival of the Four Horsemen that will herald the Apocalypse; our saffron acolytes see the vision of doom in the four wives permitted to the Muslim.

The 1991 Census showed that the Muslim population of India had grown from 61 million to 75 million between 1971 and 1981. This amounts to an increase of 23.04 per cent over the decade as a whole, giving an annual rate of increase of just over 2 per cent compounded annually. And how did the Hindu fare? Well, his number rose from 453 million to 549 million over the same decade. That amounts to a growth rate of 21.20 per cent for the decade as a whole, giving an annual growth rate of just over 2 per cent. So, the Muslim population of our country is growing at just about the same rate as the Hindu population. Will then the sons of Babur ever overtake the sons of Ram?

Despite Sadhvi Rithambara's rhetoric that Hindus are *napunsak* (impotent), the fact is that the Hindu, cursed as he is with but one wife, has been increasing the rate of growth of our country's Hindu population at just about the same rate at which the Muslim, with all his four wives, has been increasing the country's Muslim population!

While no detailed reliable information is available about differential birth rates for different religious communities, it is common knowledge that the two key factors determining birth rates are (i) the mean age at marriage of females and (ii) the rate of female literacy. Data for these two key parameters is available both state-wise and district-wise on NICNET. We also have details of the percentage of Muslims in the total population not only for every state of India but also for every district of the country. By putting these together, we should be able to discover some hidden truths about the knickerwallah hypothesis relating to the Four Wives of the Apocalypse.

Let us take the example of Madhya Pradesh (MP), where the Muslim population is only 4.8 per cent of the total, and contrast it with Kerala, where the percentage of Muslims is 21.3 per cent of the total. In MP, where less than one person in twenty is a Muslim, the total population grew by 26.28 per cent between 1981 and 1991; while in Kerala, where one out of every five Malayalis is a Muslim, the population grew over the decade by a mere 13.98 per cent. What, I ask you, were all those four wives doing? With just one wife apiece, the Hindus of MP were doubling the performance of their four-times better endowed Kerala brethren. Who says the Hindu is impotent?

Take a closer look. In the district of Malappuram in Kerala, the proportion of Muslims is 65 per cent of the district population. And the mean age at marriage of females is 18.3 years. In Rajnandgaon district of MP, where Muslims account for only 1.7 per cent of the population, the mean age at marriage of females is a mere 16.4 years! And if you object that Rajnandgaon is a largely tribal district, let us take a solid *suvarna-bhoomi* Hindu heartland district like Shivpuri, with a

Muslim minority of 1.2 per cent and a Hindu majority of 98 per cent, and compare it to Bastar, a tribal-dominated district of Chhattisgarh. Bastar district has a mean average age at marriage for females of 19 years—proving that there are enlightened tribals and less-enlightened tribals—and that, therefore, it is as foolish to talk of 'tribal' fertility rates as it is of 'minority' fertility rates. And as for Shivpuri, it disgraces the country with a mean age of female marriage at 16.3 years.

If the argument is made, as it will be made, that Kerala and MP are non-comparable, let us compare two districts in two adjacent north-Indian states, Uttarkashi in Uttaranchal and Rampur in UP. In Uttarkashi, where the Muslim population is a negligible 0.4 per cent, the mean age of females at marriage is 18.3 years. In the UP district of Rampur, where the percentage of the Muslim population is 47.2, the mean age is higher, albeit marginally, at 18.4 years. Where does religion come into this? Indeed, if you take the four districts of Uttaranchal with the lowest Muslim population in north India—Uttarkashi, Chamoli, Pithoragarh and Tehri Garhwal—all with a Muslim population of 0.4–0.5 per cent, the mean age at marriage is virtually the same as of the four districts of UP with the highest Muslim population—Rampur (47.2 per cent), Bijnore (39.5 per cent), Moradabad (38.1 per cent) and Saharanpur (31.6 per cent). In fact, the mean age at marriage in these districts is *higher* than the UP average of 17.7 years. The age at marriage has little to do with religion; it has much more to do with economic growth. All the eight districts mentioned above, half virtually devoid of Muslims and half with a large Muslim population, are in prosperous western UP. Therefore, the mean age at marriage of females in these districts is uniformly higher than the overall UP average. But as you move from the prosperous west to the poor central and the poorer eastern districts, the mean age at marriage of females falls below the UP average in every district of UP east of and including Jalaun, near Kanpur: varying from 16.2 years in

Sultanpur (Muslim population: 13 per cent) to 17.4 years in Ballia (Muslim population: 5.3 per cent).

A similar picture emerges in respect of female literacy. Whereas Kozhikode district in Kerala has a female literacy rate of 74.4 per cent (Muslim population: 34 per cent), Idukki district, in the same state, with a Muslim population of only 6.5 per cent, has a lower female literacy rate of 72.9 per cent. It is true that the lowest female literacy rate in Kerala is in the Muslim-majority district of Malappuram (66.8 per cent), but compare that to the fertile, prosperous, overwhelmingly non-Muslim (98.5 per cent) district of East Godavari in Andhra Pradesh and you find that female literacy there is a mere 43 per cent; 47 per cent in the Amritsar district of Punjab where the non-Muslim population is 99.9 per cent; down to 26.9 per cent in Ganganagar district of Rajasthan (non-Muslims: 96.5 per cent); and an abysmal 14.9 per cent in the West Champaran district of Bihar, where over 80 per cent of the population is non-Muslim.

It is, therefore, evident that even if we do not have statistics of birth rates of different communities of India, the Muslim birth rate in enlightened southern states like Kerala (high Muslim population percentage: 21.3 per cent), Karnataka (median Muslim population percentage: 11.2 per cent), and Tamil Nadu (low Muslim population percentage: 5.1 per cent) is very much lower than Hindu birth rates in unenlightened northern states like UP (high Muslim population percentage: 15.9 per cent), Rajasthan (median Muslim population percentage: 7.3 per cent) and MP (low Muslim population percentage: 4.8 per cent).

Where women are more literate, and girls get married at a later age, birth rates are invariably lower. Where birth rates are lower, rates of infant mortality and deaths of mothers at birth are also lower. The rate of growth of population is not a function of birth rates; it is the net outcome of birth rates and death rates. Therefore, what happens to the percentage of the

Muslim population in our total population has as little to do with the Koran or the shariat as with the Ramayana or the Gita. Where Muslim girls get education, as in enlightened Kerala, birth rates will come down and we will have healthy, prosperous Muslims; where Hindu girls are denied education, as in benighted MP, birth rates will go up and we will have sickly, poor Hindus. And that applies equally to Hindu girls who are encouraged to read and write and Muslim girls who are not. So, instead of all this poppycock about four wives and birth control, the Sangh Parivar would be best advised to concentrate on getting Hindu girls into school in MP and UP, Bihar and Rajasthan, while the Indian Union Muslim League (IUML) gets on with doing the same thing for Muslim girls in Malabar and the Majlis-e-Ittehadul Muslimeen (MIM) for Muslim girls in Hyderabad. In this lies good sense.

The BJP is communalizing family welfare in raising the spectre of a Muslim takeover of this country unless Muslim personal law is changed and family planning imposed on Muslims. Family planning is a national necessity. All the evidence shows that, as the economy grows, more and more Indians of all communities are resorting to family planning. The experience of booming Maharashtra—and the contrary experience of stagnant Bihar—demonstrates conclusively that the most effective contraceptive is development. Where development takes place, as in Maharashtra (Muslim population: 9.2 per cent), family planning takes off; where development gutters, as in Bihar (Muslim population: 14.1 per cent), family planning also goes down the drain. This has nothing to do with the fatwas of mullahs or the decrees of dharma sansads.

Article 370

As is the case with Jammu and Kashmir, several states of the Indian Union, including Maharashtra, Gujarat and Nagaland have, for diverse reasons, been given the benefit of the

'Temporary, Transitional and Special Provisions' of Part XXI of the Constitution. J&K is not the only state to have such special provisions. This rather obvious constitutional point needs to be emphasized because communalists often talk as if J&K has been singled out for 'appeasement'.

Although membership of the NDA since 1998 has obliged the BJP to put the issue of Article 370 on the back burner, the experience of office has not diluted its commitment, as a party, to its past political resolutions aimed at 'mobilizing nationwide support for the demand that the "temporary and provisional" Article 370 be repealed'. Professor Murli Manohar Joshi, the most unashamed voice of the Hindu right, had, as BJP president some years ago, thundered: 'Article 370 must go.' And L.K. Advani has not retracted his opposition to Kashmir having 'a special status'. The Advani argument, set out in an interview to the *Indian Express*, is that people who argue in favour of a special status for Kashmir do so only because it is a Muslim-majority state, adducing the proof that the minority community in the Kashmir Valley is 'generally described as Kashmiri Pandits not as Hindus because the Hindu denomination is taboo'!

Article 370 exists in the Constitution not because J&K is a Muslim-majority state (indeed J&K is a fascinating composite with Kashmir having a Muslim majority, Jammu a Hindu majority, and Ladakh a Buddhist majority—to all of whom Article 370 applies equally). Article 370 exists because, even fifty-seven years after its accession to the Indian Union in uniquely exceptional circumstances, close to one-third of the geographic area of the state continues to be under the illegal occupation of Pakistan.

Explaining the rationale for the 'special provisions' for J&K, to the Constituent Assembly on 17 October 1949, N. Gopalaswami Ayyangar, member of the Drafting Committee, gave four reasons:[30]

- 'In the first place, there has been a war going on within the limits of J&K state' and, notwithstanding the ceasefire, conditions there remain 'unusual and abnormal'.
  War is still going on in the state and conditions continue to be unusual and abnormal.
- Some parts of the state were still in the hands of 'rebels and enemies'.
  The same parts of the state remain in the possession of Pakistan and the government is bound by a unanimous resolution of Parliament to recovering those territories.
- Clause 1(c) of Article 370 provides that 'Article 1 of the Constitution will automatically apply. As you know, it describes the territory of India, and includes among these territories all the states mentioned in Part III, and Jammu and Kashmir is one of the states mentioned in Part III'.
  There is thus no question of the accession of the state or the full integration of J&K with the Union of India being called into question, as some propagandists sometimes misconstrue Article 370.
- Clause 1(d), however, provides that 'with regard to the other provisions of the Constitution', this will be subject to 'such exceptions and modifications as the President may by order specify'. Moreover, Clause 2 provides that for subjects beyond those specified in the Instrument of Accession, 'these additions' are matters for the determination of the Constituent Assembly of the state. The implication of these clauses read together was that the Constituent Assembly of J&K would determine the Constitution of the state as well as determine the jurisdiction of the Union over that state; hence, the Constituent Assembly of India could only provide for an interim arrangement for J&K.

The J&K Constitution continues to apply to the state and, ironically, it was BJP-appointed governor, Jagmohan, who, without even informing the Government of India, invoked the harshest provisions of the J&K (not Indian) Constitution in February 1990 to justify dissolving an elected assembly and assuming all powers himself. Article 370 is now regulated by the Constitution (Application to Jammu and Kashmir) Order, 1954, made by the president with the concurrence of the Government of J&K. The order states that Article 1 of the Indian Constitution, which describes J&K as an integral part of the Union of India, and Article 370 of the Indian Constitution, *both*, 'shall apply in relation to the state of J&K' and that other provisions of the Constitution of India shall apply to that state subject to the exceptions and modifications stipulated in that order.

The 'temporary, transitional and special' nature of Article 370 cannot be terminated until the hopefully temporary and transitional aggression of Pakistan in J&K is overcome. This means Article 370 is not a symbol of 'minorityism' as the BJP pretends. It is the expression of our determination to secure the whole of the state for India, to integrate into India all the land from Gilgit to Muzaffarabad and Skardu that was Maharaja Hari Singh's and is, therefore, by right India's.

I confess that is a distant prospect. That is precisely why Article 370 is primarily of symbolic rather than substantive value. As Advani himself testifies, in actual practice, Article 370 is something of an atrophying relic: in his interview to *Indian Express* he admits to having virtually obliterated the implications of Article 370. Then what is the quarrel about?

5

Secularism in a Time of Communal Activism

Perhaps because secularists tend to take secularism for granted while communalists look to Hindutva as a goal to be attained, communal activism, for much of the time, is countered by secular complacency, even apathy. Thus, there is no secular counterpart to the RSS shakhas, the Van Kalyan Samitis, the Shishu and Saraswati Niketans, the tribal reconversion movements of the likes of Dilip Singh Judeo in Chhattisgarh, and the *Organiser* and *Panchajanya*. It is through the assiduous spreading of their communal propaganda and the misuse of social welfare activities for sectarian ends that the communal forces prepare and ready their storm troopers to ignite and spread the communal fire when opportunity presents itself, as was most starkly evident in Gujarat after the Godhra tragedy in 2002.

Secularism is more a way of life than an ideology. There are, however, moments when the powder keg of communalism is lit. Instead of invoking secular activism only when the keg explodes, the fuse itself should again and again be defused.

Alertness is required as much at the intellectual and ethical level as in secular counter propaganda (of which the monthly magazine *Communalism Combat* is an excellent example), and above all, at the political level.

This chapter details specific turning points in the evolution of independent India when insidious communalism and communal activism were countered, or should have been countered, by secular activism: the communal challenge from within the Congress between 1949 and 1951, and Nehru's riposte to that challenge; governmental communalism in J&K in 1990; the shame of Ayodhya in 1992; the Idgah Maidan imbroglio at Hubli in 1993; and Gujarat in 2002.

Nehru: Apostle of Secular Activism

Over the decade of the 1990s and into the early years of this millennium, the BJP, representing the political face of Hindu communalism, has made enormous strides in positioning itself as the natural party of 'cultural nationalism' in juxtaposition to the 'composite nationalism' of the secular camp. Most of its gains have been at the expense of the Congress. The Congress is, therefore, caught in the dilemma of determining whether a softer line on secularism or a hard secular fundamentalism is the right response to the basic question of how it should position itself to prevent its agenda for the modern nationhood of India from being hijacked by an alternative saffron version.

This is by no means a difficult new choice for the Congress to make. It has been with the Congress since Tilak and Gokhale; since Annie Besant and Gandhi; since Lala Lajpat Rai and Madan Mohan Malaviya. The last two, in fact, saw no contradiction between being Congress leaders and chairing sessions of the Hindu Mahasabha; like Jinnah, who saw no contradiction between simultaneous membership of the Congress and the Muslim League. After independence and partition, this dilemma, in its acutest form, confronted

Jawaharlal Nehru and the Congress in the two tumultuous years from September 1949 to October 1951. It is essential to recall the events of that time to fashion a secular response to the renewed challenge from communal forces represented in the Phoenix-like rise of the BJP on the political horizon from the ashes of its defeat in 1984.

Partition, when it came, was a cataclysm. But while in the west of India it was *jhatka*, in the east it was *halal*. For in the west, in a period of a few weeks, between August and October 1947, much of Pakistan was emptied of its minorities. The exodus from Sind in January 1948 completed partition in the west.

But in the east, there was at first a mere trickle of refugees in either direction. It was not till the autumn of 1949 that the trickle assumed the proportions of a one-way flood from East Pakistan into West Bengal, Assam and Tripura. It was that flood which provided the proximate provocation for the birth of the Jana Sangh under the leadership of Dr Shyama Prasad Mookerjee—a leader without a party finding a party without a leader. The Jana Sangh began as a regional party of the 'Hindu' motherland of West Bengal reaching out to other parts of the 'Hindu' motherland, primarily through the exertions of the young man whom Shyama Prasad Mookerjee had picked as his private secretary—Atal Behari Vajpayee.

In September 1949, the pound sterling was devalued vis-à-vis the US dollar. As a member of the sterling area, India equivalently devalued the Indian rupee. But although Pakistan too was in the sterling area, it perversely decided not to devalue. India, therefore, broke off trade relations with Pakistan. And Mohanlal Saxena, the Union minister of rehabilitation, in a fit of excessive zeal, decided that if the Government of India had broken trade relations with Pakistan, it was his duty to set about sealing all shops in Delhi owned by Muslims! For his pains, he drew from Jawaharlal Nehru the sharp rebuke: 'All of us seem to be getting infected with the refugee mentality or, worse still, the RSS mentality. That is a curious finale to our careers.'[1]

Trouble was also brewing in Nehru's home state of the United Provinces. For one, the state government decided that only if forty or more children demanded it, would Urdu education be provided in primary schools. Worse were the words and deeds of Purushottam Das Tandon, president of the Congress Committee in the United Provinces. Appalled at the way 'communalism has invaded the minds and hearts of those who were the pillars of the Congress in the past', Nehru told the chief minister of the United Provinces, Pandit Govind Ballabh Pant (in a letter dated 17 April 1950):

> [The United Provinces] is becoming almost a foreign land to me. The UP Congress Committee, with which I have been associated for thirty-five years, functions in a manner that amazes me. Its voice is not the voice of the Congress I have known, but something which I have opposed for the greater part of my life.

To the other chief ministers—many of whom were responding to the siren call of Purushottam Das Tandon—Nehru wrote on 1 April 1950: 'So long as I am Prime Minister, I shall not allow communalism to shape our policy, nor am I prepared to tolerate barbarous and uncivilized behaviour.'

Nehru had fiercely put down a proposal mooted by Dr B.C. Roy, the chief minister of West Bengal (encouraged, it was widely believed, by the deputy prime minister, Sardar Vallabhbhai Patel) that ten Muslims be expelled from West Bengal for every Hindu driven out of East Pakistan. He was not about to treat the minorities of India as hostages for the good behaviour of Pakistan and he was certainly not about to lower his secular standards to the level of the communal prejudices of Pakistan in retaliation or reciprocity. His own answer to stemming the influx of frightened refugees was the Nehru–Liaquat pact of April 1950.

Never before and certainly never after has there been an agreement as unique as this in the history of international relations. Focusing on the injustice to innocents inherent in holding minorities hostage in a political dispute, Nehru and Premier Liaquat Ali Khan of Pakistan bilaterally agreed to unilaterally ensure the security of their respective minorities. When, however, Nehru went to Central Hall to address the Congress Parliamentary Party, the reaction was so negative that, despairing at his own impotence to stem the tide of communalism even within his own party, Nehru attempted to resign as prime minister. His intention was, in the manner of Gandhi in 1947, to tour both parts of Bengal to bring sense and sensibility back to our people. It was with some difficulty that an alarmed Congress Party, with Sardar Patel in the lead, persuaded Nehru to resile from his personal wishes in the matter. Setting aside his personal prejudices, Sardar Patel backed Nehru, visiting Calcutta to calm Bengali opinion and securing support for the agreement from all intransigent quarters.

However, the tussle continued between what we today would call 'soft Hindutva' and what I would term 'secular fundamentalism'. It reached a climax in the election of the president of the Congress at the AICC session held at Nasik in September 1950. The leading contenders were Acharya Kripalani, representing the well-established secular viewpoint, and Purushottam Das Tandon (looking, as someone said, like a Prophet from the Old Testament), the patriarch of the Congress in the United Provinces. In his letter to Pant cited earlier, Nehru had said of Tandon: 'Purushottam Das Tandon is continually delivering speeches which seem to me to be opposed to the basic principles of the Congress.' To Tandon himself—an associate of many years' standing—Nehru wrote on 8 August 1950, just a month before the Nasik session: 'I think the major issue before the country today...is to solve satisfactorily our own minority problems. Instead of that, we become more intolerant towards our minorities...Unfortunately, you have become a symbol of this communalist and revivalist outlook.'

Faced with an apparently vociferous Hindu claim to emerge as the dominant community in 'Hindu India', and with the first Lok Sabha elections in the offing, the majority of the Congress leadership (albeit a bare majority but a majority nevertheless) at the Nasik session opted for Tandon as president of the Congress—the 'symbol' of the 'communalist and revivalist outlook' defeating the secular alternative.

The outcome of the Nasik session was a body blow to all that Nehru stood for. He fought back with a tenacity that had been well known but with a skill for political infighting that few had hitherto suspected him of possessing. Within a year (Congress Working Committee meeting of September 1951), Purushottam Das Tandon was compelled to tender his resignation, and Jawaharlal Nehru, as the new president of the Congress, proclaimed his secular credo at a public meeting in Delhi on Gandhi Jayanti, 1951: 'If any person raises his hand to strike down another on the ground of religion, I shall fight him till the last breath of my life, both as the head of the Government and from outside.'[2]

That, it seems to me, sums up all that needs to be said about the role of governance in the maintenance of secularism. Consider the component elements of the statement:

- The focus is on 'the ground of religion';
- The culpable person is 'anyone'—no one is exempt— who 'raises his hand to strike down another on the ground of religion';
- The fight is to the finish: 'till the last breath of my life'; and
- The fight goes on whether the secularist is in government or outside.

Nehru also had to tackle the persistence with which Dr Rajendra Prasad and K.M. Munshi insisted on associating themselves with the reconstruction of the Somanatha temple, notwithstanding their official positions as president of the Union and Union food minister respectively. To Nehru, the Somanatha temple was a matter of personal faith and, therefore, outside the purview of the involvement of the state, especially as its rebuilding could be seen, and was being projected, as an act of revanchism—similar to the destruction of the Babri Masjid and the insistence on building the Ram Mandir 'there and only there', with the garbha griha of the mandir being placed at the precise spot where the mirab of the masjid stood.

The Somanatha temple lay in the princely state of Junagadh, which was integrated with the Indian Union after a brief military engagement—'police action'—in November 1947. Sardar Patel was among the first to visit the site, accompanied by K.M. Munshi, where it was announced that the temple, repeatedly looted by Mahmud of Ghazni in the eleventh century AD and finally razed to the ground by Aurangzeb in the seventeenth century, would be restored at government expense. It was none other than Mahatma Gandhi who attempted to deflect them from that intention.

However, after Gandhiji was martyred in January 1948, K.M. Munshi claimed that government sponsorship of the reconstruction of the Somanatha temple had been agreed to at a Cabinet meeting in December 1947. He got the Central ministry of works and housing to start proceeding accordingly. When an infuriated Nehru came to know of what was afoot, he, as prime minister, denied that any such decision had been taken. Cabinet minutes were sent for and no confirmation of Munshi's claim was forthcoming. So, all government involvement or assistance for the rebuilding of the Somanatha temple was stopped forthwith. In consequence, a private trust was floated to finance and build the temple. As the editorial in *Hindustan Times*—otherwise sympathetic to the restoration of the temple—on 11 May 1951 made clear: 'The Government [is] contributing nothing to the reconstruction of the

[Somanatha] Temple...Even the Saurashtra Government [is] incurring expenditure only in connection with the usual services which all governments render in time of fairs and melas.'

The inauguration of the temple was set for May 1951. President Rajendra Prasad insisted on attending. Nehru sought to dissuade him in the great cause of keeping religion out of the official visage of secular India. The president remained adamant. So, a formal meeting of the council of ministers was convened to advise the president not to go. The Constitution obliged the president to accept the 'advice'. When Rajendra Prasad persisted in wanting to go, he was told that if he went it would have to be in a private capacity and not as president of India.

Nehru was, in fact, most upset about such 'revivalism' which cuts at the very roots of our secular polity. In his communication about the Somanatha temple to the chief ministers on 2 May 1951 he made it clear:

> You must have read about the coming ceremonies at the Somnath Temple...It should be clearly understood that this function is not governmental and the Government of India as such has nothing to do with it...We must not do anything which comes in the way of our State being secular. That is the basis of our Constitution and Governments, therefore, should refrain from associating themselves with anything which tends to affect the secular character of our State.[3]

And, after the ceremonies were over, Nehru wrote again to the chief ministers:

> Our frequent declarations that we are a secular State are appreciated abroad and raise our credit. But they are not wholly believed in...The recent inauguration of the Somnath Temple, with pomp and ceremony, has created a very bad impression abroad about India and her professions (of secularism).[4]

Nehru based his stand on the 'collective subconscious' of the country. Munshi sneered back: 'I can assure you that the "collective subconscious" of India today is happier with the scheme of reconstruction sponsored by the Government of India than with many other things that we have done or are doing.'[5] The so-called 'sponsorship' by the Government of India was a deliberate distortion, contemporaneously picked up and repeated ad nauseam by the BJP.

The first elections to the Lok Sabha came a few months later in February 1952. As Professor Bipan Chandra points out, Nehru made secularism 'one of the basic issues of the campaign', confronting communalism 'on a mass ideological level'. The Jana Sangh and its associate, the Hindu Mahasabha, secured less than 2 per cent of the vote and no more than two seats in the Lok Sabha, both from West Bengal: Shyama Prasad Mookerjee's and N.C. Chatterjee's. The Congress swept the polls, definitively putting behind it the Purushottam Das Tandon deviation and committing itself for the next four decades to the Nehru line on secularism virtually without challenge. It was a triumph, at one and the same time, of the essential secularism of the country's religious majority, as it was a refutation of the appeal to majority communalism—'this narrow-mindedness in the human mind in India, this terrible thing' as Nehru had described it in a speech at Allahabad University on 3 September 1949—which not only provided the mainspring of the Jana Sangh's view of India but had, just eighteen months earlier at Nasik, apparently also inspired a majority of Congressmen and women. A secular Nehru had much greater appeal to the masses of India than the appeal of a 'Hindutva' line. Yet, Nehru did not consider secularism to be a winning electoral card. It was, for him, something far more basic, far more fundamental, far more important than passing political victory. In 1954, he declared, 'So far as I am concerned, I am prepared to lose every election but to give no quarter to communalism or casteism.'[6]

The imperative need for such secular fundamentalism, in contrast to the softer options, is manifest in the terrible consequences that the latter engendered at two different eras— in the Congress acceptance of separate electorates as far back as 1916, which in many ways provided the ideological foundation for the partition, and the inability of the Congress to provide a clear ideological platform in Gujarat in 2002 in the aftermath of the worst state-sponsored riots in the history of independent India, where the party lost more than just an election. The contrast with the gains arising out of the enduring legacy of Nehru's undiluted secularism could not be more apparent.

Jammu and Kashmir: The Consequences of Governmental Communalism

In May 1989, Governor Jagmohan invited me and my family as his guests for a holiday in Kashmir. He was an excellent host. He sent us everywhere that tourists go—boating on the Dal Lake, Dachigam, Pahalgam, Gulmarg. There was some security, but not much. No one doubted that with a few minimum precautions we could have a good time without fear. We did. In July 1989, General K.V. Krishna Rao was appointed governor of the state. In October that year, Kashmir had the largest number of tourists it has ever seen in autumn, when the leaves of the chinar turn to gold. In November 1989, the Lok Sabha elections were fought. Kashmir was hardly an issue. Things were normal there. In December 1989, the V.P. Singh government was sworn in. Mufti Mohammed Sayeed was appointed home minister. The Kashmiri militants, who till then had been lying low, reacted to his appointment by kidnapping his daughter, Rubaiya. To secure Rubaiya's release, the V.P. Singh government set free a fistful of hard-core terrorists—in Lal Chowk of all places, the commercial hub of Srinagar—and that too in full glare of Doordarshan.

Given the total non-cooperation of the Central government

under V.P. Singh with Farooq Abdullah's state government, the governor, General K.V. Krishna Rao, tendered his resignation. Chief Minister Farooq Abdullah followed suit. The BJP, which held the key to the survival of the V.P. Singh government, then insisted on its nominee, the selfsame Jagmohan, being sent to Srinagar in January 1990. Rajiv Gandhi summoned me back to Delhi from Tamil Nadu, where I was exploring the possibilities of a Rajya Sabha nomination or a Lok Sabha constituency, to be on hand to monitor further developments in Kashmir. These developments through February 1990 included Jagmohan unilaterally dissolving the elected J&K assembly without informing, let alone consulting, the Central government, under the powers accorded him by the J&K Constitution. In early March, I accompanied Rajiv Gandhi as note taker to the infamous all-party meeting with Governor Jagmohan.

Jagmohan's performance shocked everybody except the BJP representative Jaswant Singh. Leave alone the Congress, the Central government ministers in the delegation, led by Deputy PM Devi Lal and including Law Minister Dinesh Goswami and Railway Minister George Fernandes, were appalled at what Jagmohan had done to the state in the few brief weeks he had been in office. Devi Lal summed up the general sentiment when he said, '*Ganimat hogi ki yeh aadmi hamein airport tak surakshit pahunchaye!* [It would be a blessing if this guy can get us back to the airport in safety.]'

Within a week of the visit, the Valley had been emptied of almost all its Kashmiri Pandits. Jagmohan denied any hand in this, but without the governor's knowledge it would have been impossible for the Pandits to be evacuated en masse. Two months later, the same Central government which had sent him there called him back. This once-upon-a-time Sanjay Gandhi acolyte is now a senior member of the BJP. His approach to the whole issue—looking upon his task as protecting the Kashmiri Pandits from the Valley Muslims, instead of treating it as a matter of protecting the Valley people from terrorists—added a vicious new dimension to the issue, from whose communal clutches the nation is still struggling to free itself. Fifteen years on, the Kashmiri Pandits are still refugees in their own country. Their only hope is that a secular government is in office in the state.

There are many dimensions to the J&K issue, but in the context of these confessions I am going to concentrate exclusively on the terrible consequences of approaching the problem with a communal perspective, as a communal problem rather than a political one, as a matter of relations between the majority Muslims and minority Pandits of the Valley rather than as a matter of Centre–state relations, requiring special handling in view of the distinctive and special problems of the state (which is the essential rationale for Article 370, as we have already seen in the previous chapter).

In an interview to *Sunday* magazine in July 1990, described by the magazine (more to sell itself than because it was true) as 'Rajiv Gandhi's most honest interview ever', Rajiv Gandhi categorically stated that the situation would not have come to the sorry state it was in had a Congress government been at the Centre and Farooq in Kashmir. As already mentioned, Kashmir was not an issue in the elections in November 1989. There had been no migration from Kashmir in October–November that year. It had had its best tourist season in October. How did it all change in a matter of months? At the all-party meet, Jagmohan told Rajiv that he wanted to restructure the administration. Because, he said, the administration was 'totally' infiltrated by the secessionists. When asked what he meant by 'totally', he said, one hundred per cent.

The administration was not like this three months before that. The Kashmir administration was picking up terrorists. After all, who picked up the terrorists who were released in exchange for the home minister's daughter? They were picked up by the Kashmir intelligence, by the Kashmir police. How could the same people who were busy arresting terrorists and picking up large caches of weapons become terrorists in a matter of weeks? Telling us that the Congress and the National Conference (NC) were totally redundant and that they had forfeited their 'representative' character, Jagmohan said that he was going to replace them by a 'new political force'. When asked what the new political force was he concluded by saying that the Jama'at-i-Islami had to be finished because it was anti-Indian and pro-Pakistani and that the Jammu Kashmir Liberation Front (JKLF) had to be brought in as the new political force in Kashmir. Those were his exact words. He wanted the JKLF there. He wanted the arena cleared. I had the record. It was given verbatim to President Venkataraman.

How did it come to this? This was the same Valley—and the same people—who turned to us in 1947 to save them from Jinnah's murderous marauders. This is the same Valley—and the same people—who, in 1965, put paid to Operation Gibraltar, the fatuous brainchild of that armchair aggressor, Zulfiqar Ali Bhutto ('armchair' because he never went to any front himself, only sent others to certain death in the pursuit of his vainglorious ambitions). It was Bhutto who infiltrated hundreds of saboteurs, bristling with arms, money and propaganda material, into the Valley, to stir the villagers of the Valley into raising the banner of revolution. And it was the very target of these threats and blandishments—the villagers of the Valley—who identified each of these agent provocateurs, picked them up, and handed them over to the security forces.

It is upon this Valley—and this people—that Governor Jagmohan and his administration launched a war of attrition. For, there was nothing sophisticated or selective about their hunt to flush out the terrorists. Everyone in the Valley—man, woman or child, of every faith and every political persuasion—was indiscriminately the target of continuous curfews and swingeing security operations. The administration seemed animated by the mistaken belief that if it smothered, smashed and starved the Valley into submission, the people, exhausted by the severity of the security onslaught, would yield up the terrorists in their midst.

This is not to say that Farooq made no mistakes. He did. But the consequences of his errors were at once containable and reversible (and, moreover, not without precedent), and they simply paled in comparison to the turmoil in which Kashmir was plunged since the National Front (NF) government took office, and especially after it sent Jagmohan to the Valley as the governor.

The turmoil, after December 1989, was the outcome of a ghastly misreading by the NF government—and the motivated malice of its 'outside supporter', the BJP—of the causes of the tension in the Valley. This was startlingly evident in the agenda paper prepared by the Union home ministry for the National Integration Council meeting held on 11 April 1990. The paper may have been the ministry's but the pen was clearly the BJP's.

For the agenda paper identified 'communalism' as the basic cause (and not an incidental consequence) of all that has gone wrong in Kashmir. The paper focused solely on the exodus of the Hindu minority from the Valley, glossing over (or is it deliberately downgrading?) the hordes of other Kashmiris, including thousands of Muslims, who fled from both terrorism and the tender ministrations of the new dispensation. Whatever the defects of the Farooq years, all these Kashmiris—Hindu, Muslim—stayed in the Valley from March 1987 to November 1989, but, from December 1989, were left with no alternative but to take to their heels.

Since 15 December 1989 curfew continued to be imposed continuously for months on end, lifted only for a few brief hours on cold, wintry mornings and reimposed before the commencement of the normal working day. There was little or no food in Srinagar. Infants were going without milk. Life-saving drugs were virtually unavailable. Inevitably, the economy collapsed. With no one able to go out to work, manufacturing activity came to a standstill. The banking system folded up. The export trade dried up. And tourists—the holidaymakers on whom the livelihood of lakhs of Kashmiris depended—were nowhere in sight.

It was not 'communalism' but these factors—plus the terrorists emboldened by the ransom they successfully extracted for the release of Rubaiya—that resulted in the continuing turbulence in the state. The people of the Valley were no strangers to trouble but the trauma to which they were subjected during that phase was without precedent. The exodus of Kashmiris from the Valley—Hindus, Muslims or others—was not because Kashmiris of different faiths, who had lived together in harmony for hundreds of years, were suddenly unable to stand each other, but because ordinary living was rendered virtually impossible by the authorities in charge at the time.

Insisting that the administration 'has not broken down but been taken over', Jagmohan made it clear that he intended to 'dismantle and rebuild it' from scratch. Of the thousands of Kashmiri officials working in his administration, he initially identified about thirty-odd for rustication from government. Then, another score or so were removed. But the perception of a 'takeover, not a breakdown' meant that no Kashmiri official was fully trusted. Those under suspicion were suspended or dismissed (which is okay). The others under general suspicion— meaning everybody else—were marginalized, deprived of authority and robbed of responsibility (which is not okay). Vacancies were not filled: in response to an advertisement for recruiting hundreds of constables, only about a dozen applications were received and barely two or three turned up for the interview. This was not because the local youth were not in search of work (on the contrary, they were and continue to be in desperate need of employment), but because they dared not show their willingness to become the agents of alien governance. There were no such inhibitions even in the worst days of the Farooq regime.

Because the concept of 'dismantling and rebuilding' emanated primarily from the governor himself, every Kashmiri was made to feel like a second-class citizen in his own state. This never happened under Farooq or, indeed, under any of his predecessors. It was the inevitable consequence of the BJP finding the right agent to bypass the vacuous Central government and begin at the top: the building of the Hindu Rashtra from the crown of India, top down!

The governor's political prescription—the generation of 'new' (and presumably patriotic) political forces in the Valley to the detriment, indeed suppression, of the existing nationalist political forces—was equally bizarre. Jagmohan's appointment had led to the immediate resignation of the Farooq government and, therefore, to the snapping of nationalist political links to the people of the Valley. Next, Jagmohan dissolved the state assembly without telling anybody, not even the prime minister. But, for this madness, the governor explained, he had a method. By dissolving the assembly, he was sending a signal, he said, to the misguided gun-toters of the Valley that he, the governor, would give them the 'azaadi' they sought: the azaadi to get elected! (In fact, he gave us the names of the persons and parties he had in mind—a nightmarish disclosure, I might add, but it would be a breach of confidence to share these details with my readers.)

Was he authorized, the governor was asked, to extend such an invitation to those who had neither eschewed violence nor accepted our Constitution? No answer. What criteria did he use to determine that the NC and the Congress were 'unrepresentative'? None of your business, he said, the J&K Constitution entitled him to make the determination entirely at his own discretion. How did he propose to ensure the election of the gun-toters and jailbirds to whom he was promising azaadi? No answer. When, in any case, did he think he could hold these elections? No reply. What if the NC–Congress coalition were to win the next elections? God forbid.

What if the elected state government, from which the NC and the Congress were to be excluded, resulted in a coalition of hotheads proclaiming a unilateral declaration of independence? That apparently had not been worked out. When asked who all he was in touch with, his response was a staggering 'nobody'— he knew what was good for Kashmir, and the Kashmiris had better swallow it, whether they wanted it or not.

The governor's strategy wrecked the emotional integration of Kashmir with India. There can be no abatement of the turbulence in Kashmir if the Kashmiris are not trusted and if the traditional tolerance of the Kashmiri is not relied upon. Stoking the fears of the Hindu minority and aggravating the anguish of the Muslim majority is no solution. The answer lies in firm police action directed at the terrorists—and not the general populace—combined with continuing communication with the other side, through the political infrastructure and intelligence network, with a view to negotiating a settlement based upon an unambiguous affirmation of the minimum conditions for the negotiations and a clear articulation of the goals to be achieved. Neither sabre-rattling at Pakistan nor nonsense about abrogating Article 370 nor the suspension of political activity in the state is the answer.

The Pakistani attempt at subverting the Bengali character of East Pakistan failed because a nation built on religion does not understand how to forge unity out of diversity. The crisis in Kashmir assumed its present proportions only after a similar attempt was made to base policy on religion during January to May 1990 at the instance of the BJP through Governor Jagmohan. In those four dreadful months, when religion, not Kashmiriyat, was cast as the determining factor of the Kashmiri identity, Kashmir did indeed become 'East Pakistan'.

The solution lies in nurturing the delicate plant of Kashmiriyat, not Hinduizing it or Islamizing it. To do that, India (including Kashmir) has to again become the fortress of secularism it was in the heyday of Pandit Nehru and Sheikh

Abdullah. It is the rejection of the vicious viewpoint of the two-nation theory that alone justifies the integration into India of not only Kashmir but Muslim-majority Malappuram district in Kerala and, indeed, our 150 million Muslims as a whole.

And unity in diversity means being aware of the particularities of each diversity. In the case of J&K it means Article 370. It also means massive Central assistance. It finally means a Kashmiri administration run by and for the Kashmiris. Governor Jagmohan, and the forces he represented, made it abundantly clear in their four months in office that they intended to snatch away Article 370 so that this critical particularity of Kashmiriyat is erased. They also made it clear that any continuance of Central assistance was contingent on the effacing of a Kashmiri identity in favour of what they chose to consider as a 'Bhartiya' identity. Specifically, they proposed to do this by altering the religious settlements like the Zionists in the occupied territories of Palestine. And, so, when the governor proclaimed from the rooftops (or, rather, from his eyrie surrounded by a forest of security men) that not one Kashmiri civil servant, not one Kashmiri constable, not one Kashmiri domestic help was to be trusted, the civil servant, the constable and the domestic help in question inevitably decided to furnish His Excellency with proof that his trust was of no value to them. That is how militancy and terrorism were given a fillip during the Jagmohan raj. For, if you declare war on an entire people, the people will, of course, declare war on you.

In the four long decades of the progressive political and emotional integration of J&K with India, from Jawaharlal Nehru/Sheikh Sahib to Farooq/Rajiv, things were under control precisely because the process of integration was allowed, indeed encouraged, to take place gradually, naturally, progressively. The process was not artificially or externally accelerated. The BJP–Jagmohan attempt to rush integration led to the explosion of January 1990. There was, and has been since 1951, an elected assembly in J&K. Of course, it has been an inadequate democracy. The opposition to Farooq Abdullah in the 1987 elections in the Valley believed they would win. They did not. They alleged rigging. There is always some rigging in an inadequate democracy. But even if the maximum allegation is conceded, it would have affected no more than sixteen seats in the J&K House, as conceded by Governor Jagmohan at the all-party meeting in Srinagar in March 1990 after he had dissolved the state assembly.[7]

The answer to the allegations of rigging in the 1987 elections lay in ensuring a greater measure of fairness in the next round of assembly elections that were scheduled to be held in 1992, just twenty-four months after Governor Jagmohan took office. Instead, the governor chose to unilaterally dissolve the suspended assembly while V.P. Singh's government at the Centre looked on helplessly (if reprovingly). What little remained of representative democracy in the Valley was, thus, snuffed out. This played straight into the hands of the militants. Jagmohan having run away with the ballot box, the nationalist politicians of the Valley were left unprotected to face the terrorist bullet. They, therefore, fled the Valley, like lemmings leaping off the precipice. Jagmohan encouraged the Hindu Pandits to join them. The Valley was then converted into the killing fields, with the militants and their Pakistani backers on the one hand, and Jagmohan and his armed forces on the other. The victims have been the Kashmiris who remained behind. Innocent Kashmiri Muslims butchered by the Pakistan-sponsored jehadis and Kashmiri Muslim terrorists far outnumber casualties in counter-insurgency terrorist operations.

It must be stressed that the restoration of Kashmiriyat in Kashmir presupposes the return of the Kashmiri Pandit to his home, his lands and his property. The Kashmiri Pandits left the Valley in droves in 1990 because they were corralled and herded out like cattle by the cowboy-governor of the day. Therefore, all those who have unwillingly fled the Valley, the thousands of Pandits as much as the hundreds of Muslims,

Buddhists, Sikhs and others must be brought back to their homes. Only then can we have a Kashmiriyat which embraces all Kashmiris, whatever their religion.

Jagmohan argues with passion and deep conviction that the Kashmiri Pandits fled the Valley for three basic reasons: one, that they had been under constant threat of liquidation ever since 1947; two, that the threat had assumed menacing proportions from 1986 (the Anantnag disturbances); and, three, that the situation had become unsupportable during January to May 1990, the period during which the exodus occurred.

I hold that if Jagmohan's thesis is right, it follows that Kashmir can be safe for the Kashmiri Pandits only if the Valley is exorcized of all its Muslims. Or, alternatively, if the Muslims of the Valley are reduced to a minority by the enforced settlement of a Hindu majority in the Valley—a goal that cannot be achieved so long as Article 370 of the Constitution holds sway. Since Jagmohan is too human to actually want to exterminate the Valley's Muslims, he advocates the marginally less genocidal course of the abrogation of Article 370. The thesis that the Kashmiri Hindu cannot live with the Kashmiri Muslim is also, it would appear, espoused by the Panun Kashmir movement, which claims to speak for the Kashmiri Pandit-in-exile. They, or at any rate some of their office-bearers, are reported to have called for the partition of the Valley, the carving out of an exclusive homeland for the Kashmiri Pandits 'east and north of the Jhelum river', the territory to the west and the south of the river to constitute, presumably, a ghetto for such Kashmiri Muslims who choose to remain.

It is for fear of such consequences of Jagmohan's line of reasoning that it becomes essential, not as an essay into the past but as a prescription for future action, to examine whether the three turning points in Hindu–Muslim relations in the Valley as identified by Jagmohan bear any relationship to the truth.

I believe it is nonsense to maintain that ever since August 1947 the Kashmiri Hindus have been hounded by a deep sense of insecurity in the Valley. For, if what he says is true, Kashmiriyat is a myth, the Kashmir problem is a Hindu–Muslim problem, and a solution can only lie in an ethnic cleansing of the Valley as Milosevic attempted in Bosnia. Such a view on the Hindu fundamentalist side coincides, in all important particulars, with the view of the most fundamentalist and extremist of the Islamic militants. The only question that remains to be settled is whether the Valley should become a Muslim ghetto or a Hindu ghetto.

I prefer to share the view expressed at the height of the militancy in Kashmir by H.N. Jattu, president of the All-India Kashmiri Pandit Conference, as quoted in the *Hindustan Times* of 8 February 1990, that the Kashmiri Pandit community suffered as much as the other communities, including the Muslim majority. I also share Jattu's view that the Kashmiri people, Hindu or Muslim, had to suffer because of misrule and maladministration. He says nothing about Hindu–Muslim incompatibility. I also agree with the solution he then urged to the problem: strengthening the secular forces among all communities, including Muslims. The problems of Kashmir have always been, before and since Jagmohan's cut-off day of August 1947, the problems of all Kashmiris, Hindu or Muslim. Singling out the Kashmiri Pandits, and then compartmentalizing them from the Kashmiri Muslims, constitutes the very root of Jagmohan's wrong analysis.

By the time we get to February 1986 and the disturbances and desecration in Anantnag, Jagmohan's utterances become positively hysterical. In his book, the unfortunately titled *My Frozen Turbulence in Kashmir*, Jagmohan reproduces the full text of a letter he wrote to the home minister, and copied to the prime minister, on 5 March 1986, in which he compares the plight of the Kashmiri Pandits of Anantnag to the German Jews bound for the gas chambers during the Second World

War![8] This, despite not one Hindu being killed in the Anantnag riots. As Anil Maheshwari reported in the *Hindustan Times* of 28 February 1990, the hue and cry raised over the Anantnag communal riots in 1986 was entirely unnecessary as not even a single casualty was reported.

Was it the governor's function to lead this hue and cry? Was it the governor's function to be so emotionally disturbed and psychologically unfit as to compare a riot without a casualty to the deliberate gassing of six million Jews? Should there not have been some sense of proportion, some balance, some perspective to the governor's assessment of the situation? No wonder no one in North or South Block could take these hysterical cries of 'wolf' seriously.

It is this totally distorted perspective of the place of the Kashmiri Pandit in the Kashmiri ethos that Jagmohan brought to bear on his second disastrous term as governor—the term during which the Valley was denuded of its Pandits. What exactly happened during the five months from January to May 1990 when Jagmohan was given the run of the Valley?

Instead of relying on any other source, let me quote Jagmohan himself. On page 478 of his book, Jagmohan cites his own additional director-general of police, Amar Kapur, as saying that 134 innocent persons were killed by the militants in the period between December 1989 and May 1990 of which seventy-one were Hindus (which means sixty-three were Muslims!). The Kashmiri Pandits Conference is quoted as saying that the director-general of police and the additional director-general thought there was no effective way of saving their lives except by shifting them to Jammu.

The fact remains that it was not the actual killings but the atmosphere of fear created by the governor which exacerbated the situation and led to the exodus of the Pandits. That the governor, whose job it was to still these fears and infuse confidence in the minorities, failed woefully in his task and, indeed, contributed critically to the panic, is evident from

Jagmohan's own purple prose, quoted from his book in a box item in *Sunday* entitled 'The Strangest Night': 'Voices of alarm, of concern, of fright, sometimes muted voices of men too terror-stricken to speak. "Tonight is our last night," moaned one voice. "By morning we—all the Kashmiri Pandits—would be butchered."'

The fact is they were not.

Jagmohan goes on: 'Send us aeroplanes, take us out of the Valley, evacuate us at night if you do not want to see our corpses in the morning.'

The fact is that, according to Jagmohan's own additional director-general of police, of the 125,000 Kashmiri Pandits in the Valley, only seventy-one were found, over a period of 166 days, as 'corpses in the morning'; and that during the same period no less than sixty-three Kashmiri Muslims were also found as 'corpses in the morning'. In these circumstances, should the governor have visited the home of only one Hindu victim of terrorism, Satish Tikoo? Should the governor also not have been seen in the homes of Kashmiri Muslim victims of terrorism?

Then comes Jagmohan's punchline:

> I could hear the terrible slogans and exhortations that were emanating from hundreds of loudspeakers fitted on the mosques…it appeared that a number of recorded tapes were being simultaneously played at a very loud pitch, causing horrible effects in resonance and permeating the atmosphere with terror and fear of imminent death.

So, is Jagmohan saying that it was a cacophony of loudspeakers that made 100,000 or more people refugees in their own country?

No, the reality must be understood if we are to find a solution to the problem. If the Kashmiri Pandit was driven out of the Valley because Kashmiri Muslims will not coexist with

Kashmiri Hindus, the two-nation theory is right and Kashmir cannot be part of India, not, at least, until its Muslims are driven out or reduced to a hapless minority. But if the Kashmiri Pandit can live in peace and harmony with a Kashmiri Muslim majority, as he has in fact done for ages, what we need to insist on in our negotiations with the Hurriyat and the Pakistanis is that our bottom line is that Kashmiriyat must be restored so that the Kashmiri Pandit is enabled to return to his hearth and his home in the Valley with honour, in safety and full security. We must make it clear that this is not 1947 and India will not stand for the kind of ethnic cleansing that accompanied the creation of Pakistan under the aegis of a British-run administration; that we are not going to allow a Kashmir without Hindus. In short, that without the guarantee of the right to return for all Kashmiri refugees, whatever their religious persuasion, there can be no end to the travails of the Valley. For as Kashmir's revered poet, Lal Ded sang: 'Oh! Foolish man! Think not in terms of Hindu and Mussalman.'

Ayodhya

Sunday, 6 December 1992, was the blackest day in my life. Yes, of course, there have been personal tragedies much worse. But at the level of public life, and certainly since we put the partition behind us, there has never been a darker day. And I say this fully remembering our terrible despair as the Chinese crossed the Thagla Ridge and, like a knife through butter, cut through our defences all the way from the Chip Chap River through Sela and Bomdila, advancing up to Tezpur, from where our pusillanimous district magistrate fled, making a bonfire of his treasury. But that was a defeat inflicted on us by an outsider. The Babri Masjid was a defeat inflicted on us by our own people.

I was far from alone in my outrage. Millions of our fellow citizens, political and apolitical, shared the shock and the anger and, yes, the fear at what we were doing to ourselves. No dancer, it would seem, could dance to anything but our secularism; no painter paint but to pour out his anguish; no architect or designer rest till he had devised some structure to replace not just the structure that had been brutalized but our very being that had been vandalized. On the evening of the destruction, Prabhu Chawla, whose sympathies had always seemed to lie with the destructionists, unambiguously condemned this barbarity on television. My cousin, the senior member of my generation, chartered accountant to the VHP, who had often asked why I was so vicious about his clients, rang to tell me that he was broken-hearted. Every itsy-bitsy Rotary Club organized a seminar to say 'no' to such atavism. And in Parliament there was total unanimity that the Sangh Parivar be politically boycotted, no alliance with them ever again being the refrain. It seemed like the very soul of a nation crying out its despair.

L.K. Advani now says 6 December 1992 was among the worst days of his life. He has even called upon the journalists who were on the platform with him to certify how chagrined he was as the masjid came down. It is miraculous what impending prosecution can do to the mind. So, let us go back to the beginning—Lal Krishna Advani's 1990 Rath Yatra in a converted Toyota van from Somanatha to Ayodhya, interrupted by his arrest at Samastipur.

The BJP's call for an 'alternative' culture was given by Professor Murli Manohar Joshi, when he served at the start of the 1990s as the president of his party. The problem with the BJP's 'alternative political culture' is that while it knows what it is not (it is emphatically *not* the Nehruvian culture) it does not quite know what it is: is it to be rath-based or not? For, the exquisite irony of the BJP's dilemma is that it is yet to decide whether to bind itself to rath or wrath! They have been so badly let down by the community in whose name they believed they were riding a Hindutva wave that within months of his setting out from Somanatha to avenge himself on all Muslim invaders from Ghazni to Babur, Advani was reduced to admitting pathetically that the Rath Yatra had adversely affected his personal image.[9] Comfort himself as best he might by pretending that it was only in the eyes of the country's political elite that his stock had gone down and not in the eyes of the masses, the fact is that the masses too were neither enthused by the Rath Yatra nor amused by the communal poison it spread.

For although the Advani juggernaut, as it rolled from Somanatha to Ayodhya, looked set to crush our secular polity beneath its wheels, in the end it only crushed the V.P. Singh government. The thousands, perhaps lakhs, who turned out to gawp at the Advani *leela* included an overwhelming majority that had come merely for the fun of it. The people of India lead terribly boring lives. In our villages, it is a dull, unrelenting grind. In mofussil India, there is an arid sameness to one uneventful day following another. So, when the circus comes to town—whether it is magician Gogia Pasha's or politician Lal Krishna Advani's—everyone comes pouring out of their tedious tenements for the hustle and the bustle, for the jostling and the hubbub, for the chance to catch up with friends and acquaintances, for the opportunity to give the children an outing, for the extravagance of a newspaper funnel brimming over with *chana jor garam*! The BJP mistook this convivial picnic for an upsurge of grass-roots support. And since ours is a composite culture where for thousands of years the rituals and practices of our religious communities have been rubbing off on one another, it is not in the least surprising that Advani should have spotted, from time to time, a Muslim in the milling, madding crowd. Added together in the course of a 10,000-km ride, lasting close to a month from incarnation at Somanatha to incarceration in Samastipur, that tots up to the 'thousands of Muslims' that Murli Manohar Joshi had visions of seeing flocking to the rath.

In the end, it all amounted to a big zero—because our people have no desire to mix their religion with politics. Yes, they take their religion seriously. As, indeed, they do their politics. But that is precisely the reason why they do not mix the one with the other.

The direction the Narasimha Rao government should have gone after Advani himself admitted to the damage his antics had caused was, ironically, indicated by Advani himself. In the first flush of the Rao government taking office in 1991, Advani had said in the Lok Sabha that there was one way in which the matter could be brought to a conclusion: move from where Chandra Shekhar and Rajiv Gandhi had taken matters and proceed from there to use Article 143 of the Constitution.[10]

Narasimha Rao should have seized the opportunity to clarify what the Rajiv Gandhi initiative of November 1990 was and what was the change wrought in that initiative by the then prime minister, Chandra Shekhar, in January 1991 which needed to be rectified for the matter to be brought to a conclusion. Instead, Rao began a negotiation with an assortment of BJP surrogates, including a bevy of sants and sadhus, thus reopening the window of opportunity through which Advani and his cohorts squeezed in to bring down the mosque on 6 December 1992.

In November 1990, after the fall of the V.P. Singh government, Rajiv Gandhi suggested to Chandra Shekhar, who had taken over as prime minister, that a commission of enquiry be established to determine whether, as a matter of historical fact, a Ram temple was indeed destroyed by Babur's general, Mir Baqi, in 1528 to make way for the Babri Masjid. The commission was to comprise five sitting judges of the Supreme Court, selected by the chief justice. I was present when this meeting took place. The alternative suggested was a reference by the president to the Supreme Court under Article 138(2)[11] of the Constitution, as the findings of the Supreme Court would then be binding on all concerned. A reference under

Article 143 was specifically *not* suggested because the Supreme Court view would then constitute merely an advisory opinion binding on no one.

Rajiv Gandhi made this proposal because all representative bodies of Muslims whom Rajiv had contacted had assured him that, according to the shariat, it was *haraam* (sacrilegious) to destroy an existing place of worship in peacetime to construct a masjid in its place. Thus, if a judgment were secured that, as a matter of historical fact, there was a mandir at the site of the Ram Janmabhoomi which Mir Baqi had deliberately destroyed in peacetime to make way for a masjid, not only would the Muslims have no difficulty in renouncing their claim to the premises, they would, in fact, be under a scriptural injunction, in terms of Islamic jurisprudence, to do so. If, on the other hand, it were held that, as a matter of historical fact, Baqi had not destroyed a mandir in peacetime to make way for a masjid, it would knock the bottom out of the VHP/Sangh Parivar claim and thus extinguish the communal dimension that was and is sought to be added to the resolution of what was and remains, in essence, a property dispute involving the Sunni Waqf Board and other claimants to the site.

In the light of the subsequent 2003 Supreme Court acceptance of a (much-disputed) finding by the Archaeological Survey of India that there are traces of what might have been a temple several layers below the ground at the Ram Janmabhoomi site, it is important to clarify that the question, as raised by Rajiv Gandhi, was not whether at some previous point in time there had or had not been a temple at the site. The point to be established was whether there was a temple extant at the time of Mir Baqi's arrival in the area and whether Mir Baqi had then destroyed the mandir in peacetime in order to build his masjid. That is a question still to be put to the test—although no evidence has turned up to suggest that there was in fact a temple there in 1528 or that Baqi destroyed it to make way for a masjid. There is, moreover, nothing to indicate that the mirab of the Babri Masjid was raised at the precise point where the garbha griha of a previous mandir stood (which is, of course, the import of the BJP/VHP/Sangh Parivar slogan '*Mandir* wahin *banayenge!*'). Indeed, the irrefutable historical fact is that Acharya Tulsidas penned his immortal classic, *Ramcharitmanas*, in Ayodhya—in the shadow, as it were, of the masjid, and that too within a few years of the construction of the masjid. But nowhere does he lament or make any mention whatsoever of a 'magnificent' Ram temple having been destroyed. Even if a temple had existed on the spot at one time, that temple had been destroyed or had fallen into ruins long before Baqi's arrival on the scene and is thus not germane to the issue of whether Baqi destroyed a mandir to build thereon a masjid.

Rajiv Gandhi's proposal was accepted in principle by the Chandra Shekhar government and a team of authorized representatives of the Babri Masjid Action Committee (BMAC)—including my friend, Shahabuddin, who is the source of my information—did in fact arrive at the home ministry in January 1991 with all the evidence they had been able to gather to establish that Mir Baqi had not vandalized an existing mandir to build the Babri Masjid. The BMAC knew, of course, that neither the VHP nor the BJP nor any other organ of the Sangh Parivar had submitted any evidence to buttress their claim; the fact that the BMAC nevertheless turned up at the home ministry is an indication of their earnestness to accept the Rajiv formula. But the BMAC team was shocked to learn that the Chandra Shekhar government had slyly changed the terms of reference and instead of requesting the president to make the reference under the binding provisions of Article 138(2), was proposing to make the reference under the non-binding provisions of Article 143. They, therefore, returned from the home ministry, refusing to submit their evidence.

However, the BMAC's evidence was examined by a team

of four historians of repute belonging to Delhi University—Professors D.N. Jha, Suraj Bhan, R.S. Sharma and Athar Ali. Professor Jha revealed through a letter to the editor published in the *Times of India* on 28 July 1992 that they had duly submitted their report to the minister of state for home affairs, Subodh Kant Sahay, on 13 May 1991. No steps seem to have been taken then or since, by the Rao government or any successor government to bring the Jha team's report to the attention of the judicial authority(ies) concerned. Retrieving this is important if the Archaeological Survey of India's report is considered to be of relevance by the Lucknow bench of the Allahabad High Court which is seized of the basic property dispute.

Advani, in his 1991 Lok Sabha intervention, did not suggest a commission of enquiry or a Supreme Court adjudication but an advisory opinion of the Supreme Court under Article 143. Rao should have pointed out to him that there is a world of difference between the two. Detailed discussion might even have shown, as recent jurisprudential opinion indicates, that a reference under Article 138 was not, in fact, possible. But a commission of enquiry comprising sitting judges of the Supreme Court would have served the same purpose.

Tragically, that course of action was not pursued. In the final denouement before the Babri Masjid was demolished, a meeting was convened in November 1992 at which Advani suggested a reference to the Supreme Court under Article 143. This was not acceptable. The masjid fell. And strangely, there was some talk in Congress circles of an ex-post facto reference to the Supreme Court—but oddly enough under the earlier rejected Article 143. Nothing, however, came of it once the courts froze everything at the site, thus ruling out the fulfilment of Prime Minister Rao's commitment, made on 7 December 1992, to rebuild the masjid at the very place.

After the demolition of the masjid, there have been court

proceedings relating to the persons responsible. Case number
344/94 was registered in the court of the additional sessions
judge (Ayodhya Episode), Allahabad. The Central Bureau of
Investigation's charge sheet against L.K. Advani and others
included offences under seven different provisions of the Indian
Penal Code. The prosecution submitted that L.K. Advani,
Murli Manohar Joshi and Uma Bharti, along with twenty-
seven others, 'committed a criminal conspiracy' through the
period 'October 1990 to 6 December 1992'. Among other acts
of desecration, said the prosecution, 'it was decided to raze the
Babri Masjid to the ground'. It alleged that the BJP, in concert
with three other organizations—the Bajrang Dal, the VHP and
the Shiv Sena—made plans to demolish the disputed structure
of the Babri Masjid. Moreover, 'a suicide squad of the Bajrang
Dal' was 'trained in the Chambal Valley' to demolish the
mosque.

Next, 'on 5 December 1992', said the prosecution in the
charge sheet, 'a secret meeting was held at the house of Shri
Vinay Katiyar' (the BJP member of Parliament for the area)
'which was attended by Shri Lal Krishna Advani' at which 'a
final decision to demolish the disputed structure was taken'. It
was also the prosecution's contention 'that when the disputed
structure was being pulled down Shri Advani asked Kalyan
Singh [the chief minister of UP] not to tender his resignation
till the disputed structure had been completely pulled down'.
As for the now-chagrined Uma Bharti, the prosecution said she
had 'instigated the kar sevaks' with slogans like *'ek dhakka aur
do, Babri Masjid tod do'* and *'khoon kharaba hona hain, ek bar
ho jane do'*.

In court, Uma Bharti argued that she had made no speech
instigating anyone to pull down the masjid; on the contrary,
she insisted that she had asked them to climb down. On behalf
of Advani and Joshi it was contended that no criminal conspiracy
had been hatched, they had not made any 'instigating speeches'
and that the report of the observer, Tej Shauker, 'is silent about

the accused persons, Shri L.K. Advani and Shri Murli Manohar Joshi'.

The additional sessions judge (Ayodhya Episode), Jagdish Prasad Srivastava, delivering his judgment on 9 September 1997, observed, 'The court has to see whether there is any evidence available on record to sustain the charge sheet and whether there is a just basis for the framing of charges.' On the basis of what the law calls the application of the judicial mind to the evidence tendered and contested before the court, the judge held that 'it is clearly established that the accused person [Advani] acted in the demolition of the disputed structure'.

Moreover, the honourable court said that it was 'crystal clear' that the BJP, in cohorts with the Shiv Sena and the Bajrang Dal, 'hatched a criminal conspiracy due to which the disputed structure was pulled down'. Thus, 'on the basis of the evidence available on challan', the court found that 'prima facie evidence under Section 120-B is established' against thirty-eight of the forty persons accused, including Lal Krishna Advani, Murli Manohar Joshi and Uma Bharti.

The court further found that 'prima facie offences' under six other sections of the IPC, read with Section 149 of the IPC, had been made out 'against accused persons Shri Lal Krishna Advani (the first named and, inter alia, Murli Manohar Joshi and Uma Bharti)'. The court also found 'on the basis of evidence produced by the prosecution' that these three, in addition to several others, had also committed 'a prima facie offence under Section 120-B' read with five other sections of the IPC. Therefore, concluded the honourable judge, 'they are charged under the aforesaid offences' and 'directed to be presented in the court...for the framing of charges'.[12]

The charges, however, could not be framed because a criminal revision petition, no. 255 of 1997, was moved in the Lucknow bench of the high court, praying that 'the impugned order' be set aside, and that till a decision is taken on this, the proceedings in the session court be stayed. The high court set aside the charges on a technicality which it said could be easily rectified by the state government. The UP government has yet to rectify the technical error. When it does, the prosecution of Advani and other senior members of the BJP will resume. I am content to await the final judgment.

Meanwhile, one last comment before we move to other dimensions of secularism in a time of communal activism. Has the leopard changed its spots? Is it perhaps time to reassess the nature of the enemy? Is the Hindutva brigade still the same as it was when they rolled out the Rath Yatra from Somanatha?

The question arises because, in his years in office from 1998 onwards, Vajpayee repeatedly asserted that secularism, not Hinduism, was the fundamental basis of our nationhood. And Advani has, in his 1999 Durga Das Memorial Lecture in New Delhi and since, most cogently deplored the resort to communalism.

Advani would have us believe that it is consistent to decry what happened at Ayodhya with praise for what brought it about. This is like Clinton saying it was noble of him to have invited a mere intern into the Oval Office, 'unfortunate' that it led to the consequence it did. The new, chastened Advani told an open-mouthed Parliament in December 1999 that the destruction of the Babri Masjid 'should not have happened'. Of course, it should not have happened. But would it have happened if there had been no Ayodhya movement? Yet the same Advani who, in the Lok Sabha, quotes himself as having written weeks after Black Sunday that he was 'dejected and downcast', tells his listeners at the Durga Das Memorial Lecture, delivered the same day, that he remains 'proud' of the movement that caused him such dejection.

Confronted with this kind of double talk, the bewildered reader is left with no alternative but to look for the forked tongue in the fine print. It is only if one does so that one begins to see by what verbal legerdemain Advani is able to reconcile the irreconcilable. It is necessary to do so before

Advani lulls the country into imagining that the argument between Hindutva and Bhartiyata is just arcane coffee-house sophistry over words, definitions and their meaning.

First, why was Advani 'dejected and downcast' after Ayodhya? Was it because it broke his heart to see the masjid being razed, gumbaz by gumbaz, to the ground? If so, why, as the tallest leader present, did he not rush up to the vandals and stop them? If he had done that, he could have spared himself all the anguish and remorse.

Advani could reply with justice that he is no Mahatma and, therefore, could not be expected to do the Gandhian thing. Fair enough. But he does preen himself as a 1990s Sardar Patel. Could he then not have just ordered his minion, the chief minister of Uttar Pradesh, to send in the army and get the goondas off the 'disputed structure'? True, P.V. Narasimha Rao was no Sardar Patel and had, therefore, wrung his hands, saying that he had stationed the army at Faizabad for decorative purposes only, and that if Kalyan Singh wanted the army in, all he had to do was say the word. But the Sangh Parivar's Sardar was on the spot. If he had in him an iota of what made the original Sardar the 'Iron Man', all he needed to do was treat Kalyan Singh the way the Sardar treated the maharaja of Alwar, i.e. let the silly fellow know who was who. But Advani is not made of iron, and the rust is in his soul.

The fact is that Advani was 'dejected and downcast' not because the Babri Masjid was brought down brick by brick before his very eyes, but because that did not pay him the expected dividend. He thought he would be hailed as the 'Hindu saviour', the 'avenger' for 1200 years of non-Hindu dominance. Instead, nothing has turned the Hindu voter so decisively against the BJP as the demolition of the Babri Masjid. It was the antithesis of everything which makes the Hindu way of life so unique.

Advani should recognize that nothing threatens a community so much as the denigration of its identity and the demand that it subsume its identity within another for its legitimacy to be acknowledged. That, and not the secular cultivation of a minorities' vote bank as Advani alleges, is the root cause of the sense of insecurity among the minorities. Do not ask me; ask the Christians and the Muslims why it is that they feel insecure about the BJP and its Hindutva. When Advani asked the minorities to trust him because there were fewer riots when the BJP was in power than in the past, the minorities were not convinced because they know that the BJP got into office by assiduously stoking communalism in its worst form, that their sister organizations were the ones who engineered riots to come to power. No wonder then that the BJP was quite unable to win over the minorities' vote in the latest Lok Sabha elections. This claim, in fact, amounts to political blackmail of the Thackeray kind: put us in power and we will stop wrecking peace and tranquillity; don't, and you will see what we do to you! Is our democracy to succumb to such blackmail? Anyone doubting this is invited to read the Srikrishna Commission report; or reflect on the horrors of Advani's acolyte, Narendra Modi's Gujarat.

Gyan Vapi Masjid/Kashi Vishwanath Mandir

The Places of Worship Act, 1991, has put beyond the pale of the law any attempt to alter the religious character of any place of worship as it was on 15 August 1947 (except the disputed site and structure at Ayodhya which was excluded from the ambit of the Act as the matter was sub judice at the time the law was enacted). With persistence worthy of a better cause, the VHP and the Sangh Parivar (and even the BJP, although somewhat sotto voce) have made the Gyan Vapi Masjid at Varanasi the next target of their attentions.

Since Aurangzeb is generally regarded as the most fanatical of the Mughal emperors, notwithstanding the more complex reality revealed by serious historical research on the subject, he is an easy hate figure to invoke. And because it was Aurangzeb who demolished the Kashi Vishwanath Mandir to build the Gyan Vapi Masjid, communal forces are attempting to keep alive the controversy surrounding the masjid.

The truth behind the destruction of the Vishwanath Mandir has been in the public realm since the publication of Dr Pattabhi Sitaramayya's *Feathers and Stones* in 1946. In the 1985 Khuda Baksh Memorial Lecture in Patna, Bishamber Nath Pande gave a lucid account of its history.

It appears that while Aurangzeb was passing near Varanasi on his way to Bengal, the Hindu kings in his entourage requested a day's halt which would enable their queens to go to Varanasi, have a dip in the Ganga and pay their homage to Lord Vishwanath. Aurangzeb agreed. After the ranis had performed the rituals and had offered the puja at the Vishwanath temple, all of them, except the maharani of Kutch, returned. A thorough search was made of the temple precincts but the rani was nowhere to be found. When Aurangzeb was informed of this, he sent his senior officers to search for the queen. To their horror, they found the missing rani in the basement of the temple, dishonoured and crying, deprived of all her ornaments. The rajas were outraged and demanded exemplary action. On the grounds that the sacred precincts had been despoiled, Aurangzeb ordered that the idol of Lord Vishwanath be removed to some other place, the temple be razed and the mahant be arrested and punished.

Sitaramayya's narrative differs from Pande's in only one small particular. According to Sitaramayya, after Aurangzeb had ordered the demolition of the temple, since such a scene of robbery could not be the House of God, the queen who was rescued insisted that a masjid be built on the ruins. It was to please her that the masjid was built.

Uma Bharti has never satisfactorily answered a question I put to her a decade ago in Parliament. If for 300 years, I asked, the azaan sounded in the masjid has always been heard in the mandir, and if the temple bells of the mandir have echoed in the masjid, should not the coexistence of the mandir and the masjid be celebrated as a symbol of secular India. Why would you want to demolish the one to celebrate the other?

Hubli

Following the outrage at Ayodhya in 1992, Uma Bharti, Sikandar Bakht and Abbas Ali Bohra were accused of stoking a communal fire in Hubli, Karnataka, over raising the Indian flag at Idgah Maidan which had been granted on lease to the Anjuman-e-Islam by the Hubli–Dharwad municipality in 1921, seventy-two years before the communal violence was unleashed. The Anjuman-e-Islam, a social service organization, had applied for the lease of an open ground adjacent to a local mosque, universally known as the Idgah Maidan. The municipality granted the Anjuman a lease for 999 years at a rent of a rupee a year. The leased land measured 1991 square yards and is registered at CTS no. 174, ward no. 3; approved by the Government of Bombay on 11 January 1922; lease deed signed on 17 May 1930. That is how long ago it all happened. No one objected then. Indeed, for close on half a century, from 1921 to 1960, no one expressed any objection.

The Idgah Maidan was the Idgah Maidan, a place of religious congregation for the Muslim community on the days of its holiest festivals, a status conferred by the local authority, confirmed by the provincial government, and sanctified by decades of custom and usage. In actual fact, come one or the other of the Eid festivals, Hindus freely commingled with their Muslim brethren to celebrate what was, in effect, a festival for everybody.

The Anjuman had, in 1960, applied to the local authority for permission to put up a building on the premises, the upper floor to be used as an educational institution, the lower floor for about half-a-dozen shops (which were eventually given on rent to four Hindus and three Muslims—could anything be more secular?). The permission to put up the building was granted by the divisional commissioner, Belgaum, and endorsed by the Government of Mysore (as Karnataka was called in 1960). All perfectly legal. All perfectly in order.

Enter the dissenters. They did not like what had happened, and went to court—which, of course, they were perfectly entitled to do. Also, of course, alas, the law's delays are notorious. Just as the sessions judge, Faizabad, failed to do anything decisive about the Babri Masjid from 1950 till the setting up of the special bench of the Allahabad High Court in 1989, so too did the munsif's court in Hubli dawdle over the Idgah Maidan dispute for a full dozen years, from 1960 to 1972. Meanwhile, the building complex came up. Hundreds of children were educated on the top floor. Thousands of Muslim, Hindu, Christian and, for aught I know, atheist consumers fulfilled their shopping needs on the ground floor. Eid continued to be celebrated. The plaintiffs were alone in their fretting.

On 7 December 1972, the munsif held that the permission granted to the Anjuman by the divisional commissioner to put up a complex was invalid. The Anjuman appealed to the additional civil judge—which they were as much entitled to do as the plaintiffs were to approach the munsif. The additional civil judge partially upheld the munsif's view. The Anjuman then went to the Karnataka High Court. The high court took twenty years to deliver its judgment. Meanwhile, hundreds more children were educated on the top floor. And thousands more Muslim, Hindu, Christian and, for aught I know, atheist consumers continued to fulfil their shopping needs on the ground floor.

The Karnataka High Court judgment, delivered on 16 June 1992, upheld the judgment of the additional civil judge and ordered the demolition of the educational-cum-commercial complex within forty-five days. The Anjuman appealed to the Supreme Court for a stay. Their special leave petition was admitted. The stay was granted.

The Anjuman was, of course, perfectly entitled to go to the Supreme Court. Even as the plaintiffs were perfectly entitled to submit their special leave petition to the same Supreme Court, praying for the grant of 'customary rights' to the use of the Idgah Maidan by the general public—the essential precondition for hoisting the national flag—which the Karnataka High Court had refused to concede. The Supreme Court allowed the special leave petition on 19 April 1993. There the matter rested when Bharti got into her act.

At that stage, the legal validity of the Anjuman's 999-year lease had been upheld by every authority from the munsif to the high court and was *not* under challenge in the Supreme Court. Second, while the munsif, the additional civil judge and the high court had all ordered the demolition of the building complex, the Supreme Court had ordered a stay on the demolition. Until (and unless) the stay was vacated, no one had the legal right to demand any demolition. Third, the issue was sub judice, not only because the Supreme Court had admitted the Anjuman's special leave petition, but also because— and this is the pertinent point—the Supreme Court had admitted the plaintiffs' special leave petition. *Both* sets of litigants were before the court. The Supreme Court was yet to pronounce on either set of applications. And fourth, frankly, who cared a damn? This was one more dispute over property like lakhs of other such disputes cluttering our machinery of justice. If we can all wait decade after decade for the wheels of justice to grind slowly to their end, without killing each other or sowing disaffection against each other, why not wait for justice to take its course in this case also?

One of those who had been raising the flag issue in Hubli was Devendra Naik. Before every 15 August and 26 January, Devendra Naik had been approaching the munsif's court for permission to hoist the national flag on the Idgah Maidan, only to be turned down each and every time by the same court that has held the Anjuman's building complex to be illegal. How could the Sangh Parivar insist that the munsif's order on demolition be enforced while violating the same munsif's order not to raise the flag on the disputed property?

That stopped neither Bharti nor Sikandar Bakht nor Abbas Ali Bohra from insisting on raising the flag. In the melee that followed, five innocent people were killed. Foiled in Hubli by the police, the communalists went hundreds of kilometres away to Shimoga to beat up innocent Muslims who had nothing to do with the Idgah Maidan in Hubli or the Anjuman-e-Islam.

The key point of law to note is *not* that the munsif, the additional civil judge and the high court had ordered the demolition of the complex, or even that the Supreme Court had stayed the order. The key point is that the high court had specifically held that the Idgah Maidan was the property of the municipality and, therefore, no 'customary rights' to the property could be claimed by the general public. In other words, no one—not the Sangh Parivar, not Devendra Naik, not even the Anjuman—could raise a flag on the property without the sanction of the municipality. Bharti and her companions did not have such a sanction.

Even more to the point, it would have been totally illegal for the Anjuman to raise a flag on the property unless ordered to do so by the municipality. Indeed, the whole of the Anjuman's case would have been jeopardized if they were to treat their privately leased land as public property. Why should they have jeopardized their thirty-four-year-old legal battle merely to satisfy the 'patriotism' of those who had taken them to court? Especially as the Anjuman does *not* have any objection to the national flag. They run a number of schools. Two-thirds of their students are non-Muslims, mostly poor Hindu children belonging to the SC/ST and other backward classes (OBCs).

Every Independence Day and Republic Day, all the schoolchildren—Hindu, Muslim or other—in each one of the Anjuman schools gather to raise and salute the national flag.

Which is more than what can be said of the Sangh Parivar. For the core of the Sangh Parivar is the RSS. And never in the history of independent India, on not one single Independence Day or Republic Day has the RSS ever unfurled the national flag on any of its premises anywhere in India. They raise only their saffron banner, the Bhagwa Dhwaj.

Why, then, was Uma Bharti rousing emotions in Hubli? Why has she never launched a campaign to fly the national flag on every RSS premises on every Independence Day and Republic Day?

Gujarat

On 27 February 2002, a train overflowing with kar sevaks returning from a show of strength at Ayodhya stopped for three minutes at the wayside station of Godhra in Gujarat. At Godhra, there was a fracas between some Muslim vendors and the lumpen elements on the train over payment for some tea and snacks. The enquiry is still to establish what precisely happened thereafter. What is known is that the emergency chain of the train was pulled twice in quick succession and when the train stopped the second time at a railway signal about a mile outside the station, on the edges of a very poor but densely populated Muslim habitation, one of the coaches (S–6) caught fire and fifty-eight women and children, but as far as is known no men, perished within seconds. The forensic laboratory says the fire could not have been started by pouring inflammable liquid into the coach from outside. The chief minister of Gujarat, a hand-picked nominee of L.K. Advani, insists that it was the largely Muslim mob which gathered outside the train when it stopped at the signal which started the fire with the deliberate intent of burning to death innocent

Hindu women and children returning from a pilgrimage to one of Hinduism's holiest sites.

There followed a carnage in several parts of Gujarat, directed at innocent Muslim homes and families, which lasted not three days as claimed by the chief minister but for three dreadful weeks and continued sporadically for the better part of three months. While Advani (who is elected to Parliament from the same state) praised the chief minister's handling of the situation, most independent observers squarely implicated the state government for fanning the flames of hatred which resulted in at least a thousand Muslims (unofficial figures are two to three times higher) being butchered and Muslim properties worth millions being torched. Of course, there were some Hindus killed and everyone suffered the economic cost of the rioting, but the worst sufferers by far were innocent Muslims who lived hundreds of miles from Godhra and had nothing to do with whoever was responsible for the Godhra outrage.

Believing that the Hindu–Muslim divide engineered by him and his government would redound to the electoral advantage of his party, the chief minister dissolved the state assembly nearly a year in advance of the due date and pressed for immediate polls. Civilized opinion in the state and the country was horrified by this naked exploitation of hatred for narrow partisan advantage. Fortunately, the Election Commission, backed by the Supreme Court, rejected the state government demand for immediate elections. After a complicated legal and constitutional tussle, the elections were eventually scheduled for December, about two months in advance of the due date. It was an election for the soul of India, an election that would show whether we would continue to be true to our millennial history of open-minded tolerance and the symbiotic interaction of the various religious, linguistic, cultural, ethnic and racial communities that go into the making of contemporary India or go the opposite way.

The battle in Gujarat thus shaped up as a battle between Bharat and the Bharatiya Janata Party.

I could not believe that in a battle between Bharat and the Bharatiya Janata Party, Bharat would lose. So, armed with that heart-rending masterpiece, *Gujarat: The Making of a Tragedy*, I visited Gujarat to contribute my two-bits worth to the election campaign there in December 2002. It was hard to tell that it was election time in Ahmedabad. There were hardly any posters or banners, flags or buntings, nor any raucous loudspeakers. And in deference to the strictures of the Election Commission, the walls were bereft of election graffiti. In this dull, sanitized setting, there was only one hoarding which caught my eye. It asked what is 'in stock' and what is 'not in stock' in today's Gujarat. Available, it said, are American soft drinks, French perfume, English shoes, imported jeans, and Italian pizza. 'Out of Stock', it went on, are electricity, water, law and order, peace, justice, and, above all, employment.

In the battle between Bharat and the Bharatiya Janata Party in Gujarat in December 2002, it was Bharat that lost. Or was it? For the roots of contemporary communalism in the state are not ideological but economic. Not slow economic growth but a model and pattern of growth which have won the hearts of the Washington consensus. Over a decade of reforms since the early 1990s, Gujarat has been the fastest-growing state in the country and poverty levels are among the lowest in the land. Much of this development derives from globalization. No other state has been blessed with as much foreign investment or as many multinational joint ventures as Gujarat. And Gujarati entrepreneurship has been the exemplar of what Indian private enterprise can do.

Gujaratis have been globalized since long before the word became fashionable. Across the darkest reaches of Africa, it was Gujarati enterprise which followed the British flag. After the end of the empire, Gujaratis migrated to Britain and America, beginning as petty shopkeepers and ending, often within a year, as the most dynamic entrepreneurs of their host countries. Golders Green in London is now a mini-Gujarat. American highways are dotted with 'potels'. It is the NRG more than any other NRI who is swelling our foreign exchange coffers. And the most renowned industrialist of post-independence India has been Gujarat's Dhirubhai Ambani.

What then has gone so horribly wrong? Why has the globalization of Gujarat translated into the making of the most riot-prone state in the country? Why is it that communal violence has been at its most vicious in the only state of the country to rival China's rate of growth?

The answer seems to lie in the nature and pattern of economic growth in Gujarat. Gujarat's march into industrialization began nearly a hundred years ago with the textiles industry. While Mahatma Gandhi was calling for a return to hand-spun and hand-woven cloth as the centrepiece of the struggle for independence, so much so that the spinning wheel was the symbol and insignia of the freedom movement, Ahmedabad, the capital of Gandhi's home state, emerged, along with Bombay, as the premier centre of a modern cotton textiles industry. It is that industry which has collapsed over the past several decades. The economic decline of Ahmedabad and its employment-intensive textiles industry has been matched by phenomenal growth in the petroleum refining and petrochemicals sector. This has boosted growth rates to rival China's but has failed to add to employment. Growth in Gujarat has been jobless growth. Capital-intensive hi-tech projects generate high income but little employment. The magic figures are excellent for GDP but terrible for employment, especially with labour-intensive textiles in the final stages of terminal decline. Worse, much worse, is that the largest urban employer of them all—power looms—are down to a tenth or less of where they were at the beginning of the decade of reform. Neither Asia's biggest refinery at Jamnagar nor the privatization of Indian Petrochemicals Corporation Limited

(IPCL) can mask the grim state of Ahmedabad's shuttered textile mills. Those thrown out of employment from the textiles industry cannot find alternative jobs in refining or petrochemicals.

It is from this restless army of the unemployed—rendered unemployable by the march of 'progress'—that the murderous perpetrators of unspeakable crimes against the utterly innocent are hired. In the week of the poll, the lead story in the Ahmedabad edition of the *Sunday Times of India* dated 7 December 2002 quoted an analyst on Modi's appeal, which it said attracts the unemployed youth, frustrated by the ways of the world. The 'ways of the world' are not accidental. Globalization has boosted income, not employment. If we do not go in for a strategy of revival and start-up of high-employment, labour-intensive industry, the horrors of Gujarat will visit us oftener than teams from the IMF and the World Bank.

With its factories shuttered and its power looms silenced, Ahmedabad wears the exhausted look of the Depression towns of Europe and America and Japan in the 1930s. It was the Depression which led to the horrors of Hitler and Mussolini, Franco and Tojo. It is Ahmedabad's prolonged Depression that has led to Narendra Modi. The perennially poor are not communal; they are too involved with eking out an existence to provide the recruiting field for fascism. That is why the communal virus has not entered the bloodstream of either earthquake-devastated Kutch or drought-ridden Saurashtra. Nor has it overtaken Surat, whose diamond-cutting industry is deeply labour intensive, nor Vapi where small industry rules the economic roost. It is not the perennial poor but the non-perennial poor—those who have known better lives and now find the good life snatched from them for no fault of their own—that are the fodder on which communalism feeds.

We need an economic agenda to fight the spread of communal violence. That requires giving top priority not to fancy new-tech industry, but to the revival of closed textile mills and the restoration of handlooms and power looms to primacy in our economic programmes. What we need is not disinvestment in favour of the obscenely rich but investment in favour of the despairing poor. Even after centuries of industrialization, the United States, Europe and Japan have determinedly protected their textiles industry because the 1930s taught them the social and political consequences of depression in textiles. All their principles of liberalization and globalization have been thrown out of the window when it comes to textiles. The market for them ends where the textiles industry begins. Now the dismantling of their barriers on imports is in sight. It is an opening which India must avail of.

But no economic policy will succeed unless we carve Gandhiji's prayer in our hearts as surely as it is carved in marble at the entrance to his cottage at the Sabarmati Ashram: 'Give us the ability and willingness/To identify ourselves with the masses of India/O God! Grant that we may not be isolated from the people.'

The Indian Union Muslim League (IUML)

When I invited G.M. Banatwala, the IUML member of Parliament, to participate in a training camp on secularism organized by the Congress Party's political training department, not a few were outraged at a Muslim Leaguer being asked to give lessons in secularism. My argument that the Congress had been in alliance with the IUML in Kerala for decades did not wash even with some of my fellow Congress MPs from Kerala. I, therefore, pose the question: is the IUML a communal body? Or is it no more than a communitarian body? That is a key distinction we must bear in mind. Communitarian-ism is not communalism unless it chooses to become communal.

Let us begin with Jawaharlal Nehru's thundering denunciation of the League during his visit to Malabar in

December 1955. Nehru asserted that no political organization was required to safeguard the rights of the minorities when our Constitution itself protected those rights. *Chandrika*, the organ of the Muslim League, countered that the Constitution also safeguarded the rights of labour. Did that mean trade unions were not required to safeguard workers' rights?

Panditji conceded that the Constitution guaranteed any group the right to organize itself, but regretted that the right had been exercised to found a political organization based on a religious community. He said his party would fight the Muslim League in the political arena and defeat it democratically. *Chandrika* welcomed the challenge to assert its point of view within the framework of a political democracy. It too believed, it said, in participative democracy and the right of the Muslim League, as much as of the Congress or any other party, to seek the mandate of the people. In the event, the Muslim League has proved unassailable in its Malabar pocket, even as it has failed to make any headway anywhere else in the country. It exults in the one as much as it recognizes the reality of the other.

Nehru then held that it was 'barbarous' on the part of the Muslim League to divide the country communally, in its quest for freedom. He described the Muslim League as 'a barrier in the path of freedom' and a 'negation of history'. *Chandrika* replied that since the Congress leadership itself had agreed to the Muslim League's demand for partition, it was improper and inappropriate for it to deride the Muslim League now on that score. In the same editorial, *Chandrika* went on to reiterate that not only was the two-nation theory irrelevant, but there were fundamental differences between the Indian Muslim League and the Pakistan Muslim League, foremost of these being that the Pakistan Muslim League did not stand for the protection of the minorities.

This unambiguous assertion needs to be read in conjunction with the declaration of M. Mohammed Ismail in his presidential address to the League on 14 February 1959 that the Muslim League was anti-communal and fully national in its outlook and attitude and that it stood for the integrity, freedom, honour, strength, prosperity and happiness of the country and for harmony and unity of all sections of its people.

Ismail's personal patriotism was put to the test when the Chinese invaded India in the autumn of 1962. On the occasion of *Putra Daan* Day, Ismail offered his son, J.M. Miakhan, to the nation, to be used or sacrificed, as the nation saw fit, for the national cause.

So much for the background. Now, to the question on hand: is the IUML communal?

Certainly, on the historical question of whether undivided India should have been partitioned, the IUML view is that partition was justified. It further holds that in undivided India, the two-nation theory provided the ideological justification for partition, and that this was not only Muhammad Ali Jinnah's view but also that of the RSS/BJP progenitor, Veer Savarkar.

Whatever one's view on the need or otherwise for partition, the politically significant question today is whether we accept partition as a fact and, thus, Pakistan as a reality, or whether we propose the revanchist step of annulling partition (as also the Bangladesh liberation war of 1971) and reabsorbing Pakistan and Bangladesh into an Akhand Bharat. There was a time once when the restitution of an Akhand Bharat was on the Jana Sangh agenda (and still is a dream of Balraj Madhok's lunatic fringe) but no one else, the BJP included, believes that the India of yore can be brought about as a political entity.

The more germane point is: does the IUML wish to merge India in Pakistan? Does the IUML want Malappuram district in Kerala to make a unilateral declaration of independence? Has the IUML ever adopted a resolution equivalent to the Anandpur Sahib Resolution? Did the IUML oppose the merger of Hyderabad, the accession of Kashmir, the takeover of Goa, the agreement with the French over Pondicherry? Was the

IUML with the country or against it in the arguments in the UN over Kashmir, the war with the Chinese, Operation Gibraltar—Bhutto's war of September 1965, the liberation of Bangladesh? How many IUML leaders—or followers—in the last fifty-six years have been caught, tried or convicted of treachery? Correct me if I am wrong, but to the best of my knowledge, the answer is none.

In an editorial in 1955, *Chandrika* asked anyone to prove if, from 15 August 1947 to the moment when the editorial was written, the Muslim League or its leaders had done or said or thought anything against the interests, development, and progress of the country. In almost five decades since then, the IUML has passed every test of patriotism with flying colours.

Next, the question of whether a political party has the right to restrict its membership to one community. Personally, I am a Congressman precisely because my political train does not believe in first-class and second-class compartments: we do not define ourselves in terms of regions, races or communities. But I do not deny the right of the Asom Gana Parishad to concern itself exclusively with Assamese of only pure ethnic Ahom origin. If the Bodos want to talk only of Bodoland and the Dravidian parties of Tamil Nadu of the Dravidians alone or the Telugu Desam of Telugu pride (as if there were no other sort of pride), so be it. But it does seem extraordinary, in that case, to be so censorious of the IUML taking up the Muslim community as its area of primary concern.

In any case, the IUML has amended its constitution in recent times to incorporate within its fold not only 'any person who is a Muslim' but also 'any other person who is a citizen of India'. As E. Ahamed, another member of Parliament belonging to the IUML, hastens to explain, while League membership is now open to non-Muslims interested in the welfare of the Muslim community, the League remains 'essentially an organization of a religious minority'. Does that, in itself, make it communal?

Perhaps the answer to that is 'it depends'. If being interested in the welfare of a community is a sufficient definition of communalism, the IUML is without a doubt 'communal'; but, in that case, any organization whose ambit is less than all-India, must be dubbed 'communal': the Jharkhand Mukti Morcha because it seeks mukti for the Jharkhandis and not for all of us; the Gorkha National Liberation Front because the 'nation' it seeks to 'liberate' is Gorkhaland, not India; the Maharashtravadi Gomantak Party because it wants Goa for Maharashtra.

Communalism is not about whether you are for one community or the other. Communalism is about whether you would promote the interests of one community at the expense of another. The distinction is crucial. It is the BJP that wants Hindu Raj. It is not the IUML that wants Muslim Raj. It is the BJP which says all Indians must regard themselves as 'Hindus'. The IUML asks no one but the Muslims to regard themselves as Muslims. The BJP says the country's culture is the culture of Hindutva. The IUML says the country's culture is the composite of all who have contributed to it—the Hindus, of course, but also of all the others, including the Muslims. The BJP wants to regard the period of Muslim rule as an epoch of shame. The IUML looks back on our history—Islamic and non-Islamic—as a matter of pride. The BJP wants to demolish the Gyan Vapi Masjid. The IUML wishes to preserve the Birla Mandir!

The IUML approach to social reform within the Muslim community is based on the shariat and *ijtehad*, the one immutable, the other showing the way to reform. My lifestyle, the mores which inform my family life, and my personal ethic are what even Swapan Dasgupta would concede as 'liberal', even eclectic. I could never make it to the IUML.

Yet, I cannot think of a more effective way of buttressing the hold of the orthodox element on Muslim thinking than anti-Muslim Hindus taking it upon themselves to lecture

Muslims on reform. It is anti-Muslim Hindu interference in Muslim affairs that is the single biggest stumbling block in the community's march to progress. It diverts attention from community reforms to preserving the identity of the community. A community under siege cannot undertake reforms; it has then to protect itself. Patriotism is not the prerogative of any one community. Nor is any community's patriotic intent to be held suspect and the community asked to furnish proof of their patriotism. And reforms within any community should come out from within the community. It cannot be enforced from outside. The Hindu Code Bill was drafted by Hindus; not imposed on us by Ibrahim Suleiman Sait. The Hindus listened to the voices of Hindus like themselves, Swami Vivekananda, Mahatma Gandhi; it was not the Ali brothers or even Maulana Abul Kalam Azad who told the Hindus how to better themselves. Justice and fairness demands that all other communities be similarly left free to work out their own agendas for reforms.

6

Secularism and the Indian Religious Minorities

Perhaps because nearly 85 per cent of India's people belong to the Hindu religion, a disturbingly large number of Hindu Indians rarely pause to think about the role and significance of the minorities in our composite society. The space for comment on the minorities is, therefore, substantially usurped by the minority baiters. It would, therefore, be appropriate to succinctly look at the main minority communities in the country and then draw conclusions about the importance of not merely tolerating the minorities in our midst but celebrating the rich religious diversity of India; hence, the central importance of communal harmony and national integration to our continued existence as 'one nation'.

Muslims

The Muslims constitute about 12 per cent of our population. On every index of development—income, education, health, share in government services, share in private enterprise, role in self-employment, membership in legislatures—the level of their achievement is substantially below their share of the population. The only index on which they figure higher than 12 per cent is poverty. Why?

I submit that the root cause, the basic, primordial cause of Muslim backwardness in India is Pakistan. The partition in 1947 robbed the Muslims of India of leadership. I do not mean political leadership, for surely a Maulana Azad or a Rafi Ahmed Kidwai or even a Syed Shahabuddin represented and represents the true interests of the Muslims of our subcontinent more than did a mere Jinnah or a Liaquat Ali Khan. I mean leadership at the grass roots, at the local community level, in schools and universities, in village *chaupals* and dhabas, in the bazaars and the mandis, even in the mosques and the madrasas.

Those whose personal wealth and income, level of education, social mobility and economic ascension would have ensured political clout, economic strength, social cohesion and moral authority for the Muslim community as a whole, abandoned their less well-endowed brethren to make their own private fortunes in an alien land. The Muslim middle class of pre-partition India virtually vanished as the muhajir took off for a new home.

True, the fate the muhajir have met in their Dar-ul-Islam (House of Islam) is infinitely worse than any disadvantage they left behind in the Dar-ul-Harb (House of War). After all, it is in India that the faithful can go to their Friday namaz in the confidence that they will return alive to their hearths and homes; in Karachi, going to the neighbourhood mosque for the weekly prayer has become a daunting, dangerous gamble with death. However, it is cold comfort for an Indian Muslim to know that he is better placed than his relatives in Pakistan so long as he is not at least as well placed as the Indian Hindu, the Indian Christian or the Indian Parsi here at home.

At the same time, it is important to look at the issue in terms of absolute levels of achievement of the community in question and the country as a whole rather than in terms of competitiveness among communities. When we do that, I think we shall find that the disparity in achievement is much more marked among Muslims whose mother tongue is Urdu than among Muslims whose mother tongue is Tamil or Malayalam, Marathi or Gujarati, Bengali or Assamese. Indeed, in so far as Tamil Muslims are concerned, the position is almost the opposite of the Urdu-speaking Muslims of India. They tend, as a community, to have not only the same level of education as Tamilians in general, but also much higher standards of living owing to long-standing economic ties with Singapore, Hong Kong, the Gulf and other parts of the world, reinforced dramatically in recent times by remittances from West Asia. The same goes for the Malayali Muslim and, to a limited extent, for the Marathi and the Gujarati Muslim. Acute backwardness is most pronounced among Urdu-speaking Muslims.

I suggest this is because Urdu-speaking Muslims are to a substantial degree denied the opportunity (or, at any rate, denied adequate opportunity) of schooling in their mother tongue. The Tamil Muslim knows no Urdu; his mother tongue is Tamil. Therefore, access to education in his mother tongue is as equal for the Tamil Muslim as for a Tamilian of any other religious community. This has not been the case with the Muslim community in the cow belt since partition. Two factors have been mainly responsible for this.

One, state governments in Uttar Pradesh, Bihar and other states of the Hindi heartland have prescribed unrealistic levels for the minimum number of Urdu-speaking children required to provide elementary education in Urdu. Consequently, Muslim children wanting an education often have no alternative but to opt for elementary education in Hindi and go on to secondary and higher secondary education in Hindi rather than in Urdu medium. Second, for Muslims who cross the schooling threshold, the disincentive to raise their knowledge of Urdu to university standards is compounded by the knowledge that university education is virtually unavailable in Urdu, in any subject other than Urdu language and literature. Those who stay with Urdu are thus either relegated to low levels of literacy or left with little alternative to the madrasa stream. Equally, teachers who are comfortable with Urdu find opportunity for advancement in the national mainstream trimmed and so confine themselves more and more to their narrow little worlds; the narrowness is then transmitted to the children under their care. Thus, after independence the Muslim middle class has tended to be alienated from its mother tongue; Urdu has been forced into the ghetto, the mushaira and the mujra. Little wonder then that the post-partition Muslim middle class is disproportionately smaller than the share of Muslims in the total population; little wonder too that the Urdu-speaking Indian Muslim is disproportionately less represented in the Indian middle class than the non-Urdu-speaking Indian Muslim.

The solution follows from the analysis. If we want to accord Urdu-speaking Indian Muslims the same opportunities for progress which non-Urdu-speaking Muslims have grabbed after independence, we must begin with education. First, whatever the expense involved, at least 80 to 90 per cent of Muslim children whose mother tongue is Urdu must be provided the opportunity, given to children of other communities, of securing their schooling in their mother tongue. This does not mean they will not learn Hindi and English as additional languages; they must. What it means is that schooling be made available in the Urdu medium.

Second, a special effort needs to be mounted in madrasas to teach a range of subjects in Urdu without altering the basic religious character of the madrasa. Thus, the spiritually inclined Indian Muslim child or parent will be able to retain the essential religious basis of traditional education, if they so desire, while having an opportunity for modern and scientific learning.

Third, the national school midday meal scheme must be universalized and strengthened. Education in Tamil Nadu has been transformed since MGR completed this Kamaraj-initiated revolution in the state in the early 1980s. Muslim girls are as much part of the education scene in Tamil Nadu as their Hindu or Christian counterparts. So, the impact of education on birth rates in *all communities* has been dramatic; Tamil Nadu has become the first large state of the Union (after the minuscule Goa and tiny Kerala) to achieve a net reproduction rate of below unity as far back as 1991, as a result of which Tamil Nadu's population in 2010 is likely to be less than the figure generated by the 2001 census. The Kamaraj–MGR midday meal scheme is the root cause of this remarkable transformation. It has to be extended all over the country to all children, including Muslim children of both sexes, in conjunction with the availability of schooling in their mother tongue.

Fourth, university education must be made available in Urdu. This will encourage Muslim children to enter higher secondary schools in the Urdu medium since they will then be confident about avenues for higher education in the language.

Next only to education comes participation. The fundamental Muslim issue in India is not the fatwas of their imams or the number of wives they may keep. It is their grossly inadequate participation in the life of the nation. The affluent and the middle-class Muslim decamped to Pakistan in 1947, leaving behind in our charge the Muslim poor, ill-equipped financially or organizationally for the transition to modernization, and fearful of losing their identity as Muslims. The failure of our secular state lies not in the appeasement of Muslims but in our failure over five decades to provide them with even a modicum of their rightful place in nation building. Less than 3 per cent of our higher civil/police services comprise Muslim officers and even in the meanest grades of government employment, Muslims account for about 4 per cent of the total number employed. The situation gets worse in the economic sector—nationalized banks and public sector enterprises take an even smaller percentage of Muslim employees. And, in the private sector, there is a shameful absence both of Muslim executives and Muslim entrepreneurs. Worst of all, the politics of the country is marked by a desperately inadequate representation of Muslims in our elected institutions.

It is our failure to ensure equal opportunity in secular vocations for the Muslim minority that has strengthened the hold of the Islamic clerics on the community. Yet, in precisely the kind of language one might expect clerics of any religion to employ, Atal Behari Vajpayee, with his penchant for playing with words, posed a question to the Muslims of India in August 1996: did they want *Babri ya barabari*? (Babri or equality?) It is a curious question, which does not even have the merit of being particularly witty. I thought the equality granted by the Constitution of India to our Muslims was unconditional. Who is Vajpayee to make 'barabari' for our largest minority conditional on their surrendering Babri to the Sangh Parivar?

Through our Constitution, equality has been granted to a society that is unequal. For millennia, the structure and stability of our society has rested on sanctified inequality. It is only in this century that we have consciously decided to work towards deinstitutionalizing these inequalities. The first step was proclaiming a societal decision to rid society of inequality. That is the pledge of the Constitution.

The next was to evolve a programme of affirmative action in favour of the disadvantaged for which there was no precedent in our history and, at the same time, no parallel in the world. The distinctive Indian innovation was to provide, in the same Constitution that guaranteed equality, the conditions for securing such equality through discrimination—not discrimination against the weakest, which was the historical experience, but discrimination in favour of the disadvantaged, which was the charter for the future.

It is the package of measures evolved over time for protective discrimination in favour of the minorities that is opprobriously labelled as 'appeasement' by the BJP. Their slogan of 'justice for all, appeasement of none' is, in effect, a meaningless slogan because what the Constitution recognizes as 'justice' is what is described by the BJP as 'appeasement'.

Protective discrimination in favour of the SC/ST is the righting of a historical wrong and therefore meets little opposition from the dominant elements of our society, especially because this dominant element is little affected in practice by such protective discrimination. However, protective discrimination in favour of the minorities was aimed at protecting them from the consequences of immediate history. A strong, self-confident minority in a united, independent India might not have required the kind of special constitutional recognition and protection that the new republic was expected to give the minorities. But in the specific circumstances of partition immediately preceding independence, the minorities left behind in India needed the assurance that their identity would not have to be bartered as the price to pay for equality. This the Constitution did; it is what the BJP is trying to undo.

Christians

By one of those strange ironies that make the researching and reading of history such fun, the stoking of the Hindutva world view in the nineteenth and early twentieth centuries can be traced to the attempt by Jesuit missionaries from the sixteenth century onwards to understand Hinduism better so as to undermine its hold on the Hindu mind.

Beginning with St Francis Xavier translating the invocation 'Om Sri Narayanaya Namah' into Latin in 1544,[1] the first Sanskrit text to reach Europe, a host of others carefully studied the similarities between Latin and Sanskrit, thus bringing Sanskrit texts to the attention of European scholars, who then recycled these texts to India, in English and other European languages. It was through these that the newly westernized and educated elite among Indians in the second half of the nineteenth century and through the first half of the twentieth discovered the glories of their own heritage.

It was a two-way traffic. Father Thomas Stephens wrote the *Christ Purana* in the sixteenth century and pioneered the first-ever Konkani grammar. Abraham Roger translated Bhartrihari into Dutch in 1651 while Father Heinrich Roth introduced the Devnagari script to Europe. Father Francis Pons of the French Carnatic Mission composed a Sanskrit grammar in French. Father J. Ernst Hanxleden prepared a Portuguese–Sanskrit dictionary and wrote a Sanskrit grammar in Latin. Father Gaston Couerdoux drew attention to the parallels between Sanskrit and Greek. Abbe Dubois translated Spanish into Tamil and Tamil into Spanish. There were many more.

These missionaries fuelled the Orientalism (denounced in West Asia by Edward Said) of Anquetil du Perron who translated fifty-one Upanishads into French and Latin and published them between 1786 and 1802 (the translations were of the Persian version commissioned by Dara Shikoh, Aurangzeb's elder brother). Then there was Charles Wilkins, who published a Sanskrit grammar in 1785 before going on to translate the Bhagawad Gita into English in 1785, the *Hitopadesa* in 1787, and an early version of *Shakuntala* in 1795. Henry Thomas Colebrook made the existence and nature of the *Rig Veda* known to Europe in 1805, and Lieutenant Colonel Boden translated the Christian scriptures into Sanskrit with a view to enabling his countrymen to convert the natives of India to Christianity.

Sadly for Boden, after 500 years of Christian missionary activity in India, less than 2 per cent of the natives switched religion. But the interest of the missionaries in Indian spirituality, language and literature sparked the great interest in India's heritage which was fanned through the nineteenth century by Alexander Hamilton, the first to teach Sanskrit in Europe; the brothers Friedrich and August von Schlegel who made Sanskrit studies a discipline in German universities; Horace Hayman Wilson, first professor of Sanskrit at Oxford, 1833; and Sir William Jones, founder of the Asiatic Society in Calcutta, 1784.

Above all, it was the work of Friedrich Max Müller, whose research activities at Oxford were funded by the East India Company, that put paid to Macaulay's sneer about there being more to be found on a single shelf of any good European library than in all the wisdom of the East.

Ironically, Max Müller was a proselytizing Christian who had a great deal of contempt for the India of his day. In a curious paradox, therefore, he praised the 'India that was' quite as lavishly as he denigrated the India he saw in his own time as degenerate and whose redemption, he seemed to think, lay not in a return to past glory but in conversion to the Christian and Western way of life. India took what he had to say in praise of India most seriously and, except for Arun Shourie, ignored his barbs altogether.

By the mid-nineteenth century, the way out of the pitiable political condition of a subject nation seemed to lie in demanding equality, democracy and freedom for one of the greatest civilizations in world history, as the West itself was describing us. Some of the greatest minds of Europe— Schopenhauer, Goethe and H.G. Wells (as also, alas, Nietzsche!)—awakened in the Indian mind, pride in India and in being Indian, which characterized the nationalist revival of the second half of the nineteenth century and generated the Indian renaissance animating the freedom movement.

There were two broad reactions to this nineteenth-century celebration of the glory of India, particularly after the turmoil of the First War of Independence in 1857 had settled down. On the one hand were those like Ranade and Gokhale,

Rabindranath Tagore and Subrahmanya Bharati, Gandhi and Nehru who wove the numerous strands of this heritage into what Sunil Khilnani has so evocatively called *The Idea of India*—the title of his well-known book. Others, including Swami Dayananda, Bal Gangadhar Tilak and Sri Aurobindo, developed an alternative view positing the Hindu rather than the composite elements of that heritage. And Swami Vivekananda's prolific writings and speeches provided grist to both mills. It was from the 1920s that Savarkar, Hedgewar, Golwalkar and those of their persuasion brought in the Other—especially the Muslim but also the Christian, particularly the foreign missionary—as the hate object against which to venerate the Hindu heritage.

What has rendered complex contemporary India's relationship with its Christian community is the 2000-year-long association with Christianity through the Syrian Christian Church of Kerala, and 500 years of symbiotic interaction with the Jesuits in particular, followed by myriad Christian denominations flooding the country behind the imperial flag, and the dimensions of the Anglo-Indian community before and after independence.

It is among the tribals of the central belt of India, from Orissa through Bihar, Jharkhand and Chhattisgarh to Madhya Pradesh, Rajasthan, Gujarat and Maharashtra that the missionaries have done their most noble—and most controversial—work. Living in virtually impossible conditions of deprivation, removed from any contact with what passes for the conveniences of modern civilization, these intrepid missionaries braved difficulties of every kind to bring health and education to the doorstep of the most shamefully neglected people of India, its tribals. The work was not entirely selfless. The object of their endeavours was harvesting souls for Jesus Christ, in which they had a measure of success. Many tribal communities did adopt the Christian religion. Many more did not. The nobility of the Church was and is to be seen in the good work going on relentlessly, irrespective of whether or not the beneficiaries were willing to convert to Christianity.

Unfortunately, some missionaries fell in with the contempt which some of the greatest scholars of Indian civilization, like Max Müller, had for contemporary India and the contemporary state of the Hindu religion, its customs, usages and practices. Therefore, they resorted to deprecating Hinduism and extant tribal practices to project the superiority of the alternative Christian ethic and beliefs. This was in keeping with the general imperial disdain of all things native. But it caused ire among many sections of the majority population. Mahatma Gandhi was among those who, notwithstanding his warm personal friendship with Christian missionaries like the Reverend Charles Andrews (perhaps the closest friendship Gandhi had with anyone), expressed himself frequently and cogently from the days of his South Africa sojourn through his leadership of the freedom movement against the practice of persuading or cajoling people to convert from one religion to another. He urged instead that people of every religion be persuaded to rid themselves of all that was wrong and evil in their own communities. Towards this end, he set a personal example by taking up quite as passionately as his political work, the 'constructive work', as he called it, of reforming and restructuring social ills among the Hindus, campaigning against untouchability, restrictions on entry to temples, taboos pertaining to polluting influences of the lower castes and a host of other causes while advocating widow remarriage and the dignity of labour. He refrained from criticizing other communities, leaving it to their good sense and initiative to determine what reforms, if any, needed to be brought into their respective ways of life.

Others endowed with less breadth of vision and depth of understanding than the Mahatma picked up his criticism of missionary activity and ignored the larger setting in which he placed the criticism. Instead of urging and setting the example of social reform, they made Christian missionaries and Christianity their target. Among these was a hidebound, intolerant Congress activist, B.S. Niyogi, who made it his life's mission to root out Christian missionary activity. He got his opportunity when, overruling the objections of Jawaharlal Nehru, the chief minister of Madhya Pradesh appointed a commission in 1954 under Niyogi's chairmanship to report on missionary activity. The essence of the report was that missionaries were involved in spreading 'poisonous propaganda' against the majority religion. The Supreme Court ruling regarding forced conversions based on threat or blandishment is to be seen in the context of the Niyogi report. The report itself is half a century old. The number of foreign missionaries has dwindled to a mere thousand now as compared to thousands in the heyday of proselytizing. Most missionary work is now being undertaken by Indian nationals. They have the constitutional right (available also to foreign missionaries) to propagate their religion, a right being equally exercised by Hindu organizations such as the Ramakrishna Mission, Maharishi Mahesh Yogi, and the Divine Life Mission of Swami Sivananda, among many others, who are engaged in the propagation of the Hindu religion. Thus, the issue should be regarded as settled.

Unfortunately, communal forces continue to target the Christian community and missionary activity. In recent years, we have had large-scale destruction and torching of churches in the tribal areas of Gujarat. The Staines tragedy in Orissa underlines the anti-Christian and anti-missionary role being played by BJP-affiliated outfits like the Bajrang Dal. And Dilip Singh Judeo, now the de facto leader of the BJP in Chhattisgarh, is notorious for his wholesale 'reconversion' of tribals from Christianity to Hinduism. I have put the word 'reconversion' in quotes because most tribal communities, to begin with, are not Hindu and therefore cannot be 'brought back' to the Hindu fold. They are, in fact, double converts—from tribal beliefs to Christianity and from Christianity to Hinduism. Moreover, the RSS has imitated the Christian missionaries in undertaking social work among the tribal communities in the name of the Vanvasi Kalyan Samitis. This is excellent work and needs to be commended—except that the ulterior purpose is to spread precisely the kind of 'poisonous propaganda' against other religious communities that the Niyogi Commission objected to with regard to Christian missionaries fifty years ago. What has escaped the notice of these zealots engaged in converting the tribal population to Hinduism is the fact that Hindu orthodoxy holds that birth alone makes Hindus, not conversions—you cannot 'convert' to Hinduism. There is thus an amusing paradox in the RSS opposing conversion from Hinduism to Christianity but abetting conversion from Christianity to Hinduism.

The most remarkable contribution of the Christian missionaries to India as a whole, both tribal and non-tribal, is in the field of school and college education. Almost all the top colleges in India were founded by, and are run by, Christian missions—notably, my alma mater, St Stephen's College, Delhi; St Xavier's, Kolkata; Loyola, Chennai; and Sophia College for Women, Mumbai, to name but a very few. Cathedral School in Mumbai, St Columba's in Delhi and St Xavier's in Ranchi are among the best schools in India. The network of Jesus and Mary schools and colleges around the country (and in neighbouring Pakistan) are among hundreds of such Christian institutions all over South Asia. As an alumnus of St Stephen's, I can testify that no one made the least attempt to harvest my soul for anyone. We were given the freedom to decide if we wanted to attend scripture class and moral instruction for half an hour every morning. Most of us, quite sensibly, spent the half hour surveying the field in the university coffee house. Missionary work in the educational field has been selfless and non-denominational. The highest tribute to the essential secularism of missionary educational activity in India came from Gandhiji himself, who invariably stayed in Delhi with Principal Rudra of St Stephen's College!

Another area of remarkable Christian missionary activity is health. A large number of missionaries are trained in primary health care and first aid. The country is dotted, as much in mofussil India as in the metropolitan centres, with hospitals started and run by Christian missions, more often than not catering largely or exclusively to the poor. Neither are Christian patients privileged nor are patients of any other faith turned away. And it is not only the living but also the dying who have received succour at the hands of the soldiers of Christ, the most renowned being Mother Teresa and her Missionaries of Charity, the very symbol of selfless secularism in practice.

I had referred earlier to the Anglo-Indian dimension. Before independence, there was a considerable body of Indians of mixed parentage, European and Indian, to whom the term 'Anglo-Indian' (earlier used for an Anglo-Saxon working in India) came to be applied. They were almost all of the Christian faith. Some among them called England 'home' and aspired to share imperial prejudices against all things native. More than half a century after independence all that lies in the distant past. Unfortunately for the diversity of our society, many Anglo-Indians have emigrated to Australia and elsewhere, but those who remain are woven into the warp and the woof of India's contemporary nationhood. We have two reserved seats in the Lok Sabha, one of which was, for years, occupied by the redoubtable Frank Anthony.

Sikhs

The Sikh community is in a small minority in India as a whole but makes up a bare majority in the area of its concentration, Punjab. Punjab originally stretched from Attock near the Khyber Pass to Palwal, south-east of Delhi. Had it remained undivided, Punjab would have been the most dominant state of undivided India. But first it was partitioned between Pakistan and India; then, the rump fell victim to Master Tara Singh's communal demands (dressed up as a linguistic demand) for a separate Punjabi suba. In consequence, the hill states were constituted into Himachal Pradesh and the Hindi-speaking plains into Haryana, leaving Indian Punjab a small if prosperous state with some economic strength, but nothing like the political clout it would have had if communalism had not sliced it like a stick of salami.

The communalism which ran riot after a clash between two sects of Sikhs, the Nirankaris and the Akalis, in Amritsar in 1978 engendered some fifteen years of the most vicious communal terrorism—and the most repressive police action—known to independent India. In a bid to strike at the roots of communal terror, operating from the precincts of the Golden Temple complex, sacrilegiously converted into a hideout of terrorists led by Bhindranwale, Prime Minister Indira Gandhi sent in the Indian army in June 1984. Operation Blue Star was a hopelessly bungled military operation, which, far from cowing Bhindranwale and his cohorts, or smoking them out with gas, as was the original intention, resulted in virtual war. The temple was besieged for days together, with Bhindranwale's fierce resistance leading to armoured personnel carriers moving into the premises, mortar, guns and rockets flying, uncounted dead and injured—and an entire community outraged at the damage done to their principal place of worship (even though Indira Gandhi ensured that the Harmandir Sahib itself was left virtually undamaged, whatever the military cost). Tragically, Indira Gandhi paid with her life for her attempt to restore the sanctity of the Golden Temple by driving out the terrorists who had taken it over. When now we see Punjab calm and normal and totally free of communal tension, one can only wonder in bewilderment at the insanity that overtook the state for close on two long decades.

As the Sikh/Punjab 'problem', if ever there really was one,

has been settled, the one issue that every right-thinking Indian, and particularly every right-thinking Congressman, has to answer for is the senseless violence directed against innocent Sikhs in the immediate aftermath of Indira Gandhi's assassination on 31 October 1984. The responsibility for the massacre has been placed at the door of her elder son, Rajiv Gandhi, who was sworn in as the prime minister on the evening Indira Gandhi died. At the core of this charge is Rajiv Gandhi's alleged justification of the killings supposedly implicit in his comment 'when a big tree falls, the earth shakes'.

In the maelstrom of misinformation that has covered the events of November 1984, the impression has been created that Rajiv Gandhi said this the day he took office, thus provoking the outbreak of the carnage next day. In fact, on the day he took charge, he went on nationwide television and radio to plead: 'We should remain calm and exercise maximum restraint. We should not let emotions get the better of us, because passion would cloud judgement. Nothing would hurt the soul of our beloved Indira Gandhi more than the occurrence of violence in any part of the country.'[2]

Next day, on television, Rajiv Gandhi was shown admonishing Congress workers walking past the bier, shouting the slogan, '*Khoon ka badla khoon*'. But that did not stop the pogrom. We now know that thousands died that day and the next. Not till the evening of 2 November did the army undertake the flag marches that restored a measure of calm. Rajiv Gandhi himself threw security to the winds and undertook a personal tour of some of the worst-affected pockets. Rajiv Gandhi was back on TV/radio on the same evening:

> ...some people are casting a slur on [Indira Gandhi's] memory by indulging in acts of hatred and violence. This must stop forthwith...This violence is only helping the subversive forces...Communal madness will destroy everything India stands for. As Prime Minister of India, I cannot and will not allow this.[3]

And true to his word, the communal violence was brought to a stop. After 3 November, there were no further incidents. Indira Gandhi's birth anniversary fell nearly two weeks after the madness had ended, on 19 November. It was at the Boat Club meeting in New Delhi to commemorate the anniversary that Rajiv Gandhi said towards the fag end of his speech: 'But, when a mighty tree falls, it is only natural that the earth around it does shake a little.'[4]

For that sentence, he has been excoriated. Fairness demands that the sentence be seen in context and with a view to determining whether it reflected the theme of his remarks. Did it at all constitute an exculpation of, or incitement to, mass murder? Here are key sentences from the paragraph in which the offending sentence appears:

> Some riots took place in the country following the murder of Indiraji. We know the people were angry and for a few days it seemed that India had been shaken. [Then follows the sentence about the 'mighty tree'.] But, from the way you put a stop to it, from the way India has been brought back to the path of unity with your help, and is able to stand united again, the world can see that India has become a genuine democracy.[5]

The question remains: why was the army not deployed immediately? Why were reinforcements brought in from Meerut only after as much time had elapsed as it took the Indian sepoys in May 1857 to march from Meerut to Delhi? I put the question to Major General Jamwal, who was commanding the troops in the Delhi area. I learned from him that in order to forestall a coup d'état, it has been part of defence policy to avoid having any large body of troops in or in the vicinity of the capital. So, when asked to come to the aid of the civil authority, he felt that if he did not have enough troops at his disposal, army action would prove ineffective and that would seriously aggravate the situation. The troops were sent for after the government gave him the necessary orders on the evening of 1 November. The troops arrived the following day and were immediately deployed. The situation was almost instantaneously brought under control.

There is no doubt that the government erred grievously in not assessing the situation immediately after the outbreak of trouble on the evening of 31 October. The worst of the killings might have been averted had the government ordered additional troops to move from Meerut to Delhi twenty-four hours earlier than it did. For this failure, the lieutenant governor of Delhi paid with his resignation. But such administrative inaction cannot be an excuse for political failure. Sonia Gandhi has, therefore, publicly apologized for the terrible events of 1–2 November.

Whatever the grievous lapses of the first forty-eight hours of Rajiv Gandhi's government, the record thereafter must be looked at to maintain perspective. After 3 November, whatever the provocation, no harm was allowed to come to any Sikh innocent. When in May 1985, a series of transistor bombs was set off all over the capital, I was personally witness to Rajiv Gandhi calling every one of his Delhi MPs and charging them with personal responsibility for ensuring that there was no communal violence. There was none—neither then nor subsequently—notwithstanding the endless series of killings of Hindus that overtook neighbouring Punjab. By April 1985, Sant Longowal was released and in July an agreement was reached with him. Tragically, Longowal was assassinated for moving towards peace and, even more tragically, the implementation of the accord was aborted by the failure to arrive at an agreement over the territories to be transferred to Haryana in exchange for Chandigarh going to Punjab. In the fifteen years that have elapsed since Rajiv Gandhi demitted office, no successor government has been able to move matters forward. That, however, is not the issue here. The issue is that after 3 November 1984, the protection of the life, limb and property of the Sikh community all over India was assured, even if terrorism in the name of the Sikh community continued to rear its terrible head for much of the next decade.

Another issue with regard to the riots, which has often been raked up, pertains to the lack of legal action against the heinous perpetrators of the crimes against the Sikh community in the immediate aftermath of the massacre. Without attempting to justify the delay, it is necessary to put judicial action in communal carnages in perspective. Unjust and unfair though it is, when it comes to communal violence, delays in judicial proceedings have been the norm. Professor Bipan Chandra has emphasized that for decades, state inactivity has been the prime reason for the spread of communal violence and there are hardly any cases of perpetrators of such violence ever being punished.[6] We have seen contemporaneously, in the Best Bakery case in Gujarat, how difficult it is to meet the requirements of the letter of the law in cases of communal violence.

As part of the Rajiv–Longowal accord, the Justice Ranganath Mishra Commission of Inquiry was established to investigate the violence directed at the Sikh community in November 1984. The commission categorically asserted that there were no grounds to maintain that the violence was in any way organized. Organizing something of this magnitude would require time, men and money. In this case, it pointed out, that the riots started so soon after the death of the prime minister clearly indicated that it was the spontaneous reaction of the people at large and there was no scope for any organizing. However, with the police delaying its response to the situation, what began as an impulsive reaction developed into one of the darkest tragedies in the history of independent India. Even though nineteen instances were catalogued where people associated with Congress (I) had been named as having organized the riots, the commission held that their participation did not imply that the party was culpable. It concluded that the violence was not organized by the Congress (I) or any official who matters in the party although many of the participants were sympathizers from the lower ranks of the party.

The Mishra Commission report did not please those who insisted that the massacre was a pre-planned Congress conspiracy to punish the Sikhs for the assassination of their leader. Judge Dhingra, an additional sessions judge of Delhi, was among them. In sentencing eighty-nine of ninety-three persons arraigned before him in September 1996, Judge Dhingra remarked that the massacre was a conspiracy planned by those who were in power in the country at the time, and the real culprits—the administration, the police and their political masters—who had engineered the riots were still to face trial for their various acts of omission and commission.

Notwithstanding his sweeping obiter dicta, not one of the eighty-nine he sentenced was found guilty of murder. They were sentenced for crimes relating to the destruction of houses by fire and explosives (Section 436 of the CrPC), rioting (Section 147) and violation of curfew orders—but not murder, although all ninety-three were arrested in connection with the massacre of 400 Sikhs in a single pocket of Trilokpuri colony, by far the worst-affected area of Delhi. The additional sessions judge's unsubstantiated generalizations about 'political masters' who 'engineered the riots' and made 'these people their tools' has not stood the test of higher judicial scrutiny.

Four prominent Congress leaders—Lalit Maken, H.K.L. Bhagat, Sajjan Kumar and Jagdish Tytler—were singled out by civil society activists demanding justice. Maken has been assassinated. Bhagat, Sajjan Kumar and Tytler (a Sikh who has taken the surname of the Englishman who brought him up after he fled to India from Pakistan as a young boy during the partition riots) were all brought to trial. All of them have been exonerated of all the charges brought against them. Meanwhile, the findings of the Nanavati Commission, established by the

NDA government to go over the same ground that Justice Mishra has already covered, are awaited.

Those who insist that there was a Congress conspiracy to avenge Indira Gandhi have not been able to establish their charges twenty years after the assassination. While no proof of this charge has ever been proffered, those who believe that their personal convictions are proof enough to convict those they deem guilty are not prepared to acknowledge that, perhaps, there was no conspiracy. Any such conspiracy would have been inconsistent with Rajiv Gandhi's words, his actions in the immediate context of the violence, his subsequent actions to forestall trouble, and the vigilance he maintained in the matter.

By the end of Rajiv Gandhi's tenure as prime minister, 47 per cent of the police stations in Punjab had not reported a single terrorist incident in over a year. Terrorism in Punjab was extinguished by the mid-1990s, but, alas not before Rajiv himself fell victim to a human bomb. November 1984, terrible as it was, was an aberration. The Sikhs are amongst the most honoured and valued of our minorities, with a share in national life deservedly out of proportion to their numbers.

Parsis and Jews

In addition to the Muslims, Christians and Sikhs, who constitute the relatively larger sections of the minorities, India is also home to the Parsis and the Jews. Though their presence is negligible when seen as a percentage of the total population, they are as much a part of the composite culture that makes India as are the other larger minority groups. Their presence over the centuries has contributed to enriching the secular ethos of the nation in no mean manner and as such their integration into the fabric of a secular India continues to be a matter of importance.

In the ninth century AD, substantial numbers of Zoroastrians fled Persia and were given refuge in the coastal areas of Gujarat. They were always treated with the utmost compassion and no one interfered with their religious customs. As a hard-working and largely business community they prospered. During the nineteenth century, they attained considerable prominence, partly because the Tatas emerged as the major industrial group in the country, but more because of the pioneering role in the freedom struggle of Dadabhai Naoroji, the first Indian to get elected to the House of Commons, and Pherozeshah Mehta. There is no sphere of India's life in which the Parsis have not shone—business, the arts, literature (Keki Daruwala), science (Homi Bhabha), the judiciary (Chief Justice Barucha), the civil service, the army (the unforgettable Sam Manekshaw), and politics (my own very favourite political exemplar being Minoo Masani, prominent member of the Constituent Assembly).

It's a pity that globalization has claimed the community. While India has been, and perhaps still is, the largest Parsi country in the world, Canada seems to be their preferred destination in the twenty-first century. Their presence in India is dwindling and it is imperative that we make the best of what we have.

As far as the Jews are concerned, one of the loveliest synagogues in the world is to be seen at Kochi in Kerala. It stands mute testimony to the long and enduring connection between India and the Jews, an entirely tension-free relationship of close on two millennia. Unfortunately, from the Indian point of view, Israel has proved something of a magnet for our Jewish community. Like the Parsis, it too is a dwindling community, if not quite in danger of vanishing entirely. It is appropriate that I end this section with a few lines from Nissim Ezekiel's poem 'Jewish Wedding in Bombay' which not only reflect how welded the Jewish community is into India's cultural mainstream without losing its identity, but are also, to my mind, the most apposite lines to the theme in this book:

There was no brass band outside the
synagogue but I remember a chanting
procession or two, some rituals, lots of
skull-caps, felt hats, decorated shawls,
and grape juice from a common glass
for bride and bridegroom.

I remember the breaking of that glass
and the congregation clapping which
signified that we were well and truly
married according to the Mosaic Law.

My father used to say, these orthodox
chaps certainly know how to draw the
line in their own crude way. He himself
had drifted into the liberal creed but
without much conviction, taking us all
within him. My mother was very proud of
being 'progressive'.

Our Minorities: Completing the Indian Mosaic

Without its mosaic of minorities and majorities, India would
not be the India we know. In most parts of the world, one
defining ethnic characteristic—generally, race or religion or
language—is the bonding adhesive of nationhood. In India, it
is our many different ethnic characteristics—particularly, race,
religion and language—which constitute the unifying agent.
The minorities are as integral to the composite heritage that
defines us a nation as is the majority. If we lose our diversity,
we also lose our unity.

Moreover, the majority has nothing to fear from the
minorities. The loyalty of minorities lies here, not there. Their
destiny lies here, not elsewhere. They are as 'Indian' as every
other Indian. The minorities are, of course, defensive about the
preservation of their distinct identity, as are minorities

everywhere, including NRI Hindus. Indeed, to the extent that they are reassured on this score, they will find it easier to make adjustments with society at large and with universal value systems. We see this in the earnestness with which the Muslim Personal Law Board has begun wrestling with complicated traditional jurisprudence relating to matters of marriage, divorce and inheritance. Progress is inevitable if they are left to themselves to arrive at intra-community solutions to these issues. It is only when those outside the community denigrate, hector and self-righteously lecture others that this process is hampered.

To dismiss secularism as 'appeasement', as the communal camp is wont to do, is to fail to recognize that it is precisely in the realm of personal law that any community finds its identity. It is within the ambit of personal law that fall the customs and usages, traditions and rituals, heritage and pride, through which any community distinguishes itself from another. To impose reform in such matters is to force a minority community into a majoritarian mould. That, precisely, is communalism.

Demanding that a minority deny its minority nature is not to seamlessly dissolve the distinction between minority and majority but to co-opt the minority into the majority at the expense of the distinct identity of the minority. When this happens, the minority identity is subsumed by the majority. That is the opposite of secularism. For secularism respects diversity and is not threatened by the difference. On the contrary, secularism celebrates the difference, the glory of diversity. At the same time, secularism recognizes that a minority, being a minority, is faced with problems that the majority may not face.

When it comes to legislation on matters relating to personal law, it has to be remembered that the overwhelming majority of legislators belong in disproportionate numbers to the majority community—'disproportionate' because their share of the membership of any legislature has invariably been larger than their share of the population at large. Thus, the Hindu Code Bills were legislated in a House consisting overwhelmingly of Hindus. Any personal law relating to the minorities brought for legislation would necessarily be before a House in which the minority community is necessarily in a minority and, to go by the record, in a smaller minority than its numbers warrant. Hence the need for caution. The marriage and divorce laws for the Christian community passed by the thirteenth Lok Sabha show that legislation for a minority community by a House in which the community is in a minuscule minority is possible, but only after the initiative comes from the minority community concerned and only after consensus is hammered out within that community. That is the road to be followed for the reform of Muslim and other personal law: the initiative coming from within the community and legislation being based on consensus within the community.

Equally, the fact of a minority being a minority warrants special measures in favour of protecting its minority character. More often than not, those who deride as 'appeasement' the constitutional protection afforded to minority educational institutions do not seem to remember that much of the debate in the Constituent Assembly was over giving protection to the special education rights of the linguistic minorities in provinces with more than one significant linguistic minority. If minorities are to be protected on grounds of language, why is it not valid to protect minority rights in other respects, especially where these relate to the preservation of identity or the promotion of community welfare?

It is now settled jurisprudential doctrine, in India and composite democracies everywhere, that special attention to the minorities ('affirmative action', as it is called in the United States) is entirely compatible with a secular state not discriminating in favour of or against any given community. Indeed, a secular state, whether in the United Kingdom or

India, would be failing in its obligations to a disadvantaged minority if it were to deny affirmative action in their favour merely because a majority community, by virtue of its being a majority community, is not in need of similar action. The line is to be drawn at action favouring a minority transgressing the rights of the majority, but to allow a madrasa is not to deny a Saraswati Niketan.

Secularism calls for sensitivity to the concerns of minority communities. Communalism stamps on such concerns, while exalting the concerns of the majority community in the name of promoting an artificial singular identity. Nationalism which aims at wiping out the diversity of our cultures, as 'cultural nationalism' seeks to do, is neither culture nor nationalism. It will sound the death knell of the quintessence of our nationhood.

7

The External Dimension

India is far from being alone in wrestling with problems of creating a secular state out of a diversity of communities. But it is almost alone, among the emerging nations over the last fifty years, in establishing and maintaining a secular state in which its minorities are equal citizens in the eyes of the Constitution and the law.

Far from taking pride in this singular achievement, the communal camp attempts to drag the Indian state in the majoritarian direction. Much of the public discourse in India on secularism within the country is not informed by an adequate awareness of how tragically states around the world have failed in fashioning a sense of national unity because they have taken the sectarian path, distinct from the secular path.

In this chapter I have attempted to analyse the dangers inherent in creating religion-based majoritarian states, whether in our near neighbourhood or farther away. This should serve as a warning to the votaries of Hindutva who are trying, without recognizing the folly of others, to forge a majoritarian state out of the diversity that is India.

Pakistan

Secularism is our domestic concern but there is an inescapable external dimension to it resulting from our relations with Pakistan. Till 1947, we were one nation, one people. Quaid-e-Azam Muhammad Ali Jinnah said we were not, and propounded the theory of two nations—Hindu and Muslim. The viceroy and Governor General, Lord Mountbatten, accepted this and made it clear to the leaders of the Indian National Congress that partition would have to be the price paid for independence. He then told Jinnah and his Muslim League colleagues that while they may get the Pakistan they demanded, it would be the 'moth-eaten' Pakistan which Jinnah had till then resisted. After thus setting the parameters for independence and partition, Mountbatten went on to abort the one-year period available till June 1948 to complete the transfer of power into a two-month interregnum till mid-August 1947. Pakistan would be declared independent on 14 August 1947 and India the following day. The date of 15 August was chosen, in an act of monumental egotism, only because it happened to be the second anniversary of Mountbatten's acceptance of the Japanese surrender. So indecent was the haste, that Lord Radcliffe, who had never before been to India and who spent but a fortnight or so cooped up in the viceroy's palace in Delhi, drew on maps, without any consideration for ground realities, the boundary between India and West Pakistan in the north-west of the subcontinent, and between India and East Pakistan in the north-east of the subcontinent. So much so that the two new nations did not even know where their frontiers lay on the day they were respectively born. It was only two days later that His Lordship accomplished his task and returned to London, never to come back. The imperial policy of divide and rule, and anomalies in Radcliffe's cartography are the root cause of much of the horror which the subcontinent has suffered in the last fifty-seven years.

There is no doubt that India's struggle to remain secular is impinged by the evolution of Pakistan's nationhood, post-1947, based on the dynamics of its claims for a separate nation during the struggle for independence. A nation divided against itself but united against India, Pakistan, by the postures it strikes and the actions it takes, provides a ready handle to those who stoke communal antagonisms in our society. India–Pakistan relations remain the real 'unfinished business' of partition. Resolving our differences with Pakistan is, therefore, not a matter only of national security or foreign policy; it is essential to the building of our secular nationhood. However daunting the challenge, we must learn to live with each other in peace, tranquillity and friendship.

For Pakistan, partition solved few, if any, of the problems of Muslim identity in the subcontinent. For India, partition has rendered the question of Muslim identity in the subcontinent partly a matter of external relations, even though it largely remains a matter pertaining to the nature of India's own nationhood. It is because the freedom movement did not resolve the question of Muslim identity in the larger identity of India that the nation had to be partitioned at the time of independence. And if more than half a century after partition, our subcontinent remains 'the most dangerous place on earth', it is because we have been far less successful in tackling the external dimension of the subcontinent's Muslim identity than in determining the domestic parameters of Muslim identity within the overall framework of India's modern nationhood.

There is now a nuclear dimension to communalism: the age-old question of how Hindus and Muslims are to share their common subcontinent is now overshadowed by the threats posed by nuclear weaponry in the arsenals of two nations united by geography but divided by history. The continuing failure even to attempt to resolve this core dilemma is as fraught with looming danger as the failure to resolve the dilemmas of Muslim identity during the freedom movement, which led to partition as the price we had to pay for freedom. This time the price to be paid for continuing to leave the question unresolved could be a South Asian Armageddon.

If it was the failure of the freedom movement to understand the internal dynamics of the parallel movement which led to Pakistan, it is India's failure to comprehend the internal dynamics of Pakistan which has legitimized in the eyes of the people of Pakistan the implacable hostility shown us by the Pakistani politico–military establishment. Of course, even as there was a major Muslim contribution to the exacerbation of Hindu–Muslim differences in the run-up to partition and independence, so is there a major Pakistani contribution to the subcontinent remaining a boiling cauldron since 1947. Yet, even as it was the desire to keep the Muslim community within the fold of the freedom movement which distinguished the Congress position from that of the Muslim League, so must it be the desire to preserve Pakistan within the framework of a harmonious South Asia which ought to animate our quest for reconciliation in the subcontinent. Instead, India's Pakistan policy has largely consisted of scratching at the scabs of our wounds. India tends to regard Pakistani hostility as being quite as immutable as the freedom movement came to look upon the hostility of the Muslim League as unalterable. Matching League hostility with Congress hostility cost us the integrity of the subcontinent. Matching Pakistani antagonism with Indian antagonism could cost us the subcontinent itself.

A durable peace cannot come from preening ourselves on the excellence of our mindset. It must begin with an understanding of the mindset of the other side, not with a view to mocking that mindset or using the revelation to validate one's own hostility, but with a view to understanding the other side's concerns, its anxieties and apprehensions, its aspirations and imperatives; then, moving towards appeasing those concerns without yielding one's own bottom line. I use the word 'appeasing' deliberately, in all consciousness and conscientiousness, in the original sense of the word—seeking reconciliation to keep the peace—rather than the pejorative connotation given to the word by Neville Chamberlain's approach to Adolf Hitler. Hitler was a monster. The people of Pakistan are not monsters. They would have been fellow Indians but for an accident of history. If we cannot conciliate our own, whom can we?

That said, it also needs saying that while Pakistan is, of course, a state, it is not yet quite a nation. The people of Pakistan know what they are not: they are not Indian and emphatically not Hindu. Alas, they are yet to determine what they are. After half a century of existence, they are still to forge a national identity. Since their nationhood has not jelled, they fall back on the parameters on which that nationhood was conceived. Those parameters were, however, designed to achieve a Pakistan not born, not consolidate a Pakistan which has existed for five decades and more.

Hence their fractious polity. It is this, at the core, which has led to dominance over the people of forces which are neither representative of the people nor responsible to them. And hence too Pakistan's proven inability to fashion a constitution or persist with a constitutional consensus. To rule Pakistan, authority comes not from the people but over the people. Consequently, the armed forces of Pakistan will always be the dominant political force in Pakistan, centre stage on occasion, behind the scenes always. That will change—or, more accurately, could change—only when, and if, Pakistan's society and polity succeed in resolving the contradictions inherent in the Pakistan that arose as an offshoot of the failure of the freedom movement to conciliate the movement for Pakistan. For, as Choudhary Khaliquzzaman, leader of the Pakistan movement in the United Provinces remarked, 'Pakistan was our destiny, not our choice.'[1]

Thus, the internal dynamics of the Pakistan which came through before it was thought through is, in essence, a dialectic between the multiplicity of theses and antitheses which characterize Pakistan's society and polity. That dialectic is still to lead to synthesis.

First, while Islam unites Pakistan, Islamization divides it. The widest and deepest rift in Pakistan is the divide between the Sunni majority and the Shia minority. Since the Fiqh Hanafi of the Sunnis is quite as sanctified as the Fiqh Jafria of the Shias, every move to 'Islamize' Pakistan widens the divide and generates tensions. What communalism is to India, sectarianism is to Pakistan. It is a sectarianism fed by a joint Sunni–Shia antipathy to the Ahmadiyas or Qadianis, scorned as apostates. The other Muslim minorities—the Ismailis, the Khojas and the Bohras—are on the fringes of the polity and, therefore, left unimpeded in the pursuit of their business interests. The non-Muslim minorities, such as the Christians and Zoroastrians, the Hindus (largely in Sind and pockets of Baluchistan) and the handful of Sikhs are, by and large, left to their own devices because they neither seek, nor would be permitted to espouse or promote, any dilution of the essential 'Islamic' nature of Pakistan's state and society. But the Sunni–Shia divide surfaces whenever religious fundamentalism is sought to be made the bonding adhesive of Pakistan's nationhood.

Islamization also exacerbates tensions between those who wish to see Pakistan modernize (that is, globalize and/or westernize) itself into a twenty-first-century state and those who believe in all sincerity and with considerable zeal that Pakistan was created to adhere to the seventh-century ideal of the Arab desert. The reformers and the fundamentalists are thus pitted against each other: the former have the advantage of overwhelming numbers, the latter the authority of the Book.

Overlaying the religious divide is the regional divide. Punjab is so dominant—demographically, economically, politically, even linguistically—that resentment is rife in the smaller provinces of Sind, Baluchistan and, to some extent, the

North West Frontier Province. At one time, the running battle of identity with Bengali-speaking East Pakistan obscured, in some measure, the internecine regional rivalries within West Pakistan. But with East Pakistan breaking away in 1971 to emerge as Bangladesh, Punjab has become the focus of resentment of the smaller provinces.

Resentment at Punjabi domination is not amenable to argument or even political accommodation. Apart from Nawaz Sharif, all leaders of the country in post-Bangladesh Pakistan—military men or politicians—have been non-Punjabi: Zulfiqar Ali Bhutto was from Sind; Zia, a migrant from East Punjab; Benazir Bhutto, a Sindhi; Junejo and Ghulam Mustafa Jatoi were both Sindhis; Pervez Musharraf, a muhajir; and Jamali, a Baluchi. Indeed, even before Bangladesh, both Yahya Khan and Ayub Khan were Pathans, and their predecessors, for the most part, either frontiersmen or immigrants from India or Bengalis. Yet, such is the domination of Punjab in numbers, economic strength, military positions, the civil services, parliament (when intermittently elected), literature and culture, that the dominance of Punjab is assumed, even when not established.

To this has been added the disillusionment of the Urdu-speaking muhajirs from India, largely resident in Karachi and other urban centres of Sind, whose forefathers were the true founders of Pakistan and were the dominant social and political group till Ayub's coup of 1958. Their influence waned over the next decade or two and was finally extinguished when Zulfiqar Ali Bhutto triumphed. Disillusionment has bred alienation, so much so that the Muttahida Quami Movement (MQM) is virtually secessionist.

Then there is the economic dimension. The political class is drawn by and large from the immensely wealthy feudal class, landlords on a scale unknown in India since the integration of the princely states and the land reforms of Jawaharlal Nehru. The rivalries of these chieftains have little bearing upon the lives of the people. Bhutto was the exception. He touched a responsive chord but his feudal ways led to his downfall. Democracy, even when allowed, has not in a quarter of a century been about power to the people. Therefore, when available, it is welcomed for its excitement and entertainment value; when not available, it is not much missed. There is no mass demand for the restoration of democracy. That is the cry of out-of-work politicians.

So, Ayub lasted eleven years. As did Zia. I have little doubt that Musharraf too will last his eleven years. An Indian policy which rests on the restoration of democracy in Pakistan is, therefore, an exercise in wishful thinking. Or an excuse for not having a Pakistan policy beyond deriving electoral advantage from the average Indian aversion to anything remotely Pakistani.

Political instability in Pakistan and the petering out of economic growth after the mid-1960s has had the consequence of a disproportionately large Pakistani diaspora which influences Pakistan's internal dynamics because what there is of Pakistani democracy is mostly diaspora democracy. Tragically, diaspora democracy sometimes tends to be catatonic democracy, bizarrely out of touch with ground realities at home.

The Gulf boom after 1973 has led to a huge Pakistani working-class presence outside the country. There, it interacts with the substantial Indian expatriate working class. The Gulf boom has also opened opportunities for middle-class professionals to interact with Indian counterparts outside the subcontinent. Moreover, the politics of exile which has characterized Pakistani politics whenever there is change of government—military to democratic or democratic to military—has assured the presence in the Gulf at all times of a large number of practising Pakistani politicians waiting for their moment to come. They have little better to do than wait for others to call on them, including Indian interlocutors who choose to seize the opportunity. Few Indians, alas, do—not even Indian academics or media persons.

Then, there is the India–Pakistan expatriate interaction, at both working-class and middle-class levels, in the United Kingdom and the United States. Thus, it is well beyond the shores of the subcontinent that Indians and Pakistanis discover the human being in each other. However, it is a resource and an opportunity that neither has cared much to draw upon. They should.

The last dynamic we should take into account is Pakistan's relations with the Muslim world, with reference to, specifically, India. The movement for Pakistan accepted a 'moth-eaten' Pakistan because they visualized Pakistan as championing the cause of the Muslims left behind in the Dar-ul-Harb. Indian secularism denied them that role. The Indian Muslim remained fiercely loyal to India even in times of armed conflict with Pakistan. The pretence that Pakistan could speak for the Muslims of the subcontinent stood exposed when East Pakistan broke away. It was given the quietus when Pakistan, after the Bangladesh war, refused to play even a humanitarian role in providing succour to the hapless 'Biharis'—the pejorative term applied to non-Bengalis stranded in Bangladesh and subjected to unspeakable atrocities.

Moreover, the Durand Line, arbitrarily drawn by Sir Mortimer Durand in 1893 for the preservation of British India's defence interests, with no regard for the fact that it separated Pathan from Pathan—often from the same clan and sometimes from the same family—has stood in the way of a friendly relationship between Pakistan and its immediate Muslim neighbour, Afghanistan, ever since Pakistan came into being. Also, once the Islamic revolution of Ayatollah Khomeini toppled the Shah of Iran, the Pakistan–Iran relationship lost its sheen to both Sunni–Shia rivalry as also to theological contention between a zealous Iran and the more relaxed version of Islam prevalent in Pakistan. Pakistan has, therefore, never succeeded in resolving the conundrum built into its birth as a nation that if religion is the basis of nationality, why should there be a border between Islamic Pakistan and even more Islamic Afghanistan, or between the Islamic Republic of Pakistan and the rather more Islamic Republic of Iran?

True, the superior English of the Pakistan Foreign Service has won them brownie points in some resolutions of the Organization of Islamic Conference (OIC), from which India stands excluded even though, after Indonesia, we are home to more Muslims in the world than any other nation. Yet, when it comes to the UN or other forums of international relations, Pakistan's anti-Hindu, anti-India fervour finds little reflection in any other Islamic state. Thus, no one, not even most Pakistanis, see Pakistan any more as the sword arm of Islam on the subcontinent.

These unresolved conflicts in the Pakistani psyche and polity lead many Indians to imagine that it is only a matter of time before Pakistan disintegrates under the weight of its own contradictions. This is a seriously flawed perception. For whatever their internecine dissensions, there is no dynamic in the direction of disintegration, except on the fringes of the polity and that too expressed mostly in diaspora frustration. Pakistan has weathered the storm of its initial decades. It is here to stay. Like many other countries, including to some extent our own, the fact that it is a 'state' is the bulwark which prevents the dismantling of the state even if one allows for grave disputes about the nature of Pakistan's nationhood. The argument over nationhood, acute as it is, can be and has been contained within the framework of the Pakistani state. Therefore, the dissolution of the Islamic Republic of Pakistan is simply not on the cards.

There are also those who believe we can take advantage of the internal divisions and bickering in Pakistan to drive a wedge between Pakistani and Pakistani. This too is a seriously flawed perception. Any interference by India in their internal affairs, covert or overt, real or perceived, serves only to unite all Pakistanis. Indian hostility rallies Pakistanis to their flag.

They are not about to return to the bosom of Mother India.

However, provided they are reassured that India is not engaged in a hostile takeover bid of their country, the people of Pakistan, by and large, are ready to normalize relations with India—but not till the issue of Kashmir is resolved. And the Pakistani establishment, recognizing this, seeks to legitimize its authority—as both Zia and Musharraf have done—by demonstrating to their people that Pakistan can work with India on normalizing relations, subject to the issue of Kashmir being resolved. Thus, Kashmir is to India–Pakistan relations in the twenty-first century what separate electorates and weighted majorities and provincial grouping were to the tussle between the Congress and the Muslim League during the freedom movement. We won freedom by remaining firm, but suffered partition on account of our rigidity. It is by remaining firm on larger goals but being flexible on lesser issues that we might still attain peace through dialogue and interaction. In any case, is there a viable alternative to dialogue?

For the pursuit of dialogue as the path to reconciliation, the lessons of the history of independence and partition are instructive.

So long as dialogue was possible, as it was from the founding of the Muslim League in 1906 to the Lucknow Pact of 1916, a Muslim identity could be reconciled with an Indian identity. When Gandhi championed the Khilafat cause, especially till the repudiation of the Khilafat by the Turks themselves after 1922, the Muslim identity was subsumed in the Indian identity. In the late 1920s, there was a short-lived revival of hope when the Swarajists under Motilal Nehru began work on an alternative constitutional order to the one being drafted by the Simon Commission but, eventually, the Nehru Report further distanced those elements of the Muslim community who put community before nation. That element constituted such a small minority of the Muslim community till the elections of 1937 that the Congress chose to put the

Leaguers in their place when provincial governments came to be constituted. The consequent widening of the Congress–League gulf led to the 'Pakistan' resolution of 1940. However, notwithstanding the failure of the Jinnah–Gandhi talks in 1944, even in 1946 the 'Pakistan' resolution was more a bargaining chip than an irreducible demand. Pakistan was, in truth, suddenly born when Mountbatten offered to pre-date independence provided the League and Congress both accepted that their differences were irreconcilable within a united India.

There are those both in India and Pakistan who regard India–Pakistan differences over Kashmir as being even more irreconcilable than Congress–Muslim League differences over an undivided India. They may be right. On the other hand, they may be wrong. We shall not know till we give dialogue a chance. Alas, while both countries are unremitting in their preparations for defence, they are hesitant and intermittent in their preparations for dialogue.

I believe we must, as a matter of high national priority, work towards that goal. I do not for a moment imagine that the path of negotiation will be smooth, quick or easily traversed. It will be a hard and agonizing path. It will be a path beset by hurdles seen and unseen, unexpected potholes, advances followed by reverses, hope giving way to despair, euphoria interspersed with darkness. The only way to travel the distance is through perseverance. India–Pakistan dialogue has always been sporadic, never sustained. To succeed, the dialogue must be uninterrupted and uninterruptible. This is why talks about talks must precede the talks themselves. There must be a proper pre-structuring of the India–Pakistan dialogue to insulate it from the inevitable ups and downs of our mutual relationship. For, it is impossible to foretell how long or how tortuous such a process might prove. This makes it all the more important that before starting the dialogue, there be a commitment to carrying through the dialogue in good faith to a fruitful conclusion.

The Shimla Agreement of 1972 shows us the way. There

is no place in it for third parties, at least not until it fails—and we must not let it fail. India and Pakistan are two mature countries with the strength of ancient civilizations behind them. They do not need the helping hand of others. They can help themselves.

Talking to Pakistan is the essence of the Shimla Agreement. Shimla took J&K out of the multilateral mode, in which it had mouldered from 1947 to 1972, and placed it squarely in the bilateral domain. Tragically, having put issues related to J&K in the bilateral mode, Indian diplomacy has wasted three decades not discussing J&K with Pakistan. That posture of 'will not talk multilaterally—will not talk bilaterally' was maintainable (or at least proved sustainable) till Pokhran-II/Chagai in May 1998. Since then, the UN Security Council resolution of June 1998, rapping us both on the knuckles for going nuclear, has, for the first time in thirty-three years, raked up the question of J&K in a Security Council resolution. We have been put on notice of multilateral intervention in J&K if a bilateral process is not put in motion.

Dialogue does not mean summitry. Keeping the prime minister out of it is a key requirement, especially in the light of Vajpayee's proven naivety at Lahore in February 1999 (where he and his team simply forgot to write 'cross-border terrorism' into the Lahore Declaration) and then his being outmanoeuvred over cross-border terrorism at Agra in July 2001. It is not high-sounding summit statements we should be aiming at but the structuring of a continuous process of negotiation. If such a process is to lead anywhere, the Vajpayee notion that a dramatic, high-level, spur-of-the-moment breakthrough is the only possible breakthrough in Indo–Pak relations needs to be discarded in favour of a long, long haul that will face many reverses and many moments of stagnation but must be persisted with and insulated from the inevitable ups and downs. Such an irreversible process needs to get away from semantics over whether J&K is a core issue or an incidental distraction. We have a readymade formula to overcome such quibbling in the felicitous expression used by the then prime minister, P.V. Narasimha Rao, in his letter to his Pakistani counterpart, Benazir Bhutto, on her winning the elections of 1993: 'issues related to J&K'. Their issue is the validity of the Instrument of Accession; our issue is cross-border terrorism. Both are 'issues related to J&K'. Both can, therefore, be covered under the rubric of the Narasimha Rao formula.

Diplomatic maturity demands that we recognize that there are Pakistani perceptions and Pakistani concerns—and that we cannot expect Pakistan to mouth the Indian line any more than Pakistan can expect India to mouth the Pakistani line. A dialogue is required precisely because of our differences. And a dialogue is most required when the situation is at its most tense. Moreover, because our differences run so deep and wide, time and patience—but, above all, goodwill and good faith—are required to bridge the gap. We do not know where the dialogue will lead and how long it will take. For if we did, there would be no need for dialogue, we could go directly to the answers. So, let us expect the opening Pakistani position to be as hard as ours. Then let us try to understand each other and persuade each other. And out of such mutual understanding, Inshallah, reconciliation, or at least accommodation, might prove possible.

Let us remember, moreover, that it is only a secular Government of India, not a government which pursues a communal agenda against Muslims at home while pretending to stretch a hand of friendship to the Muslims of Pakistan, which can negotiate and sustain any agreement with a state that proudly bills itself the 'Islamic Republic of Pakistan'.

Sri Lanka

Unlike the Indian freedom movement which, especially after the return of Mahatma Gandhi to India from South Africa, was transformed into a mass movement, the struggle for self-determination in Ceylon (as Sri Lanka was known till 1972) was essentially a matter between the westernized, well-heeled elite of the country on the one hand and the British colonial authority on the other. But this key distinction apart, there were remarkable similarities in the evolution of the freedom struggle in the two countries, especially the impact on inter-communal relations of the prospect of swaraj.

As in India, so also in Ceylon, the late nineteenth and early twentieth centuries saw the stirrings of a nationalist self-consciousness that carried the main communities together in striving for more civic, political and democratic rights. The acknowledged leader was a Tamil, Ponnambalam Ramanathan, and his colleagues included such distinguished Sinhala pioneers as F.R. Senanayake (whose family was destined to play a major political role over the next half a century) and A.E. Goonesinha, who rose to be the founder of the workers' movement in the island. The communal question was not a significant problem at the start.

But once the Ceylon National Congress (CNC) was founded by Ramanathan's brother, Ponnambalam Arunachalam, in 1919, the year Gandhi gave the India National Congress its mass orientation, the British governor, Sir William Manning, like his counterparts in India, did all he could in the six years he was in office to divide and rule by stoking internecine tensions in Ceylonese society. Just as separate electorates and dyarchy under the Government of India Act, 1919, foster communal disharmony in India, so did the constitutional reforms of 1921 have a similar consequence in Ceylon. Communal tensions in Ceylon, through the 1920s, included resistance on the part of the traditional chiefs of the Kandyan uplands in central Ceylon to domination by the low-country Sinhala gentry. There was also tension between the peasant classes and the emerging working class on the one hand and large landholders on the other. But overlaying all these was the revanchist Sinhala–Buddhist movement, led by Anagrika

Dharmapala, which pitted itself against the secular ideal favoured by the CNC. Much like Savarkar of the Hindu Mahasabha and Golwalkar of the RSS in India, Anagrika Dharmapala and his militant followers desired a community-based nationhood, as opposed to a composite nationhood, for their country. This inevitably soured relations between the Sri Lankan Tamils of northern and eastern Ceylon, and the Sinhalas. At the same time it gave a fillip to Sinhala objections to the grant of citizenship rights to Indian Tamils working as plantation labour in the central highlands. In reaction, after the CNC went back on the assurance its leaders, James Pieris and E.J. Samarawickrema, had extended to the Jaffna Association about the reservation of one seat in the Western Province for the Tamil community, a Tamil Mahajana Sabai came into existence in August 1921, fighting for minority community rights, much as the Muslim League in India was doing.

The Donoughmore Commission, appointed at around the same time and for much the same purposes as the Simon Commission in India, recommended constitutional reforms that gave a greater say to elected Ceylonese leaders in the running of their internal affairs. But, as in the battle in India between the pro-changers and the no-changers over the Government of India Act, 1919, so in Ceylon, the 'old guard' of D.B. Jayatilake and D.S. Senanayake tried to make the Donoughmore constitution work, while the young radicals of the All-Ceylon Liberal League threw up E.W. Perera, S.W.R.D. 'Sword' Bandaranaike and G.G. Ponnambalam to oppose the Donoughmore dispensation for not really leading Ceylon to true independence and genuine democracy. Further to the left of the Liberals and Goonesinha's Ceylon Labour Party, a clutch of Marxist–Leninist and Trotskyite parties came into being, including, most notably, the Lanka Sama Samaj Party, founded in 1935 by Colvin da Silva, N.M. Perera, Philip Gunawardene and S.M Wickremasinghe.

But while the right–left divide on economic policy was, in

the fashion of the 1930s, projected as the rift valley of Ceylon's polity, it was really the communal divide that came to dominate the political scene in the 1940s. G.G. Ponnambalam emerged as a persuasive spokesman for the Tamils under the banner of the All-Ceylon Tamil Congress, while Bandaranaike started his long slide to Sinhala–Buddhist chauvinism by founding the Sinhala Maha Sabha (SMS) in 1937 as his riposte to the Tamil Mahajana Sabai. According to the renowned Sri Lankan historian, K.M. de Silva, who has documented the ideological clash between the SMS and the CNC, the CNC accepted the primacy of the Sinhala–Buddhist majority in Ceylonese polity, while visualizing a state where ethnic and religious minorities retained their distinctive identities. The SMS, in contrast, insisted on a nation where Sinhala–Buddhist pre-eminence was inviolable and stated in unambiguous terms.[2]

The parallel with the Savarkar/Golwalkar concept of a Hindu nationhood based on the ideology of Hindutva and aimed at a Hindu Rashtra is striking. It underlines how Sri Lanka's fate would have overtaken India if, as in Sri Lanka, majority communalists had assumed state power within a decade of our independence. We have survived thus far because majority communalists have never succeeded in securing a political majority on their own.

The chief bone of contention between the CNC and the SMS was Donoughmore changing the Tamil–Sinhala ratio in the legislature from 1:2 to 1:5. Meanwhile, the relatively quiescent Indian Tamil of the central highlands was compelled to take on a higher political profile in the face of Sinhala opposition to 'unrestricted franchise' being granted to Indian residents in Ceylon. K. Natesa Iyer organized the Indian Tamils into the Ceylon India Congress (renamed by S. Thondaman in 1951, after Ceylon became independent, as the Ceylon Workers Congress). The stage was thus set for post-independence politics in Ceylon to acquire a deep communal colour.

Meanwhile, the Citizenship Act, 1948, and the India and Pakistan Residents (Citizenship) Act, 1949, 'taken in conjunction...disenfranchised and rendered stateless the entire "Indian Tamil" population estimated to number in excess of one million at that time.'[3] S.J.V. Chelvanayakam, the Father of Tamil Nationalism in Ceylon/Sri Lanka, prophetically warned: 'Today, justice is being denied to the Indian Tamils. Some day in the future...the same will befall the Ceylon Tamils.'

The veteran D.S. Senanayake, first prime minister of independent Ceylon, had ushered in independence in 1948 by bringing together, under the banner of his United National Party (UNP), a rainbow coalition of Sinhala grandees and Tamil and Muslim politicians. Basing himself on Article 29(2)(c) of the pre-independence Soulbury Commission constitution, which prohibited parliament from enacting any law that would confer any discriminatory privilege or advantage to any community or religion, D.S. Senanayake foiled all attempts at discarding the idea of a secular state and advocated neutrality of the state with regard to religion.[4]

In retaliation, S.W.R.D. Bandaranaike broke from the UNP in 1951 to found the Sri Lanka Freedom Party (SLFP). At the other end of the ethnic spectrum, Chelvanayakam broke with G.G. Ponnambalam to found between December 1949 and September 1951 the Ilankai Thamil Arasu Katchi, known generally by its English name, Federal Party.

Chelvanayakam soon emerged as the most ardent and charismatic champion of the Sri Lankan Tamil cause. The founding declaration adopted by his party at Trincomalee in 1951 urged 'the Tamil people's unchallengeable title to nationhood' but hedged this with 'their right to political autonomy and desire for federal union with the Sinhalese'.[5] Under the Chelvanayakam formulation, Sri Lanka was held to be composed of two nations—Sinhala and Tamil—but he did not extend this to arguing for two sovereign states. On the contrary, he posited the need for political 'autonomy' to facilitate the Tamil 'desire' for a 'federal union' with their Sinhala co-citizens. Chelvanayakam elaborated this in a speech at Jaffna College on 26 August 1952, which I quoted when invited to deliver a Chelvanayakam Centenary Memorial lecture at Colombo in July 1997. I argued that Chelvanayakam had not desired the break-up of the Sri Lankan state provided Sri Lanka persisted with the secular ideal written into the Soulbury Commission constitution of 1945, which was the framework for the new sovereign state of Ceylon. The Tamil United Liberation Front leader, the late Sivasithamparam, who chaired the meeting, made clear his intense disagreement with my suggestion that Chelvanayakam had not equated nationhood with statehood and had sought instead a federal solution which would enable two nations to live together in peace and harmony in one state. But from the Trincomalee document it is evident that the Tamils (at the time) actually 'desired' one state provided it had a federal and not unitary character.

This, however, was not to be. In the 1956 elections, Bandaranaike's SLFP delivered a shock defeat to Senanayake's UNP in a vicious election fought on 'competitive chauvinism' and 'intra-ethnic outbidding'. Bandaranaike's slogan was 'Sinhala Only' and he was backed by the Mahajana Eksath Peramuna which voiced the extreme views of the Eksath Bhikku Peramuna and the Pancha Maha Bala Mandalaya. Sumantra Bose succinctly sums up the outcome:

> Under the new dispensation pioneered by the SLFP, Sri Lankan Tamils...were being asked to live in a unitary, centralized, territorial state of Sri Lanka that was conceived as the collateral of a nation defined explicitly in terms of a Sinhalese identity...Therein lie the roots of the Sri Lankan tragedy. Those who went about the task of building the Sri Lankan 'nation'...ended up creating not one but two nations.[6]

The language of these extremist Buddhist groups, as in this quote cited by Bose, frighteningly parallels Savarkar's and

Golwalkar's: 'The history of Sri Lanka is the history of the Sinhalese race…Buddhism is the golden thread running through the history of the Race and the Land.'[7]

Having won the election of 1956, Bandaranaike tried to wriggle out of his confrontationist and communal politics by entering into a pact with Chelvanayakam which provided for 'a very comprehensive federal solution to burgeoning Sinhala–Tamil tensions'.[8]

The pact did not last even till the ink on the signatures dried. Bandaranaike found himself prisoner to the very forces he had unleashed and far from reining them in found himself reined in. By April 1958, within nine months of the pact, Bandaranaike unilaterally abrogated the agreement. It did not save him from being assassinated the following year by a Buddhist bhikku, in a conspiracy masterminded by Mapitigama Buddharakkita. The assassins' grouse was that 'Sword' was not as communal as his Sinhala–Buddhist supporters had imagined him to be. The biblical expression 'Those who live by the sword shall perish by the sword', acquired a special Sri Lankan connotation.

Dudley Senanayake of the UNP tried to negotiate a fresh pact with Chelvanayakam in 1965. That too fell through because Dudley's government was dependent for survival on the support of Chelvanayakam's Federal Party and so UNP backbenchers revolted at being portrayed as sacrificing Sinhala–Buddhist interests at the altar of political power.

From then on, the slide towards the riots of 1983 and the rise of militant Tamil terrorism became unstoppable. The slide will not end till the principal Sinhala parties end their 'competitive chauvinism' and together rise in the defence of a secular and, therefore, united federal state of Sri Lanka.

An Indian has only to look across the Palk Straits and Adam's Bridge to understand what happens to a multi-religious nation if it loses its secularism to mean-minded majoritarianism.

Palestine/Israel

A few years ago I happened to switch on my television set idly and caught a panel discussion on the 'Question of Palestine', moderated by Saeed Naqvi. Naqvi, I thought, hit the nail on the head with his opening question: what is India's interest in the Palestine issue? Unfortunately, the first panelist, in a hurry to get off his chest what he wanted to say, forgot to answer the question. Naqvi forgot to repeat it. And the other two panelists apparently thought it impolite to answer a question not addressed to them. Consequently, the discussion, much like the Jordan river, meandered in all directions, leaving the central question of interest to the Indian listener—what is India's interest in the Palestine issue?—regrettably unanswered.

So, I put the same question to others, primarily professional diplomats and politicians with definitive views, but also to the omniscient (and ubiquitous) taxi driver and the proverbial 'janab in the galli'. I am astonished, and scandalized, at the number who seem to think it has everything to do with appeasement of the Muslims and little to do with justice for all. Jaswant Singh, as external affairs minister in the Vajpayee government, has, of course, made it official BJP-speak—in Jerusalem, of all places!—that India's delay in granting full diplomatic recognition to Israel for several decades was because of the Muslim vote bank.

Our stand on Palestine has nothing to do with our Muslims and everything to do with the manner in which British colonialism came to an end in Palestine and in India at virtually the same time, leaving both in that peculiar mess which the British art of 'muddling through' bequeathed everywhere that the empire cut and ran—dividing to rule ending up in ending rule by dividing: Ireland (Catholic Eire–Protestant Ulster), India (India–Pakistan), Cyprus (Turkish–Greek), Malaya (Bhoomiputra Malaysia–Chinese Singapore), Nigeria (Christian Biafra–Muslim Yoruba/Hausa), and, classically, Palestine.

In February 1947, the Attlee government made two key announcements: one, that they would be quitting India, come what may, by June 1948; second, that they would be quitting Palestine, come what may, by June 1948. From then on, the intertwined fate of India and Palestine started moving forward in strikingly similar ways.

This is not really the place to go into the story of how, within a month of Attlee's announcement, the All India Congress Committee acquiesced to partition; how Mountbatten arrived in New Delhi in March 1947 and reached partition arrangements by June; how the exodus in both directions led to the biggest mass transfer of populations, both unexpected and chaotic, in the history of humankind—unexpected, because the British had no idea what they were ramming down the throats of our people; chaotic and unplanned, because, after two centuries of carrying the White Man's Burden, the British administration had grown geriatrically asinine.

In the last half-century, what has perhaps largely slipped out of public memory in India is the parallel tragedy of the partition of Palestine.

There would have been no 'Question of Palestine' if it had not been for Britain's chicanery and Hitler's genocide of the Jews. British chicanery in Palestine dated back to the First World War. In that war, the Ottoman empire of the Turks (which, for the previous 500 years, had incorporated almost all the Arab lands of West Asia and North Africa) aligned itself with Germany and the Axis Powers against Britain and the Allied Powers. The British found in the colonized Arabs the instrument for overturning the Ottoman empire. That legendary romantic, Lawrence of Arabia (T.E. Lawrence), united the warring Arab tribes and, with the aid of thousands of Indian troops, knocked over the effete and corrupt rule of the Turkish Caliphs, promising independence to the states of the Arab lands after the war.

The promise was for public consumption. In private, the

British and the French struck their private deals, agreeing to divide up Arabia between themselves once they had got through the tiresome business of ridding themselves of the Turks and the Germans. Most of the vilayats (provinces) of Souria (present-day Syria) and Berout (present-day Lebanon) were to go to the French; the sanjaks (districts) which together constituted Palestine were, however, to pass on to the British.

At the Peace Conference in Paris in 1919, the bewildered Arabs, who had naively believed in British promises of independence, found themselves sliced into several pieces. Lawrence of Arabia, in a paroxysm of shame at finding his British peers so betraying his Arab friends, took himself off into self-enforced seclusion (even changing his name to Ross to disguise his identity) to nurse his nostalgia for his gay adventures in the Arabian sands and babble on about the seven pillars of wisdom. It was left to the poor Arabs to cope as best as they could with the consequences of deception. The worst sufferers were the Palestinians. They became prey to sordid intrigue between elements of the British establishment (notably Arthur Balfour and Winston Churchill) on the one hand and the Zionist Organization on the other.

Till the Zionist leader, Chaim Weizmann, began playing his games with Balfour, the Zionist objective of bringing back to Palestine a sufficient number of Jews from the diaspora (into which they had dispersed 2000 years ago!) to establish a Jewish national homeland in places sacred to the myths, legends and somewhat doubtful history of the Old Testament, seemed bizarre to most and a damned nuisance at worst. Sir Edwin Montagu, himself a Jew, recorded:

> Zionism has always seemed to me to be a mischievous political creed...I deny that Palestine is today associated with the Jews or properly to be regarded as a fit place for them to live in...It is quite true that Palestine plays a large part in Jewish history, but so it does in modern

Mohammedan history, and surely it plays a larger part
than any other country in Christian history.[9]

Lord Curzon was even more blunt: 'The Zionists,' he noted,
'are after a Jewish state with the Arabs as hewers of wood and
drawers of water.'[10]

Balfour and the imperialists had, however, different ideas.
The substance of a letter secretly written in 1917 by Balfour to
the London-based Jewish billionaire Lord Rothschild was
incorporated, after the war, in the terms of the League of
Nations mandate (now notoriously known to history as the
Balfour Declaration) which named Britain as the mandatory
power in Palestine. The mandate was based on what a child
(but not a colonialist) could have seen were two irreconcilable
objectives: progress towards self-determination for the Palestinian
people, that is, the establishment of an independent Palestinian
state and, as per the Balfour Declaration, assistance to the
Zionist Organization in promoting its purposes, namely, the
import of a sufficient number of Jews into Palestine to overturn
the inbuilt majority of the indigenous Palestinian Arabs so as
to establish a Jewish state of Israel, from which the Arabs
would be excluded or to which they would be subordinated.

In short, the British drafted their mandate in such a way
as to ensure that, if and when the time came for self-
determination for Palestine, it would not be the Palestinian
Arab who would secure independence but the Israeli Jew, with
the Palestinian condemned for ever to subordinate, second-
class servitude.

No wonder the Palestinian Arab bucked. Through the
1920s and the 1930s, and right up to the 1940s, the Palestinians
insisted on 'independence now' and an end to artificial Jewish
immigration, stressing that if all the Arab states surrounding
Palestine—Iraq and Syria, Jordan and Lebanon, Egypt and
Saudi Arabia—could be granted independence, as they were
during this period, why not Palestine too? The answer lay in

what Churchill, somewhat indelicately and indiscreetly, but undoubtedly truthfully, described as the need for the West to have a 'bridgehead' on the Asian continent.

Perhaps Britain would not have succeeded in its devious designs had it not been for that other flower of Western civilization, Adolf Hitler. Hitler's anti-Semitism was by no means an aberration in European history; he merely carried to its logical (and terrifying) conclusion the fundamental defect in Western civilization, which is non-comprehension of cultural and spiritual plurality, intolerance of ethnic diversity and discrimination against minorities. (No wonder Mahatma Gandhi, when asked what he thought of Western civilization, replied that he thought it would be a good idea!)

When, two millennia ago, the Jews fled the emergence of Christianity in Palestine (remember, the Jewish dispersal to the diaspora had nothing to do with the Muslims; Prophet Mohammad was born nearly 600 years later!), they were given a warm welcome everywhere but in Europe. In India, the local rajas of the Malabar Coast ceded them territory to establish an independent enclave, free of all outside interference, so that the only Jewish state in recorded history from the kingdom of David to the state of Israel was established in India. Similarly, in the Arab world, everywhere from Iraq to Morocco, colonies of Jews in their thousands lived for thousands of years in perfect amity, equality and harmony with their Arab brethren. It was only in European Christendom—which held the Jews responsible for the martyrdom of Jesus Christ—that unspeakable horrors were visited on the descendants of Judas. Shakespeare's Shylock is the symbol of the living hell through which European Jewry passed for 2000 years from Roman Emperor Augustine's conversion to Christianity to Adolf Hitler's Nazis.

The inability of Western civilization to tolerate Jews in their midst was the basic cause of the Zionist mission to colonize Palestine with a sufficient number of European Jews to establish a Jewish homeland in Arab Palestine. That the

Palestinians, who had done the Jews no harm, would be displaced and disenfranchised was of no concern to the Zionist, himself a product of European intolerance and Western racism.

Hitler's persecution of the Jews dramatically increased the number of European Jews seeking entry into Palestine. Where, from 1900 to 1932, the number of Jewish settlers emigrating to Palestine generally hovered around a 1000 to 5000 a year, Hitler's pogroms in Germany, Poland and the entire belt of countries he had gobbled up in Central Europe, combined with British insistence on giving priority to Jewish immigration over Palestinian independence, drove up Jewish immigration into Palestine to between 15,000 and 30,000 a year, the peak being reached in 1935 with an intake of 65,854. By the time Attlee announced in 1947 that the British were going to unilaterally terminate their mandate, the Jewish population of Palestine had risen from 56,000 at the commencement of the mandate to close on 650,000 at its termination.

In a bid to resolve these irreconcilable contradictions the UN General Assembly set up a UN Special Committee on Palestine (UNSCOP). India, itself hovering on the edge of independence and partition, was nominated a member of UNSCOP. The UNSCOP report was prepared even as India was going through the joys of independence and the horrors of partition. The members divided into two groups: a majority view and a minority view. The majority recommended the partition of Palestine into a Jewish state and an Arab state. The minority—India, Iran and Yugoslavia—recommended an independent, united, federal state of Palestine, federating a predominantly Jewish unit and a predominantly Arab unit: the philosophy of living separately together.

The tragedy of Palestine is that the UN, as then constituted, ignored the wisdom of the East and plumped for the criminal incompetence of the West. Palestine was partitioned. The Palestinian Arabs rejected this denial of their independence and integrity. The Palestinian Jews rejected the boundaries of their enclave. Far from solving anything, the plan has inflicted on the world its most agonizing conflict of the second half of the bloodiest century of them all, the twentieth century.

What needs to be stressed and underlined is that the plan for the partition of Palestine was jointly pushed by Truman's USA and Stalin's USSR. They were together then as they are together now. US–Russian collaboration is not a post-Gorbachev novelty. It was imposed shamefully on Palestine in 1947.

It is the essence of Eastern civilization—specifically of Indian civilization—to synthesize and harmonize. It is the essence of Western civilization to slice and divide. The Western mind finds only one solution to problems of conflict: separate and compartmentalize (dressed up as 'self-determination'). The Western mind finds only one answer to ethnicity: domination of the minority by the majority (dressed up as 'democracy'). The Western mind finds only one response to diversity: elimination (Hitler's 'final solution') or unity through uniformity (known in America as the 'melting pot'—the dissolution of all diversity into a single identity, the 'American' mould). What the West is totally incapable of comprehending is unity in diversity.

Hence the irony of Yugoslavia. The same Yugoslavia that joined us in 1947 in opposing the partition of Palestine has itself been shattered through ethnic partition. The same USSR that opposed us in 1947 by advocating the partition of Palestine has now itself cracked on the rock of ethnic 'nationalities'.

The single biggest long-term threat to the unity and integrity of our country comes from this inability of the West to understand our 'unity in diversity' or comprehend our multifarious ethnicities coalescing into a single composite 'nationality' (and by the expression 'West' I do not just mean the silly Wasps of England and New England but that entire civilization which extends from Seattle to Sevastopol and comprises both the 'East' and the 'West' of the Cold War).

Dissidents who wish to break our unity—be they minority religious fundamentalists in Kashmir or Punjab, or ethnic chauvinists in the north-east, or linguistic fanatics in the south—are reaching out for support to the Western nations, the Western mindset. The search for support, and the extension of support to secessionists, comes in many guises—'human rights' is one, 'self-determination' is another, 'democracy' is a third. We have so far been able to resist these incursions on our sovereignty and integrity because our record on human rights, self-determination and democracy is truly second to none. But if any of these were to change, Indian secessionists would find ready allies in the militarily powerful, economically dominant, politically overweening and intellectually narrow-minded West.

It was the Western mindset which caused the tragedy of Palestine. It is that mindset which could still bring about the tragedy of India. Unless, that is, the world embraces the quintessentially Indian concept of living separately together—which is what the celebration of diversity is all about. If the Jews and the Arabs of Palestine learn to live separately together, it will be a giant step towards ending the bridgehead of Western civilization on the Asian continent. It will bring all the people of Palestine—Arab and Jew—into the Asian resurgence. That is why we in India locate Palestine not in the 'Middle East' but in 'West Asia'. That is also why a solution to the 'Question of Palestine', in terms of the original Indian vision of 1947, is the best guarantor of both sustainable peace in West Asia and the continued independence and integrity of India.

Will Saeed Naqvi please put his question again?

In April 2002, while Palestinians wrestled with the worst excesses of the Ariel Sharon regime even as we grappled in Gujarat with the worst-ever state-sponsored carnage of the minorities, Yasser Arafat's personal envoy, Hani Al-Hassan, visited New Delhi but returned to Gaza a deeply disillusioned man. The India of Jaswant Singh, he discovered, was no longer the India of Nehru and Indira and Rajiv Gandhi. Jaswant Singh had nothing constructive to offer, not even a heartfelt word of solace, in the worst conjuncture for Palestine since the catastrophe of 1948, al-Naqba as it is called in the Arab world—the conquest of Palestine by Israeli terrorists.

Ariel Sharon is the Narendra Modi of Israel. Naroda Patiya is to Gujarat what Jenin is to Palestine. And just as Naroda Patiya is only the worst of a series of grisly atrocities deliberately inflicted as an act of revenge on a hapless people, so is Jenin only the worst of a vicious vengeance exacted from blameless innocents. If the pogrom in Gujarat is justified as 'action–reaction' for Godhra, so is Jenin exculpated as 'action–reaction' for a suicide bombing at a Passover party. That those who were killed in Gujarat and in Jenin had nothing to do with those who were killed at Godhra and at the suicide bombing is regarded with as much nonchalance by the government in Tel Aviv as by the government in Gandhinagar. And even as the Sharon of 2002 is no 'aberration', so also is the Sangh Parivar of 2002 no 'aberration'. Jenin was written into the Likud victory in the Israel elections as clearly as Gujarat was written into the ascendance of the BJP in ours.

The events in Gujarat have unpleasant parallels with those in Israel, where the full weight of the state has been thrown behind the invasion of the Gaza Strip and the West Bank—the territory on which, at Oslo and Washington in 1993, the Palestinians had been promised an independent state of their own by just about now. I derided the Oslo and Washington agreements as 'Panchayati Raj in the Gaza Strip'. But if in India, elected panchayats are sometimes dismissed and disbanded, in Israel's version of Panchayati Raj, the Palestine National Authority has been bombed from the air, its citizens killed and maimed by the thousands, shops and schools and homes set on fire, their leader placed under siege with neither electricity nor water nor phone lines nor even the freedom to walk among his own people. And all this by a Sharon who publicly rues that he did not have Arafat mowed to death in Lebanon twenty years ago. This is truly al-Naqba.

Faced with human tragedy of this magnitude, Jaswant Singh went no further in asking Sharon to desist than Vajpayee did in restraining Narendra Modi. For, Jaswant Singh profoundly believes that the Israeli way is the right way. That mindset was exposed in Jaswant Singh attributing our decades-long Palestine policy to the 'Muslim vote bank'. Unable to believe that even a BJP external affairs minister could be so irresponsible, I asked for confirmation from the publicity division of the ministry of external affairs and was informed that the minister had indeed said exactly that. I gave Jaswant Singh the opportunity to retract or apologize on the floor of the House; the offer was haughtily refused. The BJP believes in its bones that there is nothing more than the 'Muslim vote bank' to Gandhi declaring in the 1920s that 'Palestine belongs to the Palestinians as England belongs to the English and France to the French'; to the 1947 Nehru formula of a federal state of Israel–Palestine; and to the half-century of unflinching Indian solidarity with the mercilessly persecuted Palestinians which preceded the advent of the BJP to power in our benighted land.

Extraordinarily, the apologist who sprang so gratuitously to Jaswant Singh's defence then was the same journalist who now writes so feelingly about the carnage in Gujarat—Saeed Naqvi. He argued that it was indeed vote-bank politics which drove our Palestinian policy because, it seems, Rajiv Gandhi had once asked him what would be the impact on Indian Muslim opinion if we were to extend full diplomatic recognition to Israel. The query was entirely justified. For Jerusalem is home to some of the most revered shrines of Islam. But is such concern for Muslim sentiment any more communal than seeking special assistance from the Chinese for Indian Hindus to circumambulate Kailash Mansarovar? Of course, there is a religious dimension to Palestine, but that is only one dimension. It is much more the question of an entire people being driven like cattle from their homeland and being denied the right of return which the Israelis have proclaimed in their constitution to all Jews everywhere and for ever. The issue here is of an alien state being imposed upon a guiltless people for the sins of European Christendom against the Jews for which the Palestinians are not culpable in the first place. Palestine is not a matter of religion; it is a matter of thwarted secular nationalism. Above all, it is a question of justice. For, without justice there can be no peace—not in Gujarat, not in Palestine.

In 1947, Nehru pointed out that the partition of Palestine was no solution; nor, he said, was it right that the Jews who had settled in Palestine be 'driven into the sea'. The answer, he insisted, lay in a federated democratic state with equal civic and political rights for all its citizens, Jewish or Arab. That, and not Oslo or Washington or the Wye River accord, is the only way to end al-Naqba.

Yugoslavia

The great Indian public, alas, was simply uninterested in the disintegration of Yugoslavia which began with the secession of Slovenia in 1991–92 and carried on inexorably through the rest of the decade and into the first decade of this millennium. Bosnia was a faraway war, taking place amid a welter of incomprehensible (and unpronounceable) places: Srebrenica, Gorazde, Bihac, even Sarajevo, seemed absurdly remote. There was virtually no media interest and practically no public debate. The collapse of Yugoslavia was deemed to have nothing to do with our own survival as a nation. So, we ignored it and went about our own business. Not only was this surprising, it was also infinitely sad. For at the heart of all that happened in Tito's Yugoslavia are matters of the most profound relevance to our nationhood and our survival as a nation state.

Yugoslavia was, like India is, a magnificent exemplar of unity in diversity. Emerging at the end of the First World War from the detritus of the Austro–Hungarian empire, Yugoslavia was forged from a multitude of ethnic diversities: Serbian Orthodox, Roman Catholic, Islam; a myriad languages, of which even the major national language, Serbo-Croatian, was a melange of the dialects of Serbia and Croatia; and a profound awareness of ethnic identities labelled as 'nationalities': Slovenia, Croatia, Serbia, Bosnia-Herzegovina, Montenegro and Macedonia.

German-speaking Slovenia was culturally affiliated to neighbouring Austria and was Roman Catholic by religion. Croatia, too, was Roman Catholic but affiliated, by a history of collaboration in the Second World War, to Germany against the Serbs. Along its borders with Hungary it contained a substantial minority of people who spoke Hungarian. To the south, Croatia stretched along the Adriatic Sea and contained the historic resort of Dubrovnik, much coveted by Germany as its outlet to the Mediterranean (which explains Germany's unusual interest in the break-up of Yugoslavia). Serbia, the heartland of former Yugoslavia, was Orthodox by religion, fiercely nationalistic by temperament and rough-hewn in character. In and around the town of Kosovo, in Serbia, was a substantial concentration of Albanian-speaking Muslims. Montenegro (the 'Dark Mountains') was, as the name indicates, a mountain fastness along the border with Albania, containing a considerable minority of Albanian-speaking Muslims scattered among a majority of orthodox Serbs. To the south lay Macedonia (capital: Skopje, birthplace of Alexander the Great), wedged between Bulgaria and Greece, both of which have cultural and historical claims on the identity and loyalty (and even territory!) of the Macedonians. And, finally, Bosnia-Herzegovina, a Yugoslavia within a Yugoslavia: a majority of Islamic Slavs concentrated in the central and southern districts but also dominant in significant enclaves along the eastern border with Serbia, enveloped on the east by ethnic Serbs, on the north and west by ethnic Croats and on the north-west by the so-called Krajinian Serbs. A total of some thirty million people following three major religions and speaking half-a-dozen major languages.

For an Indian, this seems natural; for a European, a monstrous artificial construct. And therein lies the relevance of Yugoslavia's nationhood to our own. In India, virtually any segment of thirty million Indians will display the ethnic diversity of former Yugoslavia: consider Kolkata, along with the districts of Howrah and South 24 Parganas, constituting some thirty million souls and you will see what I mean.

Flush with the triumph of its reunification in 1990, united Germany took its first major bow on the international stage in 1991 by insisting on the dismemberment of Yugoslavia. The Germans thought nothing of getting, first, the European Union and, next, the UN Security Council to line up behind them in beginning the break-up. It was the recognition of Slovenia and Croatia as independent republics, followed swiftly by their admittance to the United Nations, which began the process of one Yugoslavia disintegrating into five sovereign states.

The partition of Yugoslavia, like the partition of undivided India, brought in its wake millions of homeless refugees, countless civilian casualties of war, hundreds of thousands dead, mass rape as a deliberate act of war, and unprecedented genocide on a scale not known since the Nazi holocaust.

And while the world shuddered, India slept.

What a fall, my countrymen! In 1947, there was a similar European mono-ethnic assault on the plurality which comes naturally to Asia: the partition of Palestine. The first vote which independent India cast in the United Nations was its vote against the partition of Palestine. We had just been through the terrible trauma of partition ourselves. We were in a commission of three who were dead set against the horrendous consequences of partitioning Palestine; Yugoslavia (under Soviet pressure) and Iran (under the Shah) left us when it came to the vote; we alone had the courage of conviction to plead for a multi-ethnic, pluralistic, democratic, federated state of Palestine. Our vote against the partition of Palestine was an act of principle. That one act of principle aligned us with the Arab world against all the machinations which Pakistan resorted to in the name of Islam.

The India which spoke out on Palestine was transmogrified into an India silent on Bosnia. I suspect the reason was that there are two parallel strands to the thinking of our foreign policy establishment. One: since the OIC was pro-Bosnia, we should be anti-Bosnia. Two: since Bosnia co-sponsored Pakistan's aborted human rights resolutions on Kashmir, why should we be pro-Bosnia?

No reasoning could have been more perverted. First of all, Yugoslavia was a multi-ethnic, pluralistic, composite nation. Ergo, offensive to Europe's narrow identification of nationality with ethnicity. There is no greater danger to India's nationhood than the imposition of the European concept of ethnicity as nationhood on the composite Indian nation. The argument for separating Kashmir from India parallels the argument behind wrenching Slovenia and Croatia from composite Yugoslavia. In standing up for multi-ethnicity in former Yugoslavia, indeed, in standing up for multi-ethnicity in contemporary Bosnia-Herzegovina, we would be standing up for the Indian concept of nationhood as against the narrow Western version.

Second, by advocating multi-ethnicity we would also be securing our doors against Western intrusion in Kashmir on grounds analogous to their intrusion since 1990 in Yugoslavia and now in Bosnia-Herzegovina through the 51:49 per cent formula for the dismemberment of Bosnia-Herzegovina into a Muslim nation and a non-Muslim nation.

Third, even as former Yugoslavia was a symbol of secularism, so also is the sovereign state of Bosnia-Herzegovina based on the secular principle that Muslims, Croats and Serbs can live together. The reduction of Bosnia to a postage-stamp Islamic state would pave the way to the argument that a postage-stamp Islamic state of Kashmir would, population-wise and area-wise, be larger even than Bosnia, so why not azaadi for the Valley?

Fourth, five sovereign states have replaced one nation state in Yugoslavia because of the application of the principle of self-determination to parts of a sovereign state. It is precisely this principle which Pakistan and their nefarious cohorts, as much in the West as in the OIC, are attempting to apply to J&K. Do we wish to fall into that trap?

Fifth, the Serbs and Croats were mutually responsible for ethnic cleansing not only in Croatia and Serbia but also in Kranjina and the eastern Muslim-majority enclaves of Bosnia. Notwithstanding some (equally reprehensible) imitations of Serbian–Croatian tactics in Muslim-controlled areas of Bosnia, it was largely the Muslims of Bosnia who were the innocent victims of plunder, rape, murder and genocide. Shockingly, instead of recognizing this, official India pathetically attempted to equate Serb and Croat with the virtually defenceless Bosnian Muslim.

Was this just or fair? And should not the nation with the world's second-largest Muslim population, India, have spoken out on Bosnia, especially when we so readily jump to the defence of the Indian diaspora in Fiji or Guyana or even Sri Lanka? Does our secularism not apply to external relations? Indeed, does common humanity not apply to international affairs? Have we really assassinated Gandhi in his soul and lit the funeral pyre of Nehru's principles?

Let us never forget that if Bosnia votes with Pakistan, it is because Pakistan votes with Bosnia and India does not. India was the only non-Islamic state to vote against Israel in 1947. For half a century after that vote, neither Pakistan nor the OIC could get the Islamic world to take an anti-India posture on any issue—not even Kashmir. We drove the Arab world out of Pakistan's arms and into India's by standing up for secularism in a pluralistic society and sovereignty in international relations. We must never sacrifice larger principles at the altar of narrow— and ultimately self-defeating—considerations.

Bangladesh

East Pakistan broke from Pakistan, in a second partition of the subcontinent, in December 1971, conclusively proving that while religious passion can divide, it can do nothing to unite. And although—perhaps because—India was the principal and decisive ally of the Bangladeshi freedom fighters in their struggle for liberation, after a very brief honeymoon in early 1972, India–Bangladesh relations have always been fraught and tense. Yet, both countries maintain the fiction that while India and Pakistan are sworn enemies, India and Bangladesh are the best of friends. The international relationship between India and Bangladesh is further complicated by, and indeed rooted in, domestic tensions for which the cross-border relationship becomes both a surrogate and a paradigm.

The British espousal of partition was based on the simplistic principle that areas where the majority was Muslim should become Pakistan; where the majority was Hindu should become India. It was a messy perspective that led to a messy outcome. For what was to become of the numerous minority if the ethnic divide were to be purely religious? The solution in West Pakistan was genocide, expropriation and expulsion. Where nearly a quarter of the population of what is now Pakistan was Hindu in 1947, the Hindus are now non-existent almost everywhere in Pakistan (except in small pockets of Upper Sind). Those Hindus (and Sikhs) who were not massacred were driven out in the most massive exodus known to history and their properties expropriated. The situation in the Indian half of Punjab province was no better. Except for a pocket in the Muslim nawabate of Malerkotla, which miraculously remained entirely insulated from the surrounding madness, the Muslims were either butchered or driven like cattle across the border into Pakistan. In the east, neither the genocide nor the exile was so complete, but in consequence there has been an unending drift of population, mostly from East Pakistan/Bangladesh to India for all these decades. The Indian count of fifteen million illegal Bangladeshi immigrants includes largely Hindus and their descendants whom vicious religious animus has pushed out of Bangladesh. But increasingly, the millions entering India includes millions of Bangladeshi Muslims whom economic distress is driving into India in search of work—low-paid, menial work.

Communalism in Bangladesh is more than matched by the BJP's counter-communalism. The British formula of partition has left, as of today, close on 150 million Muslims in India. The Indian Muslim is for the most part indistinguishable from the Pakistani/Bangladeshi Muslim, especially in the east/north-east of India, since the Bengali Muslim on both sides of the border speaks the same language, Bengali, and is heir to the same composite Hindu–Muslim heritage. (The Bangladeshi national anthem *Amar sonar Bangla*—'My golden Bengal'—was written by the Bengali Nobel laureate Rabindranath Tagore, and Kolkata's longest boulevard is named after the great Bengali poet Nazrul Islam, national poet of Bangladesh!) Communalists on the other side of the border have a field day targeting Hindus on the grounds that they are illegal Indian immigrants, while communalists in India enjoy the political bonanza of fingering any Muslim, Indian or Bangladeshi, as an illegal Bangladeshi immigrant. Since the flow from India to Bangladesh is a trickle compared to the flood in the opposite direction, the problem of Hindu communalism masquerading as concern for India's security is more acute.

The only solution is to apply the balm of common humanity on the wounds left by the savage vivisection of British India. But so long as the ruling establishments in the subcontinent continue to regard human beings as pieces on the chessboard of diplomacy and military strategy, humanity will only triumph intermittently. Fortunately, left to themselves as they are much of the time, ordinary folk on either side of the divide treat each other in exemplary fashion without regard for religion—an example for governments to follow.

Lessons to be Learned from Others

As conclusive evidence that religion has nothing to do with nationhood, I would like to cite the example of Nepal and its response to that high priest of the Hindu Rashtra K.R. Malkani's wholly unwarranted proposition in 2001 that since Nepal is a Hindu Rashtra it must be part of the Greater Hindu Rashtra. In what was a kick to our national funny bone, Nepal, the only Hindu Rashtra in the world, turned its pent-up fury on K.R. Malkani. It was like the Catholics throwing eggs at the Pope for being an apostate. Or red-blooded communists desecrating Karl Marx's grave at Highgate cemetery in London.

Malkani made the same mistake in his comments on Nepal that Jinnah had made in articulating his basis of nationhood. The Muslim League confused the umma of Islam with nationhood, not asking themselves why, if Islam constituted a nation, there should be a political boundary between Pakistan and Afghanistan or Pakistan and Iran. In exactly the same vein, Malkani was unable to understand the passion for a separate nationhood in Nepal even though it is more Hindu than India.

It is not for us to prescribe secularism to others; it is for us to prescribe secularism to ourselves. But, in doing so, it is entirely relevant to search through the experience of others to discover whether religion-based nationalism is a valid or desirable option in building our modern nationhood. The experience of Pakistan as an Islamic state or of Sri Lanka as a Buddhist state does not seem to demonstrate any greater unity coming out of the majoritarian view of nationhood than out of a secular nationhood. Indeed, quite to the contrary, the Indian experience of secularism as the appropriate response to religious diversity would appear to conclusively establish that multi-religious nations like ours need a secular state to preserve and sustain their integrity and national unity.

The Palestine/Israel example starkly shows that the attempt to forge a Jewish state in a land occupied by Jews, Muslims and Christians cannot in the long run endure unless secularism triumphs over sectarianism. The Palestine National Authority has been much more successful in creating a sense of Palestinian nationhood among Palestinians of Muslim, Christian and Jewish origin than has Israel in infusing a sense of shared nationhood with the Arabs who are Israeli citizens, let alone the Palestinians on the periphery of the Israeli state.

The fate that overtook former Yugoslavia will overtake us if we allow communal conflict, especially majoritarian communalism of the Milosevic kind, which so mirrors the Hindutva view of India, to devour our secular nation. Indeed, with thirty times the population that former Yugoslavia had, any attempt to transform India from a secular state to a majoritarian Hindutva stronghold will lead to death and destruction on a scale magnified thirty times that in Yugoslavia.

The experience of the world holds many lessons which we can ignore only at our peril.

8

In Conclusion:
Why I am a Secular Fundamentalist

One is either secular—or one is not. There can be no halfway house. One cannot be sometimes secular and sometimes not. Or be secular in some matters but not so secular in others. Above all, in matters of state policy, appeasing the majority merely because it is the majority or accommodating majority sentiment at the expense of principled secularism is either soft Hindutva or soft secularism but is no substitute for secular fundamentalism.

We cannot preserve secular India by compromising the secular principle. We cannot promote secularism in practice by making secularism in practice more palatable to the communal mindset. Invariably, the attempt to accommodate the non-secular view to forge an artificial consensus has always failed, never more dramatically than on 6 December 1992, when one by one, brick by brick, hour after hour, the three domes of the Babri Masjid were demolished while a secular government dithered between secular principle and communal compulsion. Then followed thirty-six hours of secular shame as the makeshift temple was allowed to be restored by the very elements that had perpetrated the communal outrage.

In our country, the gaping divide between secularism and non-secularism is defined by whether we regard India as a Hindu country or a Hindu-majority country. The former shapes a world-view. The latter is a matter of numbers.

The communal heresy begins with two assertions. First, that equal treatment is not a question of constitutional order but of civilizational ethos. And since Hinduism is uniquely secular, the best guarantor of secularism is not a state that perches itself above the social order but a social order that is permeated with the Hindu spirit of secularism. The second assertion is that words like 'majority' and 'minority' should be expunged from the discourse because perceptions of community-based interest should be replaced by perceptions of a seamless national interest where community identity is superseded by and gives way to a larger national identity.

It is these twin assertions that inform the majoritarian ideology which I regard as communal.

If Hinduism is *uniquely* secular, all other religions—especially the Semitic religions, Islam, Christianity and Judaism—are not and, therefore, they represent the polar opposite to Hindu secularism. In the Indian context, this argument boils down to a choice primarily between broad-minded Hindu tolerance and narrow-minded Muslim fanaticism, on the one hand, and Hindu *sarva dharma sambhava* versus Church evangelism, on the other. I hope this book has shown that this merely sets up stereotypes that can neither bear the scrutiny of history nor bear out contemporary experience. It also insultingly parodies the Semitic religions. Worst of all, the portrayal of the Hindu ethos as the exemplar negates the very basis of *sarva dharma sambhava*. For, if all religions are equal, how can the Hindu religion be superior?

The second basic assertion of the majoritarian communalist is that although India must be treated as a Hindu country because it *is* a Hindu country ('just look at the numbers'!), the minorities must not regard themselves as minorities but as Indians—indeed, so says the Sangh Parivar, as Hindus. From Vajpayee and Advani down to the most junior RSS cadre, Indianness is held to be Bhartiyata and Bhartiyata to be Hindutva. In this view, our nationhood is sought to be determined on the basis of the majority being the majority, but the minority being asked not to think in terms of majority–minority but accept the terms of citizenship set by the majority. Thus, goes the argument, Muslims should think of themselves as Hindu Muslims and Christians as Hindu Christians. It is not enough that they regard themselves as Indian Muslims and Indian Christians; they must also accept that to be Indian is to be Hindu. Moreover, they should regard themselves privileged to be Hindu Muslims or Hindu Christians so that their thought processes and ways of life are purged of all that the Sangh Parivar regards as retrograde, perverse or even sinful in the religious scriptures, teachings and religion-based customs and usages of the minorities—an opportunity denied to all those non-Hindus unfortunate enough not to be Hindu Muslims or Hindu Christians!

The UNESCO Charter famously says that war begins in the minds of men. So does communalism. It is above all in the mind that communalism is to be challenged and secularism asserted. And if in the mind, secularism is not fundamental, in practice, particularly state practice, tactical compromises are effected on the grounds of political expediency which, sooner rather than later, and usually much sooner, undermine the secular order and set the precedent for using kid gloves, rather than the sharpest instruments in the state's armoury, to worst the communal menace.

In the mind, secular fundamentalism imposes three levels of commitment. First, clarity regarding the rationale of the secular ethic. Second, secular answers to communal questions, so that secular principles are not left in disarray before the communal challenge, as has so often been happening in the electoral fray and in the democratic dialectic, especially over the past two decades. Third, seamlessly merging the 'is' and 'ought' of secularism so that secularism is transformed from an intellectual conviction to a moral imperative.

It is easier to reject the repulsive communalism of a missionary and his son being burnt alive as they slept in their open jeep in tribal Orissa than it is to meet the challenge of insidious communalism exemplified in the Prologue to this book. When one of the best minds of contemporary India can so artlessly slide into dressing up prejudice as ratiocination, secular fundamentalism calls for a secular riposte. For, it is from the ball of such prejudice that is spun the yarn of communal ideology and communal politics that not only forages for reasons to 'explain', that is, effectively, to justify the carnage of Gujarat 2002 but then contrives through such reasoning to keep the perpetrators in office. Gujarat was lost to communalism because communal thinking led to communal action; and secularists lost Gujarat because they tried to accommodate 'majority sentiment' and temporized over the issue of secularism.

Yet, remember, India was won back from the horrors of partition because Mahatma Gandhi and Jawaharlal Nehru profoundly understood, even in the midst of the bestiality overtaking the subcontinent, that 'majority sentiment' is not communal. They remained unflinchingly secular when even their closest colleagues were getting infected with the virus of communal thinking. They recognized that the 'majority' in 'majority sentiment' does not refer to the 'majority community' but to the majority of Indians drawn from all communities. *Sarva dharma sambhava* is not the preserve of Hindus alone; Muslims are no more swayed by fatwas than Hindus are by the injunctions of Sankaracharyas; 'godmen' abound in every community. Indians are secular not because someone has misled them into being so but because the whole course of our millennial civilization has been that of a mighty river which, while Hindu in its origins, has been fed over the centuries, ever since its first encounter with pre-Hindu Indians, by so many tributaries of other origins that as we step into that mighty river in the twenty-first century, we are bathed in the waters of not a Hindu heritage but a composite Indian heritage.

We are secular because we are Indian, not because we are Hindu. And so, preserving, protecting and promoting our Indianness, or Bhartiyata, does not mean preserving, protecting or promoting Hindutva. The Hindu religion coexists with the other religions of India, superior in numbers but equal in all other respects, and as part of the Indian dispensation—precisely because that dispensation is Indian not Hindu, and is designed for all of us, not some of us.

It is above all in the teaching and propagation of popular history that the battle is first joined between the secular and communal forces. It is, therefore, in understanding the eternal verities of our history that secularism must be anchored. This calls for translating the academic rigour of historical research into the everyday currency of the discourse in the roadside dhaba. The university professor is unlikely to sip his tea in the dhaba. So, it is for the rest of us, and primarily for the political class, to render the abstruse findings of the professional historian into the idiom of the dhaba. To do so, however, requires a presence both in the seminar room and the dhaba. The politician by his calling is obliged to frequent the dhaba. The politician by his privilege is also welcomed at the round table. Yet, too few of our politicians combine calling with privilege to press the secular case. In contrast, the communalist spans the dhaba and the symposium. That is one reason the secularist school has lost ground. If these confessions serve as a wake-up call to even a few secularists, they would have served their purpose.

Intellectual secularism needs to be reinforced by secular activism. Personal conviction is never enough; the message has to be spread, others have to be carried along, the challenge has to be met as much on the battleground of the communalist's choosing as in dragging the communalist to the battleground of the secularist's choosing. And this has to be done both when inter-communal relations are stable as well as when they are disturbed. It was in the long Nehruvian calm from the early 1950s to the mid-1990s that secular somnolence left open the space for creeping communalism. As we have seen, that Nehruvian calm was the consequence of a principled commitment to secularism that elevated secular principle above the heat and dust of the political battle—and in consequence won the political battle. The point is important because it makes little sense to win the argument and lose the government. Nehru showed that we can win the government by winning the argument. Faint hearts after him let the argument go in the hope that the government might be kept. By the mid-1990s, the secularists ended up losing both the argument and the government. By taking up the argument, the secularists can win—and indeed have won—the government. Secular fundamentalism is, therefore, as much a political strategy as it is a moral choice, an intellectual conviction, and a preferred way of life.

A considerable body of secularists advises against meretricious secularism, that is, against wearing one's secularism on one's political sleeve. Secularism is said to offend the majority because secularism is perceived as favouring the minority at the expense of the majority. If that were indeed so, India would have gone down the majoritarian way long ago, and because the majority is so overwhelming, it would have done so definitively. But secularism is not about disadvantaging or disenfranchising or delegitimizing the majority. It is about not disadvantaging or disenfranchising or delegitimizing the minorities.

A majority of the majority has not been taken in by the tushtikaran argument because Indian secularism denies neither religion nor community identity. There is a majority and there are the minorities—but this mathematical fact does not detract from equality of treatment. Indeed, recognition of minority status reassures the minorities that their identity is not under threat and that their special problems will be attended to. Similarly, the promotion of community interest is not incompatible with secularism provided such community interest does not infringe the interests of any other community. Thus, there is nothing non-secular about government improving pilgrimage facilities to Vaishno Devi for the same reason that there is nothing non-secular about government building a Haj Manzil in Mumbai. Muslims do not go to Vaishno Devi and Hindus do not go on Haj, but that is no reason for Hindus to be denied state help or for Muslims to not be extended it.

A more subtle trap into which non-fundamentalist secularists are apt to fall is equating 'majority communalism' with 'minority communalism' and denouncing both in the same breath so as to escape the charge of tushtikaran. The argument thus gets shifted from relations *between* communities—which is what secularism is about—to modernizing retrograde social practices *within* communities—which is what liberalism is about.

The distinction is important. Liberalism, under our Constitution, works through liberals in each community persuading their co-religionists to abandon obsolete and reactionary practices. Secularism, on the other hand, is a constitutional obligation cutting across communities. Put another way, in our constitutional order, liberalism in personal law matters is an intra-community issue, while secularism is an inter-community issue.

By confusing issues of liberalism with issues of secularism, communalists succeed in shifting attention from their lack of secularism to the secularists' lack of liberalism. And since nothing so characterizes a liberal as a disturbed conscience, the liberal is stung into proving his or her liberal credentials instead of rebuking the communalist for justifying his reactionary communal mindset by invoking the reactionary social practices of the Other.

Mahatma Gandhi exemplified the reconciliation of the secular objective with the liberal objective. He remained rock solid on secularism as the fundamental principle of inter-community relations but directed all his liberalism at reform within his own community. His zeal for social reform—which took up much more of his attention and energies than political questions—was directed entirely at his own community, not in hectoring other communities to reform their ways. He left it to the abundant good sense available in every community to reform their respective ways instead of seeking to impose reform on others from without.

The way forward for the secular fundamentalist is the Gandhian way—secularism in inter-community matters and liberalism in intra-community matters, without confusing the one with the other. What is reprehensible in the Other is for the Other to rectify. He will. For liberalism is hardly the preserve of only one community. But it is unacceptable that reproaching triple talaq be the justification for launching a pogrom against the mian and his mullah.

There is another important consideration to note, a consideration which is a running theme in Jawaharlal Nehru's post-independence secular discourse but which has since virtually slipped out of the vocabulary of political secularism—the distinction between 'majority communalism' and 'minority communalism'. As a secular fundamentalist, I abhor all communalisms but regard majority communalism as by far the greater danger. For, majority communalism can undermine the very character of our secular nationhood precisely because the majority is an overwhelming majority. Minority communalism cannot, precisely because it is such a small minority. A Hindu communalist in independent India can work towards a Hindu India. It would require an advanced form of insanity for a Muslim communalist to work towards a Muslim India. Hindu fundamentalism is directed against other communities. Minority fundamentalism is inner-directed—against members of the same minority.

On the other hand, as a liberal, I would want to see all harmful, discriminatory social practices, especially gender-based discrimination which is rampant in all communities, removed as expeditiously as possible. But as a secularist, I recognize that such social reform must come from within, not without. And, therefore, I reject the argument that my priority should be to end polygamy among Muslims. I regard that as the priority for the Muslim liberal to take up, while I get on with crusading against Hindu polygamy, which is much more rampant, as the Gopal Singh Committee established decades ago.

There is a biblical injunction to refrain from pointing to the mote in the other's eye without considering the beam in one's own. In a similar manner, our Constitution prescribes that each community reform itself on the best liberal principles. So, the conscience-stricken liberal's first task is to attend to the warts in his own community, trusting that his fellow liberals in the other community will do the same. At the same time, as a liberal constitutionalist, I would urge wider resort by all—Hindus as much as the minorities—to the voluntary civil code embodied in the Special Marriage Act and related legislation.

There are two other points to be stressed—'stressed' because the issues have already been dealt with extensively in the main body of this book. One relates to special provisions in the Constitution and law for the minorities. If there can be special provisions for the minorities—as in respect of education—why not for the majority? How is such discrimination compatible with the basic secular principle of non-discrimination?

The essential secular answer is that if any such special provision infringes the rights of the majority, it certainly needs a fresh look. But there is no incompatibility if a special provision does not abridge or abort a right available to other citizens. A madrasa does not stop a Hindu parent from sending their child to a shishu niketan (although they would be well advised not to!). Second, affirmative action (such as state aid to minority educational institutions) does not amount to discrimination because it is designed to compensate for historical disadvantage. In any case, the secular order must respect the personal law of the minorities as much as it does the personal law of the majority—hence the multiple legislation which has gone into the codification of Hindu laws, a set of personal laws which are in no way incompatible with a secular order—for the good reason that the personal laws of the minorities are also not incompatible with a secular order!

Secularism also does not deny the legitimacy of communitarian interest. Communalism does—except for the majority community. This is best illustrated in the case of the IUML or Syed Shahabuddin's magazine, *Muslim India*. The IUML is avowedly concerned with the Muslim community. That makes it communitarian, not communal. For communitarian-ism to spill over into communalism, the pursuit of community interest has to be at the expense of another community—as when a masjid is deliberately despoiled to make way for an alternative place of worship. The IUML has never uttered a word against another community or advocated a single transgression of a majority community right. Indeed, the IUML broke from the original Muslim League in protest against the Pakistan branch instigating and colluding in discrimination against the minorities in Pakistan. It has actually sent a Hindu to the Kerala state assembly. The Sangh Parivar, on the contrary, spends a great deal of its energies on denigrating other communities, thwarting their interests and deprecating their identity.

Communalism seeks to absorb the other community by eliminating its separate identity. Communitarian-ism defensively seeks to preserve that identity. Secularism seeks to synthesize both without dissolving either. Applying these criteria to *Muslim India* one finds that while the magazine insistently and almost exclusively deals only with the plight of the Muslim community, there is never any word of denigration of the beliefs and practices of any other community. Look at *Panchajanya* or *Organiser* (the house magazines of the Sangh Parivar), on the other hand, and one finds an almost hysterical obsession with the minority communities to the virtual exclusion of any other consideration. *Muslim India* is communitarian; *Organiser* is communal. Secular fundamentalism recognizes the distinction.

Secular fundamentalism also draws lessons from the

experience of others. In this book, we have ranged over experiments in communalism conducted by several countries. That indicates the horrors in store for us if we make the same or similar mistakes. Equally, the rise of multiculturalism in several proud single-culture nations like France and Britain, and the shift away from the melting pot to cultural diversity on the North American continent, show how dated and reactionary is the communal preference for 'cultural nationalism' over pluralistic nationalism in our country.

I have a closing confession to make. I am an atheist, a somewhat reluctant atheist because I have seen the comfort which religious conviction brings to many. I saw my mother, to whom this book is dedicated, wither away with cancer—and was both impressed and moved by the courage of her conviction that she knew where she was going. Not having that conviction, the journey for me into the Unknown will be a perilous prospect. More importantly, being an atheist, how do I reconcile my claim to secular fundamentalism with frequent visits to places of worship—Hindu, Muslim, Christian—in my constituency as also the occasional family visit to the temple my father built in New Delhi near the Rivoli cinema next to the Shiv Mandir on Irwin Road (now Baba Kharag Singh Marg)? How do I resolve the dichotomy between my agnostic outlook and my long stays in the Sivananda Ashram where my mother spent seventeen years before ill health obliged her to come home to me?

I do feel hypocritical when all I see is a stone where others see Divinity. I feel hypocritical because my companions are worshipping while I merely go through the motions. Why then do I not walk out denouncing the whole charade?

Only because of my secularism. For secularism is not about giving primacy to my beliefs. It is about respecting the right of others to hold beliefs that I do not hold.

Appendix

Secular Answers to Communal Questions: A Catechism for Communalists

Perhaps I should first explain what a catechism is. It started as a set of questions and answers relating to the fundamental principles of the Christian Church. It has since gone on to become a technique of setting out and clearing doubts regarding the implications and applications of principles related to any subject.

In the five decades since independence, we have rarely seen as sharp a communalization of our polity as we are witnessing now. The principles of secularism no longer seem to be as self-evident as they once were. This not only calls for a reaffirmation and explanation of the fundamental principles of the secular way of life, it also warrants specific answers to specific questions which are being raised to facilitate and justify the creeping advance of the forces of communalism.

I have attempted to collate some of these questions and tried to provide some answers. I have also included questions that were raised and answered at the high-level national training camp on secularism which I organized in my capacity as chairman of the Congress party's political training department, in Bhopal in June 2000.

Why should we not have a uniform civil code?

The Constitution directs the state to progressively evolve a uniform civil code. This means, first, working towards the codification of personal law and customary usage within each community and, then, working out commonalities which would constitute the basis for discussing and agreeing upon a common code.

The provisions of a uniform civil code should not be imposed on the country by majority opinion alone. It must evolve through consensus among the different communities inhabiting our country. Fortunately, every religion provides for a process of social reform from within. In Islam, this is called ijtehad. It is utterly wrong to assert—as both minority and majority communalists often do—that there is no scope for any change in Muslim personal law. Social and legal reform is part of the everyday politics of avowedly Islamic countries. Equally, far-reaching social reforms in the Muslim community, within the tenets of Islamic belief, were an integral part of our freedom movement. Many changes and improvements have been brought about in Muslim personal law since independence. The same holds true of the personal law of other religious communities in India, including the Hindu personal law.

There is, sometimes, resistance to changes in the law or to judicial interpretations of the law. The Shah Bano case is often cited as an example of Muslim fundamentalist obduracy. But it is by no means unique. There was fierce resistance to the codification and provisions of Hindu personal law in the mid-1950s. After the codified law was enacted, it was repeatedly challenged in the courts. And even today, there are blatant violations of the law in such matters as child marriage, dowry, sati, untouchability and a host of other social evils, with the sanction and support of fundamentalists of the majority community. It is because the Hindu community, by and large, accepted changes in Hindu personal law that these changes were eventually made possible. The same holds true of other communities, including the Muslims. There is no room in such matters for holier-than-thou attitudes. Nothing is gained by denigration of others or mutual recrimination in such matters.

Personal law is a highly sensitive matter. Forcing people to change their way of life merely because they belong to a religious minority will destroy the principle of 'unity in diversity' which is the foundation of our strength as a civilization, of the emotional integration of our nation, and of our unity as a country. Progress is taking place in the social practices of all religious communities. It is, however, a fact that the pace of progress is faster in some communities than in others. Nothing could be more dangerous or reactionary than forcing the pace of change from outside. The answer lies in members of any given community being encouraged to quicken the pace of change from within.

The example is sometimes cited of Goa, where a common civil code applicable to all communities, including Muslims, has been in operation for centuries. It must be remembered that the code was imposed by a totally non-democratic, foreign, imperialist power that had captured Goa after defeating the ruling Muslim dynasty in the region. We can never replicate the methods of these proselytizing colonialists—nor would we wish to. We have to carry all communities with us in democratically evolving a uniform civil code.

Meanwhile, we already have a civil code which is open to members of all communities who wish to break away from the constrictions of their respective personal laws. It is a code which is adopted by many members of our majority community who find even the very advanced laws of the Hindu code inadequate for their personal purposes.

Progressive members within each community should be encouraged to reflect upon and promote progress within their respective communities, prevent the social boycott of persons within the community who opt for the civil code, and push for changes of a practical nature where formal changes in personal law might take time.

All religious communities—including the Muslims—deeply believe that many of their personal laws, customs and usages are divinely inspired and have been codified in their scriptures, or documents derived from these scriptures, by some of their greatest sages and seers. It is by introspection and community-based effort that this sensitivity is best taken care of.

Political activism by members of the majority community to forcibly impose changes in what the faithful believe are divinely sanctioned values will only outrage religious sentiment and thereby inflame communal passions. Social progress will come about neither by communalization of the polity nor by blind appeasement. In a democratic, multi-religious society such as ours, progress is possible only in a social and political atmosphere free of communal tension and through voluntary efforts within each section of society. Over time, this will lead to a large area of commonality which would lay the basis for a uniform civil code. In the meantime, any individual Indian remains free to stay within his or her personal law or to opt for the civil code.

What justification was there for negating the Supreme Court judgment in the Shah Bano case by an Act of Parliament?

Here I would like to draw upon what jurist and Congress leader Salman Khurshid had to say on this issue at the Bhopal training camp. In Islam, marriage is a sacred contract. The terms of the marriage are defined within the contract. The contract is also a divorce arrangement, clearly laying down the terms and conditions by which the marriage can be annulled. These terms include the maintenance to be provided by the man to the wife. But in Islamic law and practice, whatever has to be provided must be provided *within the period of the marriage*, as, after the divorce, there can be no further relationship or contact of any kind between the man and his former wife. So, Islamic law provides that before the marriage is terminated, that is before the period of the *iddat* is over, the man must pay all dues solemnized contractually at the time of marriage.

In case of transgressions of the law in specific cases, Muslim women are entitled to go to the civil courts to seek such allowances or such arrangements as have been provided for at the time of marriage but not adhered to by the husband.

But civil law and criminal law are different things and the Shah Bano case related not to civil law but criminal law, in particular, to the provisions for the prevention of vagrancy covered under Sections 125 and 127 of the CrPC. These sections provide for a maximum payment of Rs 500 per month by the man to the woman to forestall her falling into vagrancy. Further, Section 125 specifically provides that where the customary and other legal payments that have to be made upon divorce have been made, there will be no resort to the CrPC.

Shah Bano's husband argued that since he had made all the contractual payments due on divorce, he could not be proceeded against under the CrPC. The really important issue which got submerged in the subsequent controversy arising from the rulings of various courts is whether Parliament should not increase the maximum limit well beyond Rs 500.

With regard to the allegation so often made that the Muslim Women (Compensation on Divorce) Act, 1986, 'reversed' the Supreme Court judgment, the Supreme Court itself, in a ruling delivered by a bench of five judges, has held that Parliament did not reverse the decision in the Shah Bano case but, in fact, consolidated that decision.

Essentially, what the 1986 Act did was amplify the Islamic principles which provide for looking after a wife during marriage and upon divorce, and clarified that, upon divorce, certain rights accrue to the wife which go up to the time limit for the iddat, that is, the three-month period before the divorce can be made final. The Act provided that certain other arrangements have to be made which are part of the marriage settlement; that settlement also has to be made for the children for whom the husband is responsible; and that separate arrangements have to be made for any child still on mother's milk. It further provided that Section 125 was to be excluded only when all these arrangements have been made.

Of course, the law is sometimes not obeyed, as much in the Muslim community as in other communities. And, yes, there were some flaws left which people felt could be rectified in due course. But there was a huge outcry engineered against the 1986 Act alleging that Rajiv Gandhi had surrendered to the fundamentalists. The Supreme Court has now very clearly indicated that this was not the case. It was an amplification that Parliament provided, an amplification which makes available an alternative system of providing for Muslim women, without denying them any of their rights under Islamic law.

What is the logic of persisting with Article 370?

The special problems of J&K do not arise only because it is a Muslim-majority state. It is a state coveted by a foreign power which has thrice gone to war with India to capture it. It is also a state whose territory is partly under hostile foreign occupation. It is a border state whose frontiers touch both Pakistan and China. It is a state whose future as an integral part of the Indian Union is sought to be questioned by Pakistan in international forums. It is a state whose continuance in the Indian Union depends on massive assistance from the Union government, that is, from the country as a whole. It is a state in the throes of a proxy war.

It is with a view to addressing ourselves to these very special—and very serious—problems of J&K that the constitutional device of Article 370 was evolved in 1949. In the decades that have passed since then, the international aspects of the J&K question have not changed significantly. In particular, notwithstanding the Shimla Agreement, Pakistan continues to play its subversive games in J&K. Indeed, recent world developments, including the restiveness in the Central Asian republics of the former Soviet Union, have made it all the more important to handle Kashmir affairs with delicacy, sensitivity and understanding.

In the circumstances, the demand for abrogating Article 370 is totally misplaced. It would only result in the further alienation of the people of J&K at a time when the unity and integrity of India are under threat from Pakistan and their collaborators in the Valley.

In any case, there is no practical relevance to abrogating Article 370. J&K has freely accepted the application of almost all the laws of the country to the state. There is a common market between the state and the rest of the country, making J&K an integral part of the Indian economy. There is free movement of persons from J&K to the rest of the country and vice versa. There is, in normal times, no hindrance to the free flow of information between the state and the rest of the Union. The culture of J&K is a vital and vibrant component of our composite culture.

The main practical impact of Article 370 is restrictions on non-Kashmiris (please note: not non-Muslims) settling in the Kashmir Valley. This is not a matter of religion alone, as is sometimes sought to be made out, especially by communal-minded people. There are many parts of India—for example, much of the north-east, and the tribal areas under the Fifth Schedule in Bihar/Jharkhand, Madhya Pradesh/Chhattisgarh, Orissa and the border areas of Uttaranchal—where there are restrictions on settlement and the local economy is protected from outside encroachment.

This is the wrong time and wrong context in which to agitate for the abrogation of Article 370. In course of time, it will wither away of its own accord. Those who are attempting to make this non-issue into the central issue of our politics are only endangering the unity and integrity of the country at a time of grave national challenge.

Why should Hindus adopt family planning when Muslims resist it?

Our entire family planning programme is voluntary. Nobody is being forced to adopt it. All are being encouraged to do so.

The objective of family planning is not so much to restrict numbers in itself as to increase the welfare and happiness of families by assisting them in limiting their family size to what the family income can cater to. Any family or community that rejects family planning is only ensuring its own weakness and continued poverty. No community—neither the majority community nor any other community—will be able to augment its strength or rid itself of poverty if it rejects family planning.

In fact, family planning is practised by many Muslims and there are many Muslim opinion makers who are propagating family planning within their community.

It is the fear of the population profile of the country being reversed in favour of the Muslims that is behind the apprehension of those who wish to stop family planning among Hindus because there is resistance in the Muslim community—or who, alternatively, wish to impose family planning on the Muslims because the Hindus are voluntarily accepting it. The apprehension is misplaced. The majority community of India comprises 85 per cent of the population. Even if the annual rate of growth of the population of one or the other of the minority communities is a few decimal points ahead of the average for the majority, it will be aeons before any significant change is effected in the overwhelming majority status of the majority community. And any significant change that occurs in demographic ratios in this manner will only be to the detriment of the community that resists family planning because it will be a poverty-ridden, undereducated and backward community.

The myth of a threat to the majority status of the majority community is propagated only to inflame communal passions. Hindus who reject family planning to keep up with the increase in the non-Hindu population are only enfeebling themselves. Equally, non-Hindus who allow their families to increase unchecked are doing so to their own detriment. This is not a question of politics or community. It is a question of family welfare.

Why build a Haj Manzil for Muslim pilgrims at a cost of rupees ten crore when there is nothing similar at Gorakhpur for Hindus wanting to undertake a Teerth Yatra to Pashupatinath?

First, our Muslims are Indian citizens—and, as such, fully entitled to be looked after by the Indian state. Second, the need for a manzil arises because the holiest places of Islam require a journey by sea or air from India and cannot be reached by road or rail. Moreover, the holiest pilgrimage of the Islamic faith is concentrated at a specific point in time, i.e. the eve of Eid-ul-Azha. It is for these practical reasons that a manzil is required in Mumbai, which is the main exit point for pilgrimage by air or sea to the holy places of Islam.

To make such a facility available to Muslims is not to deny facilities for religious pilgrimage to Hindus. In fact, many more crores have been spent on developing travel and stay facilities to, and at, hundreds of holy Hindu religious shrines all over the country and even outside India—for example, the annual pilgrimages to Kailash Mansarovar. Facilities have even been negotiated with Pakistan for Sindhi Hindus to visit Sadhu Bela and for Punjabi Hindus to visit the shrine at Katasraj. For Sikhs, special arrangements have been made for pilgrimages to Nankana Sahib and Panja Saheb in Pakistan. Within the country, public money running to hundreds of crores has been spent—and rightly so—in catering to the religious requirements of the majority community, whether at Vaishno Devi or Kedarnath, the four *maths* established by Adi Sankaracharya, the Kumbh Mela and thousands of other melas, the great temple of Vishwanath at Varanasi or the temples of Pandarpur, Tirupati and Madurai.

If, in fact, there is any major requirement of a manzil for Hindu pilgrims at Gorakhpur, or anywhere along the Nepal border, to facilitate visits by Hindu pilgrims to Pashupatinath, there should be no difficulty in fulfilling the demand.

The fact is that the Haj Manzil issue is being exploited by majority communal elements like the Shiv Sena only to inflame communal passions. What really bothers them is not that a requirement of the majority community is being overlooked but that that of a minority community is being catered to.

Why does the government of India subsidize hajis when it does not similarly subsidize Hindu pilgrims?

On this issue I would like to draw attention to the views of Mohammed Hamid Ansari, who has served twice as India's ambassador to Saudi Arabia and has organized numerous Haj pilgrimages for Indian Muslims.

There are some tasks a government must carry out for its citizens. These include providing facilities for pilgrimages. Thus, whether it is at Badrinath or Vaishno Devi or Tirupati, or any other place where these facilities are required, the state is duty-bound to make the required facilities available. This is so even when the pilgrimage requires visiting a foreign country. That requires all kinds of assistance from the government. It is in this perspective that one must understand the problem of the Haj subsidy.

Earlier, the Haj used to be undertaken by sea. A private company, Moghul Lines, ran the service. Then, Moghul Lines was nationalized, but went into losses and, as is the case with many other state enterprises, the government decided to subsidize the losses of its own company. Thus, the initial Haj subsidy amounted to the transfer of its own funds from one pocket of the government to another. But when sea services for the Haj ended and it was decided that air services would be brought in, it was obvious that the cost of passage would be much higher. It was, therefore, argued that since it was the government itself which was denying sea passage to Haj pilgrims and forcing air services on them, the government must compensate the pilgrims for the additional expense they had to bear not of their own choice but because it was a decision thrust upon them.

Ansari opines that this was the wrong way to have gone about it. According to him, there can be no objection to the government subsidizing a government company for commercial reasons but the haji, being an individual pilgrim, should not be subsidized in this manner, particularly because it discriminates against those pilgrims who go on their own as private hajis and not on the government quota. This needs to be changed. Minorityism is just as bad as appeasement and we, therefore, need a new way of tackling the issue. But the sad fact is that when there was a non-BJP government in power, the Haj subsidy was used as a stick with which to beat the government, but in the six years the BJP was in office no new initiative was taken in this regard. In any case, even at subsidized rates, it costs Rs 75,000 per person to perform the Haj and if the pilgrim goes with his family, an expenditure of several lakhs is involved. So, it cannot be said that the subsidy is being given to poor Muslims. In fact, the beneficiaries tend to be the better-off. What has to be recognized is that if there is a commercial problem, it should be dealt with as a commercial problem.

John Dayal agrees that the state should not involve itself in issues that do not concern the state, but reasons that when the state spends crores on the Kumbh Mela and hundreds of other pilgrimages, the same logic should apply to subsidizing pilgrims of other religious persuasions. When government finance is available for the pilgrimages of other religious communities, denying the same to one community is unfair and unjust.

Why should we make such a hue and cry over secularism when no Muslim country practises it?

Simply because another country does not practise secularism is not a good enough reason for us not to do so. Do we want to copy the sectarianism of others—or would we prefer to be an example to the world of a vibrant secularism?

Each country must decide its own destiny for itself. There are many Muslim countries that wish to run an Islamic polity. There are some—like Iraq under Saddam Hussein and Turkey since Kemal Ataturk—which prefer the kind of secularism we practise. There are many Christian nations that have proclaimed Christianity as the state religion. Nevertheless, there are few in which the non-Christian population is subjected to disabilities. There is the Zionist state of Israel where Judaism is the official religion, and where the majority Muslim Palestinian population has been driven out of the country or deliberately reduced to second-class status. There is one Hindu country—Nepal—which has proclaimed Hinduism as its official religion.

Yet, almost all countries—whether or not they have an official state religion—are having to come to terms with the fact of large religious minorities in their midst. The United Kingdom—whose queen bears the official title of Defender of the Faith (Protestant

Christianity)—is a good example of a non-secular state coming to terms with secularism. In other words, all these states are increasingly having to learn from the Indian example of a multi-religious, secular society. We, for our part, have nothing to learn from uni-religious sectarian anachronisms. Those who want to convert our secular country into a Hindu Rashtra will only end up dragging our country backwards.

Does not a religion which talks of kafir and jehad pose a special threat that other religions do not?

It will be worthwhile here to first set out certain definitions. As pointed out by the dedicated secular activist D.R. Goel, the Prophet himself defined 'kafir' not as an 'unbeliever' but as one who transgresses the basic principles of humanity, one who refuses to accept the unity of God. To illustrate the point, Goel says, the Prophet gave non-Muslims the right to retain their places of worship. Indeed, there were villages/communities near Mecca where Hindus were permitted to retain their temples and justice was administered according to Hindu custom and usage. Al-Hajjaj, the governor of Iraq, whose nephew Mohammad bin Qassim was sent to conquer Sind, was also instructed to bring back with him to Baghdad, Pandits who could help translate Sanskrit scripture into Arabic. Goel also quotes Jawaharlal Nehru as saying that if contact between Islam and Hinduism had come by means of peaceful interaction between the Arabs and the Indians, rather than through so-called Turkish conquerors forcing the Khyber Pass, it might have led to the creation of a new civilization through a process of synthesis. Moreover, adds Goel, a true *momin* is defined as one who helps everybody, not just fellow Muslims, and so instead of being taken in by the debased meaning of 'kafir', the word should be understood as explained in the Holy Koran and the Hadith.

Salman Khurshid points out that 'jehad' is not about what is popularly or sometimes maliciously projected. The biggest jehad of all in Islam is the struggle which you have with yourself to overcome your weaknesses. In that sense, Mahatma Gandhi was the greatest jehadi of them all because he was constantly struggling against what he believed were his own weaknesses before teaching anything to anybody. Khurshid adds that there is another sense in which jehad is used and that is in connection with war. But not all wars are jehad;

it is only wars that are fought for justice that constitute jehad, and while there may be different interpretations given to the concept of 'just wars', so long as it is understood that what is just in word must also be just in practice, it should not be difficult to distinguish between just wars, which are jehad, and unjust wars, which are not.

G.M. Banatwala of the IUML says it is completely wrong to equate every terrorist attack with jehad because this only confers respectability on terrorism. If the attack on the Twin Towers in New York was an act of terrorism, so was the flattening of Afghanistan by the Americans. As was, he reasons, the razing to the ground of the Babri Masjid. It would be wrong to dignify or justify any of these acts by terming them jehad. We should not be equating terrorism and unjust wars with jehad as understood in Islam.

Why do Indian Muslims cheer Pakistani teams at sports meets?

Some Indian Muslims may do so. Most do not. In any case, a sport is a sport and the playing field should not be made the battleground for determining national loyalties. In England, there is a controversy raging over the question of whether Indian (and Pakistani) emigrants to Britain should cheer for the English or the India/Pakistan sides in cricket matches.

The patriotism of the Muslims of India is not to be tested in a cricket match, but when there is a challenge to the independence, unity and security of the country. Were the Muslims of Kashmir with India or Pakistan in October 1947 and May 1948? Was it not the Muslims of Kashmir who captured the saboteurs sent by Pakistan in August 1965 under Operation Gibraltar? Did not the civilian Muslim population of Kashmir back our army in 1965 and 1971? Are there not Muslim jawans and officers in our armed forces, many of whom have sacrificed their lives in the defence of the nation? Have not crores of Muslims everywhere in the country stood up for the nation in every national crisis, whether it has involved Pakistan, China, Sri Lanka or any other country?

Is patriotism the monopoly of the Hindus? In the years since independence, hundreds of Hindus have been caught spying for Pakistan. Does that mean the patriotism of the entire Hindu community is to be impugned? If not, why should the doubts and anguish and even treachery of some Indian Muslims be taken as proof that the entire Muslim community is traitor to their motherland?

Why should the cricket loyalty test be administered to Muslims when the captain of our cricket team has been a Muslim, and when as many as three leading members of the current team belong to the Muslim community?

Those who question the patriotism of the Muslim community as a whole are not themselves patriots but unthinking—and, sometimes, maliciously motivated—saboteurs of the unity and emotional integrity of our nation.

Does not the demand for azadi on the part of Kashmiri Muslims after more than fifty years of being an integral part of the Union of India—and despite the thousands of crores spent on their development, welfare and defence—show that a Muslim can never be a patriotic Indian?

In a sensitive border state like Kashmir, which is the continuous target of subversion and sabotage by Pakistan, there is bound to be a section of opinion which entertains thoughts of secession. The task before the country is not to denounce or distrust all Kashmiris, but to fight the forces of secession at the political level.

Past experience has shown that secessionist forces have to be fought politically—whether it was among the Christian community of Nagaland or Mizoram, or the Sikh community in Punjab, or the Hindu communities of Assam or Tripura, or the Gorkha community of the Darjeeling Hills, or the atheists of the Dravida Kazhagam in Tamil Nadu. How can an entire community be dubbed unpatriotic for the faults of a few?

It is those who seek to exploit the grievances of the Kashmiris to stoke communal passions everywhere in India who are really betraying the interests of the nation. It is communalism which is the highest form of treachery. The genuine problems of the people of Kashmir have to be tackled; the natural secularism of the Kashmiri people has to be restored. This was how the problems of secession were tackled in Nagaland, Mizoram, Tripura, Assam, the Darjeeling Hills and Tamil Nadu. It will be disastrous for the unity and emotional integrity of the country if the real problems are neglected and communal feelings needlessly inflamed. The unity and the integrity of the country cannot be preserved by either handing over the Kashmir

Valley to Pakistan, which is the counsel of despair now being given by some faint hearts, or by driving all the Muslims out of the Valley, as is being propagated by some of the most viciously narrow-minded communal elements in our polity.

Why are Indian Muslims worried about the Al Aqsa mosque in Jerusalem when there are so many dilapidated mosques in India?

The Al Aqsa mosque has a special place in Islamic faith. It has been damaged—and could even be destroyed—by the authorities and extremists of Israel, an avowedly Zionist state where, with state encouragement, the Jewish religion prevails over the Islamic faith.

It is but natural that the Muslims of India should join others of their faith to condemn the Zionist desecration of one of their holiest shrines. Indeed, all right-thinking Indians, of all religions, have joined hands with their brethren in the Non-Aligned Movement (which contains representatives from two-thirds of the countries of the world, including dozens where there are no Muslims at all) to condemn repeated Israeli attempts to destroy the mosque.

There have been cases of Muslim shrines being shifted to other locations in Islamic countries such as Saudi Arabia. Why not in India?

There can be no objection in principle to shifting religious shrines for well-founded, well-established practical reasons (such as traffic requirements, which is the reason cited for Saudi Arabia) provided this is legally valid and in keeping with the public interest. But we must resist and prevent any attempt at gratuitously destroying or removing religious shrines only to hurt the religious sentiments of particular communities or to inflame religious passions or provoke communal feelings.

In the specific case of the Babri Masjid—which is the context in which this question is generally raised—the issue is before the courts and it is essential that everybody strictly abide by the court verdict in letter and spirit. The VHP, backed by the BJP, has said that it will destroy the Babri Masjid and build a Ram Mandir in its place, whatever the court verdict. That position is unacceptable to secular opinion in the country.

Why do Muslims object to singing *Vande Mataram*?

It is not only the martyr Maqbool Ahmed of Sholapur who, in 1930, went to the gallows singing *Vande Mataram*; there are thousands of Muslim Congressmen who join in singing *Vande Mataram* at Congress functions every day.

There is a religious objection, on the part of some Muslim believers, to singing a song which speaks of bowing in worship to Mother India because, according to them, the Islamic faith enjoins them to worship only Allah. There are also objections to the veiled condemnation of Muslim rule in the second and subsequent verses of the song. This was made into a political issue between the Arya Samaj and the Muslim League, especially during the early decades of the last century when the running battles between the shuddhi and tabligh movements contributed to dangerously communalizing our polity.

Those who are now seeking to flog this dead horse are not really trying to honour the memory of Bankim Chandra Chatterjee but merely trying to communalize our polity again. We must not fall into their trap.

Why do Muslims seek a separate identity in India—in terms of language, dress, etc.—when they do not do so in countries like Indonesia?

As is evident to anyone who visits the Kaaba in Mecca during the holy pilgrimage, the Muslims of the world are drawn from every race, every continent, many different languages, and many different cultural and ethnic identities.

In India itself, Muslims belong to numerous different linguistic ethnic groups. It is in a religious sense that they constitute a distinct identity. To reinforce this identity, they have, historically, evolved some symbols of a common identity and means of communication which breach other linguistic barriers. Thus, Urdu is a language spoken by many Indian Muslims. But neither is Urdu an exclusive preserve of Muslims (it is the lingua franca in parts of India and some of the greatest scholars and writers of Urdu include Hindus, Sikhs and Christians) nor is knowledge of Urdu the sine qua non of being an Indian Muslim (there are many Indian Muslims with little or no knowledge of Urdu).

The search for a common language of communication and symbols of religious identity is by no means peculiar to India's Muslim community. For centuries, Hindus have breached linguistic barriers through the use of Sanskrit and, in modern times, this is being increasingly done by resorting to Hindi and even English. Some of the greatest writings of Swami Vivekananda were in English. There are also many symbols which Hindus living in different parts of India and in different countries—whether this be in Hindu-majority countries like India, Nepal and Mauritius or Hindu-minority countries like the United States and the United Kingdom—use to underline their religious identity.

To make an issue of Urdu or achkans or qawwalis is merely to communalize our polity.

Why do foreign missionaries proselytize in India when there are so many problems—like drug abuse—which they should be attending to at home?

For the same reason that Hindu missionaries from India have established ashrams in numerous foreign countries and converted uncounted numbers of Christians and others to the Hindu way of life. Religion, at its best, looks on the world and humanity as one (*Vasudhaiva Kutumbakam*, as the Hindu scriptures put it).

Foreign missionaries working in India follow a faith which is the faith of millions of Indians. Christianity is not a 'foreign' religion, nor is Hinduism the only authentic religion of India. A secular Indian gives equal respect to all the religions of India, including Christianity. Our Constitution permits the free propagation of religion. So long as foreign missionaries work within the bounds of the Constitution and the law, there can be no legitimate objection to what they are doing.

Communal elements in our majority community who object to the humanitarian work being done by foreign missionaries on the ground that they should restrict their activities to their own community and their own countries would be well advised to follow their own advice—and tend to the problems of social and economic deprivation within their own community instead of inflaming communal passions by raising the bugbear of foreign missionary activity.

Why should we permit Christian missionary activity when Swami Vivekananda and Mahatma Gandhi had denounced Christian proselytizing and the Niyogi Commission appointed by the Congress government in Madhya Pradesh had detailed the anti-Hindu propaganda carried on by Christian missionaries in the guise of spreading the Gospel?

We need to consider a few facts about Gandhi's relationship with Christianity before we bring up his name to justify any stand against Christian missionaries. One of Gandhi's closest personal friends was the Reverend Charles Andrews, a foreign Christian missionary. Gandhi was frequently a guest in Delhi with the principal of St Stephen's College, known accurately in common parlance as 'mission college'. More importantly, Gandhi readily confessed to having understood the Bhagawad Gita better after discovering the Sermon on the Mount, that is, to having become a better Hindu by becoming a better Christian. Indeed, John Middleton Murry described Gandhi as the greatest Christian teacher in the modern world. It is obvious that a communalist invoking the name of Gandhi, to denounce Christian proselytizing, is tantamount to the Devil citing the scriptures.

Gandhi's objection was to conversion without consent and conversion by inducement as also to the denigration of other religions in the name of proselytizing. Swami Vivekananda, making much the same point, also paid the mission mode a tribute by launching the Ramakrishna Mission which has for a century and more done excellent social service in India and abroad, besides welcoming into the Hindu fold those from other religions.

Conversion by threat or blandishment is illegal in independent India, as is the denigration of other religions. The right to propagate one's religion is a fundamental constitutional right given to all religions—not Christians alone. This right is, however, hedged with the statutory condition that forcible conversion is a cognizable offence and missionaries, of whatever faith, are prohibited by law from spreading disaffection towards other religions.

Niyogi had a long personal record, going back to before independence, of protesting against foreign missionary activity. As one who opposed missionary activity with missionary zeal, he was hardly a disinterested observer. In any case, the report of his commission of enquiry was submitted nearly half a century ago. It is the duty of the state to ensure that missionaries operate within the framework of the law, but there is no place in our Constitution or in law for self-appointed militia to spread terror and mayhem the way the Bajrang Dal has done by targeting the Christian community, Christian missionaries and their places of worship in Gujarat and Orissa.

It also appears that most of the excesses of the past are a thing of the past and that the overwhelming record of Christian missionary work in the country is not only positive but has worked as an incentive for similar educational, health and social work among the deprived by missionaries of other religious persuasions. In any case, as John Dayal pointed out at the Bhopal camp, there are less than a thousand missionaries of foreign origin in all of India, the youngest of whom has been in India for forty years! Most of our contemporary Christian missionaries are Indian citizens exercising their constitutionally guaranteed fundamental right of propagating their religion but most of the time devoting themselves less to harvesting souls for the Church than answering to their Christian duty of looking after those less fortunate than themselves.

Notes

1. Secularism: An Overview

[1] Rasheeduddin Khan, *Bewildered India*, p. xv.

[2] Ibid., see also p. 3.

[3] Ibid., p. 161.

[4] Ibid., pp. xii–xiii.

[5] Ibid., p. xii.

[6] Ibid., p. xii.

[7] Ibid., p. xiii.

[8] Ibid., p. 11.

[9] Ibid., p. xiii.

[10] Ibid., pp. 282–284.

[11] Ibid., p. xiv.

[12] Ibid., pp. 15–16.

[13] Ibid., p. 16.

[14] Ibid., see Chapter X: 'Violence and Communal Riots in India', especially Table IV, pp. 223–224.

[15] Ibid., p. xvii.

[16] The 2004 elections to the fourteenth Lok Sabha, which has reduced the BJP's strength from around 180 to below 140, appears to reinforce this assessment.

[17] Bipan Chandra, *Communalism—A Primer*, p. 7.

2. The Ideological Dimension

1 Kheer, *Veer Savarkar*, p. 263. See also, Andersen and Damle, *The Brotherhood of Saffron*, pp. 33–34, p. 60, footnote 45.

2 Jyotirmay Sharma, *Hindutva*, p. 62.

3 Quoted in A.G. Noorani, *Savarkar and Hindutva*, pp. 66 and 116.

4 Jyoti Trehan, *Veer Savarkar*, p. 42.

5 Extracted from Kheer, *Veer Savarkar*, and Trehan, *Veer Savarkar*.

6 A.G. Noorani, *Savarkar and Hindutva*, p. 27.

7 Jyotirmay Sharma, *Hindutva*, p. 172, quoting *Thus Spake the Prophet*, Swatantryaveer Savarkar Rashtriya Smarak, Mumbai, 1998, p. 2.

8 Jyotirmay Sharma, *Hindutva*, p. 272.

9 Golwalkar, *We, or Our Nationhood Defined*, p. 35.

10 Ibid., pp. 45, 47.

11 Golwalkar, *A Bunch of Thoughts*, p. 519.

12 Ibid., p. 70.

13 Ibid., p. 103. Arun Shourie reflects the same argument in the Prologue.

14 Quoted in Shyam Chand, *Saffron Fascism*, p. 1.

15 As quoted by the chairman of the BJP's think-tank, Balbir Punj, in the *South Asian Journal*, no. 2, October–December 2003.

16 A.G. Noorani, *Savarkar and Hindutva*, p. 65.

17 *Sunday Observer*, 13 January 1991.

18 *Organiser*, 2 September 1990.

19 Bipan Chandra, *Communalism—A Primer*, p. 52.

20 Golwalkar, *A Bunch of Thoughts*, p. 183.

21 Ram Swarup, *Organiser*, 30 June 1991.

22 Sudhir Kakar's translation of Rithambara's standard speech, *The Times of India*, 19 July 1992.

23 *The Sunday Mail*, 21 October 1990.

24 *The Sunday Mail*, 9 December 1990.

25 *The Sunday Mail*, 23 December 1990.

26 *The Sunday Mail*, 11 November 1990.

27 *The Sunday Mail*, 2 December 1990.

28 *The Sunday Mail*, 9 December 1990.

29 Ibid.

[30] *The Sunday Mail*, 4 November 1990.

[31] *The Sunday Mail*, 2 December 1990.

[32] Bipan Chandra, *Many Faces of Communalism*, p. 67.

3. The Historical Dimension

[1] Dr Sarvepalli Radhakrishnan, *The Hindu View of Life*, pp. 17–18.

[2] M.S. Golwalkar, *A Bunch of Thoughts*, p. 71.

[3] Romila Thapar, 'Somanatha: Narratives of a History', in *Seminar*, no. 475, March 1999. See also, Thapar, *Somanatha: The Many Voices of a History*.

[4] Romila Thapar, *A History of India, Vol. I*, pp. 186–187 and 217–218.

[5] Dr Sarvepalli Radhakrishnan, *The Hindu View of Life*, p. 18.

[6] Rajmohan Gandhi, *Understanding the Muslim Mind*, p. 35.

[7] Ibid., p. 36.

[8] Mushirul Hasan, *Nationalism and Communal Politics in India*, p. 1.

[9] Ibid., p. 83.

[10] Ibid., p. 89.

[11] As phrased by the *Indian Patriot*, ibid., p. 207.

[12] Ibid., p. 87.

[13] Ibid., p. 87.

[14] Ibid., p. 95.

[15] Ibid., p. 185.

[16] Ibid., pp. 184–198.

[17] Ibid., pp. 207–210.

[18] Ibid., p. 103.

[19] Bipan Chandra, *Many Faces of Communalism*, p. 67.

[20] Nehru, *An Autobiography*, p. 172.

[21] Hasan, *Nationalism and Communal Politics in India*, p. 211.

[22] Moonje Papers, 13 July 1926, cited by Hasan, *Nationalism and Communal Politics in India*, p. 239.

[23] Rajmohan Gandhi, *Understanding the Muslim Mind*, p. 113.

[24] Ibid., p. 138.

[25] Hasan, *Nationalism and Communal Politics in India*, p. 272.

[26] Ibid., p. 250.

27 Ibid., pp. 260–261.
28 The phrase is Motilal Nehru's from his letter to Annie Besant, 30 September 1928, cited in Hasan, *Nationalism and Communal Politics in India*, p. 260n.
29 Hasan, *Nationalism and Communal Politics in India*, Chapter 27, 'The Clash'.
30 B.R. Nanda, *Jawaharlal Nehru*, pp. 68–69.
31 Cited in Stanley Wolpert, *Jinnah of Pakistan*, p. 101.
32 Rajmohan Gandhi, *Understanding the Muslim Mind*, p. 140.
33 B.R. Nanda, *The Nehrus*, p. 291.
34 Gandhi to Jawaharlal Nehru, summer 1927, quoted by Nanda, ibid., p. 274.
35 25 December 1928, cited in Hasan, *Nationalism and Communal Politics in India*, p. 262.
36 Choudhary Khaliquzzaman, *Pathway to Pakistan*, p. 98.
37 Rajmohan Gandhi, *Understanding the Muslim Mind*, p. 139.
38 Hasan, *Nationalism and Communal Politics in India*, p. 281.
39 Ibid., p. 275.
40 Rajmohan Gandhi, *Understanding the Muslim Mind*, p. 141.
41 Hasan, *Nationalism and Communal Politics in India*, pp. 289–290.
42 Presidential address to the Hindu Mahasabha as quoted in Noorani, *Savarkar and Hindutva*; Kheer, *Veer Savarkar*; and Trehan, *Veer Savarkar*.
43 Rajmohan Gandhi, *Understanding the Muslim Mind*, p. 117.
44 Ibid., pp. 134–135.
45 Ibid., pp. 117–118.
46 Quoted in Rajmohan Gandhi, ibid., p. 154.
47 Ibid., p. 237.
48 *Census of India*, 1941, Vol. I, Pt I , Table XIII, pp. 98–99.
49 *The Statesman*, 14 January 1937.
50 Mushtaq Naqvi, *Partition—The Real Story*, p. 2.
51 Ibid., p. 83.
52 Ibid., p. 86.
53 Ibid., p. 85.
54 Ibid., p. 95.
55 Ibid., p. 90.
56 Ibid., pp. 199–210, Annexure II, 'Detailed Results of the 1946 General Elections in the United Provinces'.

[57] Ibid., pp. 2–3.

[58] Sana has also helped me in editing this book.

4. The Constitutional and Legal Dimensions

[1] Lok Sabha, 29 July 1992.

[2] Translated from the Hindi original by the author.

[3] *The Times of India*, 26 June 1991.

[4] *The Times of India*, 13 May 1991, emphasis added.

[5] This has recently been revoked after Jayalalithaa's AIADMK lost every Lok Sabha seat it contested in the 2004 elections.—Editors

[6] Constituent Assembly Debates.

[7] Jawaharlal Nehru, *Selected Works*, pp. 189–192.

[8] D.G. Tendulkar, *Mahatma*, vol. 8, p. 61.

[9] Rajya Sabha Debates, vol. 86, col. 186, 18 December 1973.

[10] Lok Sabha Debates, vol. 9, Eighth Series, cols 419–455, 23 August 1985.

[11] Mukul Kesavan, *Secular Commonsense*, pp. 10–11.

[12] Cited in Zakaria, 1995, p. 171.

[13] Khalidi, 2003, p. 11.

[14] Khalidi, 1995, p. 87 and 2003, p. 71.

[15] Khalidi, 2003, p. 65.

[16] Ibid., p. 65.

[17] Ibid., pp. 76–77.

[18] Chandra, *Communalism—A Primer*, p. 20.

[19] Ibid., pp. 54–55.

[20] Khalidi, 1995, Table 13, p. 184.

[21] Zakaria, 1995, p. 135.

[22] Ibid., p. 135.

[23] Mukul Kesavan, *Secular Commonsense*, p. 135.

[24] Kesavan's critique of Neera Chandoke's *Beyond Secularism*, ibid.

[25] Ibid., p. 22.

[26] Khalidi, *Indian Muslims since Independence*, p. 181.

[27] Ibid., p. 179. The quotation is from Jennings's *Some Characteristics of the Indian Constitution*, OUP, 1953.

[28] Khalidi, 2003, p. 19.

[29] Khalidi, 1995, pp. 90–91.

[30] Constituent Assembly Debates.

5. Secularism in a Time of Communal Activism

[1] Letter to Saxena dated 10 September 1949, as quoted in Gopal, *Jawaharlal Nehru: A Biography*.

[2] S. Gopal, *Jawaharlal Nehru: A Biography*, quoting the *National Herald* report of 4 October 1951.

[3] *Letters to the Chief Ministers*, Vol. 11, pp. 388–389.

[4] Ibid., p. 462.

[5] Munshi to Nehru, 24 April 1951.

[6] Quoted in Bipan Chandra, *Many Faces of Communalism*, p. 31.

[7] For a perceptive analysis of the allegations of rigging in the 1987 elections, see Vernon Hewitt, *Reclaiming the Past? The Search for Political and Cultural Unity in Contemporary Jammu & Kashmir*, pp. 152–154.

With regard to rigging and other irregularities, Hewitt proffers the guesstimate that as against the four seats won by the Muslim United Front, it would have at best won ten seats.

[8] Jagmohan, *My Frozen Turbulence in Kashmir*, pp. 496–497.

[9] Interview to *Indian Express*, 4 February 1991.

[10] Article 143 deals with the powers of the president to consult the Supreme Court. It states: 'If at any time it appears to the president that a question of law or fact has arisen, or is likely to arise, which is of such a nature and of such public importance that it is expedient to obtain the opinion of the Supreme Court upon it, he may refer the question to that Court for consideration and the Court may, after such hearing as it thinks fit, report to the president its opinion thereon.'

[11] Article 138 deals with the enlargement of the jurisdiction of the Supreme Court. Article 138 (2) states: 'The Supreme Court shall have such further jurisdiction and powers with respect to any matter as the Government of India and the Government of any State may by special agreement confer, if Parliament by law provides for the exercise of such jurisdiction and powers by the Supreme Court.'

[12] Quoted in A.G. Noorani (ed.), *The Babri Masjid Question, 1528–2003: 'A Matter of National Honour'*.

6. Secularism and the Indian Religious Minorities

[1] I would like to acknowledge my indebtedness to Rajesh Kochar, *The Vedic People*, pp. 4–10, for much of my information on Christian missionary translations of Indian literature and their contributions to it.

[2] *Rajiv Gandhi, Selected Speeches and Writings*, 1984-85, p. 3.

[3] Ibid., pp. 3–4.

[4] Ibid., p. 11.

[5] Ibid.

[6] Bipan Chandra, *Communalism—A Primer*, pp. 18–19.

7. The External Dimension

[1] As cited in Rajmohan Gandhi, *Understanding the Muslim Mind*.

[2] K.M. de Silva, 'Religion and the State', in *Sri Lanka: Problems of Governance*.

[3] Sumantra Bose, *States, Nations, Sovereignty: Sri Lanka, India and the Tamil Eelam Movement*, p. 53.

[4] K.M. de Silva, *Sri Lanka: Problems of Governance*, p. 313.

[5] Sumantra Bose, *States, Nations, Sovereignty: Sri Lanka, India and the Tamil Eelam Movement*, pp. 54–55.

[6] Ibid., pp. 54–55.

[7] Ibid., p. 60.

[8] Ibid.

[9] Avi Shlaim, *The Iron Wall: Israel and the Arab World*.

[10] Ibid.

References

Books

Andersen, W.K., and Shridhar Damle, *The Brotherhood of Saffron: The Rashtriya Swayamsevak Sangh and Hindu Revivalism*, Boulder, Colorado: Westview Press, 1987

Bose, Sumantra, *States, Nations, Sovereignty: Sri Lanka, India and the Tamil Eelam Movement*, New Delhi: Sage, 1994

Chagla, Justice Mohammed Currim, *Roses in December: An Autobiography*, Bombay, 1973

Chand, Shyam, *Saffron Fascism*, New Delhi: Hemkunt, 2002

Chandoke, Neera, *Beyond Secularism: The Rights of Religious Minorities*, New Delhi: OUP, 2003

Chandra, Bipan, *Many Faces of Communalism*, Chandigarh: Centre for Research in Rural and Industrial Development, 1985

Chandra, Bipan, *Communalism—A Primer*, New Delhi: Anamika, 2004

de Silva, K.M., *Sri Lanka: Problems of Governance*, New Delhi: Konark, 1993

Gandhi, Rajmohan, *Understanding the Muslim Mind*, New York: State University of New York Press, 1986; New Delhi: Penguin Books India, revised edition, 2000

Golwalkar, M.S., *A Bunch of Thoughts*, Bangalore: Sahitya Sindhu Prakashan, 1996

Gopal, S., *Jawaharlal Nehru: A Biography*, Vol. II, New Delhi: OUP, 1979

Hasan, Mushirul, *Nationalism and Communal Politics in India*, New Delhi: Manohar Publications, 1991

Jagmohan, *My Frozen Turbulence in Kashmir*, New Delhi: Allied Publishers, 1992

Jalal, Ayesha, *The Sole Spokesman: Jinnah, the Muslim League and the Demand for Pakistan*, Cambridge: Cambridge University Press, 1985

Kesavan, Mukul, *Secular Commonsense*, New Delhi: Penguin, 2001

Khalidi, Omar, *Indian Muslims since Independence*, New Delhi: Vikas, 1995

Khalidi, Omar, *Khaki and the Ethnic Violence in India*, New Delhi: Three Essays Collective, 2003

Khaliquzzaman, Choudhary, *Pathway to Pakistan*, Karachi: Longman, 1961

Khan, Rasheeduddin, *Bewildered India: Identity, Pluralism, Discord*, New Delhi: Asia Books, 1994

Kheer, Dhananjay, *Veer Savarkar*, Mumbai: Popular Prakashan, 1988

Khilnani, Sunil, *The Idea of India*, New York: Farrar, Straus & Giroux, 1997

Khuhro, Dr Hamida, *Mohammed Ayub Khuhro: A Life of Courage in Politics*, Karachi: Ferozsons, 1998

Kochar, Rajesh, *The Vedic People*, New Delhi: Orient Longman, 2000

Malkani, K.R., *The Sindh Story*, New Delhi: Allied Publishers, 1984

Nanda, B.R., *Jawaharlal Nehru*, New Delhi: OUP, 1995

Nanda, B.R., *The Nehrus: Motilal and Jawaharlal*, Chicago: University of Chicago Press, 1962

Naqvi, Mushtaq, *Partition—The Real Story*, New Delhi: Renaissance, 1995

Nehru, Jawaharlal, *An Autobiography*, New Delhi: Jawaharlal Nehru Memorial Fund, 1998

Nehru, Jawaharlal, *Letters to the Chief Ministers*, Vol. 11, New Delhi: Jawaharlal Nehru Memorial Fund

Nehru, Jawaharlal, *Selected Works*, New Delhi: Jawaharlal Nehru Memorial Fund

Noorani, A.G., *Savarkar and Hindutva*, New Delhi: Leftword, 2002

Noorani, A.G. (ed.), *The Babri Masjid Question, 1528–2003*: '*A Matter of National Honour*', New Delhi: Tulika, 2003

Radhakrishnan, Dr Sarvepalli, *The Hindu View of Life*, New Delhi: Unwin Books, 1926

Rajiv Gandhi: *Selected Speeches and Writings, 1984-85*, New Delhi: Publications Division, 1987

Savarkar, V.D., *Hindutva*, 1925

Savarkar, G.D., Trans. by M.S. Golwalkar, *We, or Our Nationhood Defined*, 1945

Sharma, Jyotirmay, *Hindutva*, New Delhi: Penguin/Viking, 2003

Shlaim, Avi, *The Iron Wall: Israel and the Arab World*, New York: W.W. Norton & Company, 2001

Sitaramayya, Dr Pattabhi, *Feathers and Stones*, Bombay: Padma Publications, 1946

Tendulkar, D.G., *Mahatma*, New Delhi: Publications Division, 1984

Thapar, Romila, *A History of India*, Vol. I, New Delhi: Penguin Books India, 1990

Thapar, Romila, *Somanatha: The Many Voices of a History*, New Delhi: Viking/Penguin, 2004

Trehan, Jyoti, *Veer Savarkar*, New Delhi: Deep & Deep, 1991

Varadarajan, Siddharth (ed.), *Gujarat: The Making of a Tragedy*, New Delhi: Penguin, 2002

Hewitt, Vernon, *Reclaiming the Past? The Search for Political and Cultural Unity in Contemporary Jammu & Kashmir*, Portland, London, 1995

Wolpert, Stanley, *Jinnah of Pakistan*, New York: OUP, 1984

Zakaria, Rafiq, *The Widening Divide*, New Delhi: Penguin/Viking, 1995

Newspapers and Magazines

The Statesman, 14 January 1937

The Times of India, 13 May 1991

The Times of India, 26 June 1991

The Hindustan Times, 28 February 1990 (Anil Maheshwari's article)

The Indian Express, 4 February 1991, Interview with L.K. Advani

The Times of India, 28 July 1992, Letter to the editor, Professor D.N. Jha

The Sunday Observer, 13 January 1991
The South Asian Journal, no. 2, October–December 2003
Organiser, 7 April 1991
Organiser, 30 June 1991
The Times of India, 19 July 1992.
The Sunday Mail, 21 October 1990
The Sunday Mail, 9 December 1990
The Sunday Mail, 23 December 1990
The Sunday Mail, 11 November 1990
The Sunday Mail, 2 December 1990
The Sunday Mail, 9 December 1990
The Sunday Mail, 4 November 1990
The Sunday Mail, 2 December 1990
Seminar, no. 475, March 1999, Thapar, Romila, '*Somanatha: Narratives of a History*'

Index